MAX HAINES

MULTIPLE MURDERERS

Other books by Max Haines...

Bothersome Bodies (1977)
Calendar of Criminal Capers (1977)
Crime Flashback # 1 (1980)
Crime Flashback # 2 (1981)
Crime Flashback # 3 (1982)
The Murderous Kind (1983)
Murder and Mayhem (1984)
The Collected Works of Max Haines, Vol. I (1985)
That's Life! (1986)
True Crime Stories (1987)
True Crime Stories, Book II (1988)
True Crime Stories, Book III (1989)
True Crime Stories, Book IV (1990)
The Collected Works of Max Haines, Vol. II (1991)
True Crime Stories, Book V (1992)
Doctors Who Kill (1993)

Canadian Cataloguing in Publication Data

Haines, Max
        Multiple murderers

ISBN 1-895735-06-8

1. Murderers. 2. Murder. 3. Criminals. I. Title.

HV6515.H35 1994   364.1'523   C94-932278-4

Editor: Glenn Garnett
Copy editor: Maureen Hudes B.A., B. Ed.
Cover and text design: Nargis Churchill

Printed and bound in Canada

Published by the Toronto Sun Publishing Corporation
333 King Street East, Toronto, Ontario M5A 3X5

Distributed by Penguin Books Canada Limited
10 Alcorn Avenue, Suite 300, Toronto, Ontario M4V 3B2

To Marilyn

INTRODUCTION

An epidemic of killings involving more than one victim is sweeping the civilized world. This phenomenon respects no boundaries or cultures. The incidence of such horrendous crimes and criminals is so widespread that it has become necessary for the FBI Academy at the National Centre for the Analysis of Violent Crime in Quantico, Virginia, to classify multiple homicides into type and style.

According to the Academy, murder involving more than three victims killed in one location within one event is deemed to be a mass murder. The two types of mass murder are classic and family. A classic mass murder involves one person operating in one location at one period of time. Usually, the person perpetrating this type of crime has a mental disorder and firmly believes that they must give vent to their frustrations by seeking revenge on an entire group, who usually have nothing to do with the person committing the crime. England's Michael Ryan is an example of the classic mass murderer.

The second grouping of mass murder is family member murder, which occurs when an individual kills more than three members of his own family. Sometimes this type of killer takes his own life, but not always. Gene Simmons of Arkansas paid for his crimes when he was apprehended and put to death by lethal injection.

Spree killers murder at two or more locations with no emotional cooling off period between homicides.

Finally, the most horrific of all types of multiple murderers is the serial killer. This type of human predator claims more than three victims with cooling off periods between each killing. Henri Landru of France, also known as Bluebeard, was an earlier day serial killer.

All types of multiple murderers have been with us since ancient times, but more recently their numbers have increased dramatically. Many of the monsters contained within these pages received international attention, so notorious were their crimes.

Ted Bundy, David Berkowitz, Reg Christie, Charles Manson, John Wayne Gacy and Wayne Williams have become household names. Not so familiar are other madmen such as Ed Kemper, Dennis Nilsen, Gerald Gallego, Lee Andrews and Richard Chase. The dastardly deeds of these killers and many others are detailed in Multiple Murderers.

CONTENTS

LEE ANDREWS

No one had a bad word to say about Lee Andrews. Why should they? After all, around Grandview, Kansas, he was reputed to be a bright boy with an even brighter future.

Lee graduated from high school with the highest marks ever achieved by a Kansas student. His IQ was in the near genius category. Like many big men, Lee was kind and gentle. At over six feet and 260 pounds, he was an imposing figure in the tiny community.

Lee regularly accompanied his parents and his sister Jenny to the Grandview Baptist Church. He often had long chats with his minister, the Reverend V.D. Dameron. They discussed religion and world events. Rev. Dameron, who was Lee's father's best friend, often thought that everyone should be blessed with a son like Lee Andrews.

After entering the University of Kansas, Lee became an honor student. For relaxation, he played the bassoon in the university band.

Who knows when Lee Andrews first thought that there were pursuits in life other than scholastic ones. In hindsight, the germ of the idea was probably planted in his mind when his parents' home was burglarized. Big Lee figured that with brains and imagination, he could plan and carry out the perfect crime. Why wander further afield than his own family? His parents always had a couple of thousand dollars in their bank account. Then there was the 250-acre spread his father owned. Lee figured it had to be worth $50,000. If they were to die suddenly, he and Jenny would inherit their entire estate. Of course, if Jenny were to die at the same time, Lee

1

would be left as sole heir.

For months, the ideal son fantasized about killing his family, inheriting their worldly goods and leading the good life. Right off, he would purchase a car and clothing; not jeans or t-shirts, but made-to-measure suits. He would quit university and travel the world. There would be no clues. This would be the perfect murder.

Lee considered poisoning his family, but dismissed poison as too risky. No, he would shoot them and fake a robbery. The police would be no match for him. As the only surviving member of the family, he would be the recipient of much sympathy. It was ironic. His parents had given him a .22 repeater rifle last Christmas to go with his German Luger. He would snuff out their lives with their Christmas present. Lee figured the very best time to kill his family would be during the Thanksgiving break, when he would be home from school.

On Friday, November 28, 1958, Lee prepared to commit the triple murder. As he talked to his father that afternoon, he idly glanced out the living room window. He noticed that the bread man had made a delivery to a neighbor and was slowly making his way to the Andrews home to deliver the usual weekend supply. How silly, thought Lee. There would be no one alive to eat the bread. He ran outside and told the bread man that they wouldn't be requiring their usual delivery that weekend.

Thanksgiving dinner went off without a hitch. Lee's dad made a mini speech, saying how happy he was to have his family together for Thanksgiving dinner. Lee kept waiting for an excuse to leave the room. Just as he was about to leave, his mother started to clear the dishes. This was no good at all. For his particular purposes, Lee wanted all the members of his family to be together. At last, his mother and Jenny joined him and his father.

Lee got up, excused himself and went to his bedroom. He loaded his .22 rifle and silently placed the German Luger into his pocket. His plan was now in motion. To simulate a burglary, he pushed out his screen and opened the window.

Then he opened the drawers of his dresser.

The young boy with the bright future proceeded to the living room, his purpose clear, his mind unclouded. The killings were well planned. In the living room, Jenny watched as her mother adjusted the controls of the TV. Mr. Andrews was engrossed in the daily paper.

No one paid attention to Lee. He stood in the doorway and calmly slammed four slugs into his mother. She died instantly. Jenny turned.

Lee fired three times. One of the slugs smashed into Jenny's brain, killing her before she crumpled to the living room floor. Mr. Andrews managed to rise and move into the kitchen before bullets entered his back. He staggered. Lee followed, firing as he went until his father sprawled dead on the floor. Standing over his father, Lee fired into his body again and again. An autopsy would later reveal that the dead man had been shot 17 times. The house became deadly quiet.

Calmly following his preconceived plan, Lee drove his father's car to the Kaw River and threw away his two weapons. He smiled as he heard the splash. So much for incriminating weapons.

Lee continued to his room at the University of Kansas in Lawrence. He spoke to his landlady, being careful to mention that he was there to pick up his typewriter and that it had taken him a long time to get there due to the icy condition of the roads. That took care of one witness who would place him in Lawrence at the time of the murders, but you couldn't be too sure in this business. Lee took in a movie called *Mardi Gras*, and talked for some time to a girl behind the confectionery counter. On the way home, he purchased gasoline, making sure to get a receipt. That should do it for alibi witnesses.

Lee arrived home about 1 a.m. He called police, who arrived at the house 10 minutes later. They found Lee sitting in the sun room, petting the family dog. When the police inquired as to the nature of the emergency call, Lee didn't say anything. He just nodded toward the living room.

Inside the house were the bodies of the Andrews family.

Police turned to Lee. The bright boy with the bright future didn't realize that most people, who stumble on the bodies of their sister and parents, are usually upset. Lee was cool as a cucumber. He related his story without shedding a tear. He had had Thanksgiving dinner with his family, had gone to Lawrence to pick up a typewriter, had taken in a movie and had filled the family car with gas on his way home. He volunteered that burglars must have entered the house through his bedroom window.

Investigators followed Lee to his bedroom. They expected to find the room in shambles. Instead, they noticed that while drawers were pulled out, nothing had been scattered about the room. This was the tidiest burglary the police had ever encountered. They were also surprised to learn that nothing had been stolen from the house.

The big lumbering boy didn't seem to care that his entire family had been murdered. It wasn't natural. The police questioned Lee in detail about his activities. He told them that he had been to Lawrence - his landlady would verify that. He had taken in a movie - the girl at the confectionery counter would verify that. He had purchased gas on the way home. Sure, he had a receipt.

It was all too much. The boy had left so many tracks a Boy Scout could have traced his movements. Lee was informed that he was a prime suspect in the triple murder. When he was taken to jail, he asked to speak to his father's best friend, Rev. Dameron. In minutes, the minister was brought up to date on the crime. Like police, he was amazed at Lee's nonchalant demeanor.

Lee had not planned it this way, not at all. Rev. Dameron seemed to be as suspicious as the police. It was obvious that he believed that Lee had committed the murders. When the reverend asked, "You didn't do it, did you?" Lee replied in his usual calm manner, "Yes, I did."

Now that Lee had confessed to the murder, his minister pressed him for his motive until the boy admitted that he had wanted his family's money.

The entire town of Grandview attended the Andrews funeral. Lee wasn't one of their number. Throughout his incarceration and trial, he remained calm and collected. His lawyers attempted to prove that he was insane at the time he committed the murders and that he had acted impulsively. The state produced the bread man, who testified that Lee had cancelled the usual bread delivery on the afternoon of the murders. Only Lee knew there would be no one alive at the Andrews home after the Thanksgiving Day meal.

Lee was convicted of the murders of his family and was sentenced to death. He never displayed any remorse for what he had done. On November 30, 1962, 22-year-old Lee Andrews was hanged at Lansing Prison.

DIETER BECK

Ingrid Kanike's parents never even knew their 23-year-old daughter had been delayed. She often took the train from her home in Rehme, Germany to Minden. Usually, she arrived home after midnight when her parents were already in bed and left for work in the morning before they got up.

On Friday, April 17, 1961, Ingrid took in a movie in Minden, but she never returned home. On Saturday morning, Oscar Riedel was on his way to work at a local factory near the Rehme railway station. There, lying in a ditch, was the body of a young girl. She had been raped and strangled. Ingrid Kanike would never see her parents again.

Police examined the girl's purse, which was found near her body. It contained the usual items, including some money. Investigators were convinced that nothing had been removed from the purse. They felt that someone had randomly attacked the girl after she had disembarked from the train.

It was established that Ingrid was fearful of walking home alone after midnight and always took a cab. Investigators questioned the 20 people who had arrived on the 12:07 train from Minden. Not one could remember having seen Ingrid. Cab drivers who regularly met the train were questioned. Several recalled Ingrid having been their passenger on previous nights, but they swore they hadn't seen her on the night of the murder. For some reason, on this particular night, Ingrid had chosen to walk from the station to her home rather than take a cab.

The first murder in 20 years in a town of 35,000 caused quite a stir. Girls who normally walked alone at night were now afraid to venture outdoors. Husbands and boyfriends accompanied their mates wherever they went. As time went by, the incident faded from people's minds. The general feeling was that a stranger had plucked a local girl off the streets and, after satisfying his abnormal urges, had moved on.

When the investigation wound down, Ingrid's parents consulted Dutch clairvoyant Gerard Croiset. He told them that the killer worked in a machine factory near Rehme, which was not too helpful as there were several machine factories in the area employing hundreds of men.

Four years after Ingrid's murder, another young woman was killed in a similar fashion. On May 17, 1965, Ursula Fritz, a 26-year-old secretary failed to show up at her place of employment in Herford, about eight miles down the road from Rehme. Her employer figured she had quit her job and made no inquiries. Eight days later, Ursula's landlady decided to use her passkey to open the door to the young woman's room. The rent was overdue and she hadn't seen her roomer for over a week. Once the bedroom door was open, it was obvious why Ursula had not been heard from. She was lying, strangled and raped, on her own bed.

There was no forced entry to the room. In fact, it appeared that Ursula was quite friendly with her killer, which was contradictory to her lifestyle. She had no boyfriends, certainly none that had ever been invited to her room, yet there were two glasses on a coffee table, one of which bore Ursula's fingerprints, while a smeared set of male prints were lifted from the other. Gray serge fibres from a man's suit were found on the bedclothes.

Police in Herford sent out details of the crime to all surrounding towns and cities. It didn't take long before the current crime was connected to the similar murder of Ingrid Kanike, which had taken place four years previously. Was a serial killer on the loose? That was the fear of residents of the surrounding towns.

Despite the many clues pertaining to the most recent murder, police couldn't get a lead to the killer's identity. In desperation they decided to requestion all the cab drivers who had met the 12:07 train from Minden four years earlier.

When one cabbie, August Fennel, gave a statement which conflicted with the one he had given years earlier, police pounced. Fennel admitted that he had lied in his earlier statement. His reason was simple enough. He didn't want to get involved in a murder investigation.

Under threat of being charged with obstructing a police investigation, Fennel admitted that Ingrid had entered his cab when she had disembarked from the 12:07 train. She had been accompanied by a good looking man who had instructed him to stop the cab, saying, "We will walk the rest of the way." Fennel was sure Ingrid had willingly accompanied the stranger. When Fennel was shown photos of men who had been on the train that night, he could not pick out the one who had been in his cab with Ingrid. It appeared to detectives that Ingrid must have met the man on the train.

Once again, police pored over the male passenger list, eliminating those with ironclad alibis, as well as those who were too young or too old. Finally, they were left with four men - Otto Johanns and Emil Bach from Rehme, Carl Mueller from Minden and Dieter Beck from Bielefeld. It was felt that Fennel would have recognized the first two men, whom he knew by sight. The remaining two men, Mueller and Beck, worked at machine tool plants in Rehme, which brought to mind clairvoyant Croiset's opinion that Ingrid Kanike's killer worked at such a factory. Still, there was no proof that either man was involved in the murders.

The killer struck again on February 28, 1968, almost three years after Ursula Fritz's murder. The victim was 21-year-old Anneliese Herschel of nearby Werther. Her body was found by railway track inspector Leopold Beisel beside the tracks about a mile from Bielefeld. Anneliese had been raped and strangled. She was thought to be the third victim of the serial killer who let long periods of time elapse between murders.

Police found a book of matches in the victim's coat,

advertising the Igloo Bar, Kon St., Bielefeld. The manager of
the bar remembered Anneliese. He stated that she had been
in his establishment and had left with a man on the night she
was murdered. Police showed photographs of several suspects, including Mueller and Beck, to the bar owner. He
picked out the photograph of Dieter Beck as the man who
had left his bar with Anneliese. Two other employees inde-
pendently identified Beck's photo as well.

Dieter Beck was located and taken into custody. He
unhesitatingly admitted killing all three women. Dieter had
chosen them because they were slightly overweight or not
very attractive. He figured they would be easy to meet casu-
ally and might even consider themselves fortunate to make
the acquaintance of a rather handsome young man. Dieter
told police, "I didn't want to kill those girls. It's just something that comes over me and then I can't help myself." Over
the years in which he raped and killed three women, Dieter
carried on normal sexual relations with several women, all of
whom claimed he was a considerate, gentle lover.

In June 1969, Dieter Beck stood trial on three counts of
premeditated murder. He was found guilty on all three
charges and sentenced to three terms of life imprisonment.

DAVID BERKOWITZ

Seldom has an individual criminal managed to hold an entire city in a grip of terror. Jack the Ripper did it by killing and mutilating five prostitutes in London, England, in the autumn of 1888. In more recent times the Boston Strangler assaulted and murdered 13 women. In so doing, he kept the entire city of Boston in a state of fear.

It takes a series of unusual criminal acts to make the good citizens of New York City sit up and take notice. Almost every bizarre occurrence perpetrated by man has taken place in Gotham. The natives are accustomed to the unusual.

When Bette and Tony Falco gave birth to little David Richard on June 1, 1953, they had already decided to put their newborn son up for adoption. The details had all been arranged.

Pearl Berkowitz was an active woman who, at 38, had been informed by her doctors that she could never conceive. Her husband Nathan, a hardware store owner, had often discussed adopting a child with his wife. It was Pearl and Nathan who drove David Richard home from the hospital. They didn't know the soft, cuddly bundle Pearl held so gently was a potential monster. Eighteen months later David Richard Falco legally became David Richard Berkowitz.

David grew up to be a quiet, introverted little boy. In hindsight, many friends and neighbors who knew him during his formative years later came forward with some anecdote or other illustrating a streak of meanness or cruelty in David as a child. In actuality there was probably nothing to distinguish David from thousands of other children being brought up in like circumstances.

When David was 14 his mother died of cancer, after a long and painful bout with the dreaded disease. Pearl had been a kind and loving mother, and we have every reason to believe that her son was truly affected by her death. In 1971, when Nathan remarried, David displayed open resentment toward his stepmother.

His father's marriage coincided with David's joining the army. David, who had always expressed patriotic sentiments toward his country, was shipped off to Fort Dix, New Jersey. During rugged basic training he showed some skill with a rifle. Pursuing his natural aptitude, he soon qualified as a sharpshooter.

From Fort Dix, David was sent to Fort Polk, Louisiana, for advanced training. On December 13, 1971, he was shipped to Korea, where he served with the 17th Infantry, 1st Battalion. After his tour of duty, David was posted to Fort Knox, Kentucky. On June 24, 1974, he was discharged from the U.S. Army after serving three years.

David returned to his parents' apartment in the Bronx. He was mildly surprised to find out that they were trying to sell their apartment in order to retire to Florida. By the end of the year David had found a one-bedroom apartment for himself at 2161 Barnes Ave. in the Bronx. He registered at the Bronx Community College in February 1975, where he attained a high C average. During the summer he worked for his uncle as a sheet metal worker. To all outward appearances, David Berkowitz was going to make something of himself.

Donna Lauria was an attractive, 18-year-old with shoulder-length brown hair. Donna and her friend Jody Valente were sitting outside Donna's apartment building double parked in Jody's car. It was 1:10 a.m. on a hot July morning in 1976. Donna's parents walked by and entered the apartment building. Without warning, a man appeared beside the automobile occupied by the two girls. He pointed a long barrelled revolver at Donna's head and fired. Donna Lauria was dead without ever knowing what had happened. A .44 cali-

11

bre slug slammed into Jody's left thigh. Despite bleeding profusely, her wound was not serious. No one knew it at the time, but the killer later to be known and feared as the Son of Sam had claimed his first victim.

A short time later David Berkowitz left his sheet metal job.

Rosemary Keenan and Carl Denaro, a pair of 20 year olds, had promised to meet friends at a tavern in Flushing. It was about two in the morning when they drove into the tavern parking lot. Carl was about to open the car door when a bullet crashed through the car window and lodged in his head. Fortunately the slug missed Carl's brain. His friends from the tavern rushed him to the nearest hospital, where an emergency operation, lasting over two hours, saved his life. The senseless attack on Carl Denaro and his girlfriend was not connected at the time with the Lauria-Valente shooting.

On a cool November night two teenagers, Joanne Lomino and Donna DeMasi, sat on Joanne's front steps talking about boyfriends and job opportunities. The two girls had taken in a movie and had finished off their night out with hamburgers. Now they were preparing to part. Out of the darkness a man approached the girls. He appeared to be of average height, about 30 years old, and wore a green army-type three-quarter length coat. The man extracted a revolver from his belt and began shooting.

The first slug entered Donna's neck and shattered her collarbone. She fell to the sidewalk. Joanne took a slug directly into her back. Of the five shots fired at the girls, three went astray. Donna DeMasi recovered from the attack, but Joanne Lomino will forever remain paralyzed from the waist down. The mad killer who used a .44-calibre revolver had struck again.

John Diel was a 30-year-old bartender. He and his girlfriend, Christine Freund, had a lot to talk over. They were planning to get engaged in two weeks time. Now, as they sat talking well past midnight on the morning of January 30, they had no way of knowing there would be no engagement party. Christine would be dead in a matter of hours. Two explosions interrupted their conversation, sending a shower of windshield glass cascading into the interior of the car. Diel lifted his girlfriend's limp form out of the car and gently placed her on the ground. At 4:30 a.m. Christine died in hospital from bullet wounds to the head.

The wanton attacks had all been treated as individual cases. Now the cases were cross checked, and police attributed the attacks to the frenzy of one man. Lauria, Valente, Denaro, Lomino, DeMasi, and Freund. A monster with a .44-calibre revolver was loose on the streets of New York. No wonder the police could find no motive for the individual attacks. The madman didn't even know the victims. He killed at random.

David Berkowitz applied for a job at the Bronx General Post Office. He scored an exceptional 85.5% on the post office test. David got the job on a part-time basis at $7 an hour.

Virginia Voskerichian was a 19-year-old student at Columbia University. She lived in fashionable Forest Hills Garden with her parents. One evening in March, as she walked home, the crazed killer shot her dead with his .44-calibre revolver.

Back at the Bronx Post Office David Berkowitz often talked of the .44-calibre killer to fellow employees. It seemed to be one of the few topics pleasant, quiet David liked to talk about.

Valentina Suriani lived at 1950 Hutchinson St., only a few streets from the killer's first victim, Donna Lauria. Valentina attended Lehman College, where she was majoring in acting. Her fiancé, Alexander Esau, parked his car early on the morning of April 19. Both fell under the rage that burned within the .44-calibre killer. This time he left a sealed envelope beside the bodies of his victims. The contents of the letter were not revealed by the police at the time. From it police knew that the killer had no intention of curtailing his murderous rampage.

The killer then wrote to Daily News columnist Jimmy Breslin, signing his letter Son of Sam. The letter was authentic, having been written by the same crazed mind which had composed the letter found beside Valentina Suriani's body.

In April 1977, within days of the Suriani-Esau murders, a man not connected with any victim, Sam Carr, received an anonymous letter at his home at 316 Warbuton Avenue. in Yonkers. It contained gibberish about his Labrador retriever being a menace, saying that the dog should be removed from his home. Carr mentioned the crazy letter to members of his family and then dismissed the incident from his mind. He then received another more threatening letter, but still did nothing abut it.

On April 27, someone shot Sam Carr's Labrador retriever. The dog, Harvey, had been severely wounded in the thigh. Carr was to spend over $1,000 to save his dog, but the bullet remained lodged in Harvey's thigh. After this incident, Carr took the letters to the Yonkers police. They attributed the letters and the shooting as the work of a schizophrenic, but did not connect the incident to the mass killings which were now under the jurisdiction of a task force formed exclusively to capture the .44-calibre killer.

David Berkowitz had moved. He now lived at 35 Pine St. in Yonkers. His apartment building backed on to Sam Carr's back yard.

Sal Lupo and Judy Placido frequented the same discotheque in Queens. They had never dated, but knew each other rather well and often danced together. Judy was in a good mood. She had just graduated from St. Catherines Academy that day. Now, it was after 3 a.m. Sunday morning, June 26. One of the main topics of conversation that evening was the crazed murderer who killed without reason.

Sal asked Judy if he could drive her home. Judy, still wearing her special graduation dress, was thrilled to accept the ride. Before Sal could turn the ignition key in his car four slugs poured into the interior of the car. The wound inflicted to Sal's arm was not serious. Judy had taken one bullet behind the right ear. One lodged close to her spinal cord, and the third pierced her right shoulder. All three bullets were removed from Judy's body, and miraculously she recovered. The bullets were .44-calibre and had been fired from the same weapon which had felled the other victims.

David Berkowitz did commendable work at the post office. He often told fellow employees that he sure hoped the police would catch that Son of Sam fellow. A year had passed since the first Son of Sam murder.

Sixteen-year-old Stacy Moskowitz of Brooklyn had been asked out by the best looking boy she had ever dated. Robert Violante, a recent graduate of Brooklyn's New Utrecht High, was by any standards a handsome young man. Before seeing a play, Stacy brought Robert home to meet her family.

After the play and a bite to eat, the young people parked alongside the Shore Parkway at Bay 14th St. Several other cars were parked there. Four successive explosions roared into the open car window. Robert received a bullet in the temple which exited at the bridge of his nose. He recovered, but will only have partial sight for the rest of his life. Stacy Moskowitz died later in hospital.

David Berkowitz left his job at the post office a few days later and never returned.

On the night of Stacy Moskowitz' murder, Mrs. Cacalia Davis took her dog Snowball for a walk. As she walked she fixed her gaze on a young man approaching from the opposite direction. They passed within touching distance of each other. Mrs. Davis noticed that the young man's right arm was stiff. Later she found out it was because Son of Sam carried his .44-calibre revolver up his sleeve.

Next day, when Mrs. Davis became aware of the murder which had taken place close to her home, she was positive that it was Son of Sam whom she passed on the sidewalk. She informed the police of her suspicions. When she told her story she mentioned that during her walk with Snowball she had noticed a cop writing out a traffic ticket for a car parked too near a hydrant.

Police checked on all traffic tickets issued in the early morning hours in that area. There were only three. Two had been issued to respectable citizens in their late sixties. The third was issued to David R. Berkowitz.

Son of Sam, who had terrorized an entire city for over a year was to be taken into custody because he had parked too close to a hydrant. When picked up, Berkowitz' car yielded a sub-machine gun, a rifle with several boxes of ammunition, and a .44 Charter Arms Bulldog small revolver. Later it was proven that the .44 was the weapon which Son of Sam had used for over a year.

Why had David Berkowitz killed six innocent individuals and wounded seven others? He had no choice. You see, the devil who lived in Sam Carr's Labrador retriever Harvey commanded him to kill.

David Berkowitz was adjudged unfit to stand trial by reason of insanity. No doubt he will spend the rest of his life in custody.

KEN BIANCHI
ANGELO BUONO

Yolanda Washington couldn't support her baby on the money she earned as a waitress. That's why she turned to prostitution. Her beat was Sunset and Vista in Hollywood, California. Yolanda did pretty well at her profession, averaging somewhere between $500 and $1,000 a week. Not bad for a 19-year-old. It beat depending on tips in a restaurant.

On October 17, 1977, at 11 p.m. Yolanda let herself be picked up. Next day her body was found on a Los Angeles hillside. She had been strangled to death before being tossed out of a car. Semen samples indicated that two men had had sexual relations with her before death.

Judy Miller was only 15, but was already a part-time prostitute who sold whatever charms she possessed along Hollywood Blvd. in order to keep herself supplied with pot and pills. On October 31, Judy disappeared from her usual haunts. Her nude body was found near La Crescenta just outside of L.A. She had not been thrown from a car, but had been carried to her final resting place. Footprints indicated that two men, one holding the body by the arms, the other by the head, had carried Judy to where she was found. Judy had been gagged, bound, and strangled. She had also been raped. Police did not connect Judy's death to that of Yolanda Washington's.

Lissa Kastin, 21, unlike the first two victims, was neither a prostitute nor a drug user. She worked as a waitress, and also for her father's construction firm on a part-time basis. Her real ambition was a career in show business and Lissa was making some headway. She and some other girls had formed a dance group and were good enough to obtain bookings in several local clubs. Lissa's body was found on the side of a hill in Glendale. She had been bound, raped, and strangled to death. Physical evidence at the scene of the crime indicated that two men were responsible. Detectives met to discuss the similarities of the three recent murders.

The killing spree continued. Jane Evelyn King, 28, an actress and part-time model, was murdered on November 9. Her body was discovered two weeks later near the Golden State Freeway.

Two friends, Dolores Cepeda, 12, and Sonja Johnson, were last seen near the Eagle Rock Shopping Centre on November 13. Their bodies were found on a hillside near downtown Los Angeles.

No one remembers who coined the phrase The Hillside Strangler, but the name stuck. Women of all ages took precautions against the madmen who raped and strangled without mercy. Throughout Los Angeles women walked in groups, husbands picked up wives after work, while many women carried weapons and warning devices. The Hillside Strangler was the main topic of conversation in L.A., but still the killings continued.

On November 19, Kristina Weckler, 20, an art student, was strangled to death before being deposited in Highland Park. Lauren Wagner, 18, was murdered November 28.

A break in the pattern occurred with the murder of 17-year-old Kimberly Martin. Despite her tender years, Kim was a hardened, experienced prostitute. Because of the Hillside Strangler's well-known penchant for prostitutes, Kim decided to protect herself in the pursuit of her risky profession. She secured employment with a nude modelling agency, which was in reality a front for a call-in prostitution service.

Girls like Kimberly would wait for calls from the agency, and would be sent out to perform their unique services. The advantage to Kim would be the screening done by the agency before giving her the assignment. Supposedly this procedure would eliminate the weirdos.

Kim obtained an assignment from the agency on December 13. Her body was found on a hillside near downtown L.A. While investigating the murder, detectives obtained the address of Kim's last assignment. It turned out to be a vacant apartment in the Tamarino Apartments.

The apartment had been wiped clean of fingerprints, but police believed that Kim's murderers had waited for her in the unoccupied apartment. They felt that the victim had been bound and beaten before being led out of the apartment to be strangled elsewhere.

Police questioned all the tenants in the apartment building, and found out that several tenants had heard noises coming from the vacant apartment on the night of Kim's disappearance. No one had investigated.

Many of the tenants detected that the police officers questioning them were unnecessarily gruff and abrasive in their manner. Several officers felt a degree of animosity towards people who did not want to get involved. If someone had reported the scuffle, the vicious killers might have been caught in the act.

It was refreshing to interrogate clean-cut handsome Ken Bianchi, even though he hadn't heard any noises. He was most co-operative and understanding. Bianchi seemed concerned about the safety of his pregnant live-in girlfriend, Kelli Boyd. Ken hardly ever let Kelli walk alone on the streets after the questioning.

Death took a holiday over the Christmas season. It wasn't until February 17, 1978, that 20-year-old Cindy Lee Hudspeth's nude body was found strangled in the trunk of her car in Glendale. No one knew it at the time, but the notorious Hillside Strangler, whose exploits were now being reported throughout the world, had struck in L.A. for the last time.

Kelli Boyd gave birth to her baby. She and Ken Bianchi named the boy Sean. After the baby was born Kelli informed

Ken that she was returning to her home town of Bellingham, Washington, to give her baby a proper home with her family. Ken was heartbroken. He loved Sean and couldn't believe Kelli would leave him. Kelli explained that Ken didn't earn enough to support a family, and besides, he seemed more concerned with visiting and playing cards with his cousin Angelo Buono than raising a family.

Kelli left. Ken wrote letters and poems, pleading for another chance. Kelli relented, and Ken joined her in Bellingham to begin a new life. The good citizens of the community, located just south of Vancouver, had no way of knowing it at the time, but the Hillside Strangler was now among them.

On Friday, January 12, 1979, two Western Washington University students, Karen Mandik and Diane Wilder, were reported missing. Both girls were responsible, serious students, whose absence caused immediate concern. Their known movements were carefully traced. On Thursday Karen, who worked part-time at a department store, left the store and picked up Diane, who was her roommate. The girls had a chance to earn some easy money that night. A wealthy family who were travelling in Europe normally had their home fully protected by an alarm system operated by a highly respectable protection agency. Apparently the alarm system had failed, and Karen had received an offer of $100 to house-sit for two hours while the alarm was being repaired. Karen brought Diane along for company. When Karen failed to return to the department store, police were notified.

Detectives found out that Karen had received her generous house-sitting job from Ken Bianchi, a young man whom she had met some months before when he worked as a security guard at the department store. Ken had moved to a good job with a protection company.

Detectives learned that Bianchi had lied in order to get the use of a company van on the night of the girls' disappearance. He had told a fellow worker that he was taking the van into a garage for repairs, but the garage had no record of repairing the vehicle. Karen's phone number was found on a piece of paper in Ken's home.

At 4:30 p.m. on the day following the missing person's report, the two girls were found murdered in Karen's car, parked in a wooded side street. They had been strangled. Detectives immediately arrested Ken Bianchi while they continued to amass evidence against him. By now the similarities between the Bellingham double murder and the handiwork of the Hillside Strangler was recognized. Clean-cut Ken Bianchi was quite possibly a monster in disguise.

On March 21, 1979, Bianchi gave a highly detailed confession of the murders while in a hypnotic state. He claimed that he was not Ken when he murdered but was controlled by his other half, Steve. Bianchi claimed that while he was Steve he and his cousin Angelo Buono had killed all ten Hillside Strangler victims in Los Angeles. He later confessed in minute detail to the double murder in Bellingham.

Doctors were divided in their opinion. Was Ken Bianchi a bona fide example of a multiple personality, or was he conning the doctors in an attempt to save his skin?

As the investigation into Buono's past was being undertaken, the judicial system as it applied to Bianchi was slowly grinding to a conclusion. For the Bellingham killings he received two consecutive life sentences. He was then shunted off to L.A., where he received several additional life terms. Bianchi's lawyers had made a deal. Their client escaped the death sentence in return for his testimony against Buono. It is doubtful that Bianchi will ever be a free man again.

Ken Bianchi has repudiated all his confessions since his conviction and has become a shaky and less than credible witness for the state against his cousin Angelo, who has steadfastly maintained his innocence. Since Bianchi has admitted and subsequently denied involvement in all of the murders, he is obviously a liar, which weakened his usefulness as a prosecution witness against Buono.

Despite the lies, the evidence against Buono proved to be overwhelming. He was tried, found guilty, and sentenced to nine life terms in prison with no possibility of parole.

ARTHUR BISHOP

The area in and around Salt Lake City was caught in a grip of fear. Was it possible that here, in the very centre of the Mormon faith, a mad serial killer was preying on little boys?

On October 14, 1979, four-year-old Alonzo Daniels left his apartment, as he did most days, to play in the backyard. Mrs. Daniels, who had a clear view of her son from her kitchen window, observed Alonzo imitating an airplane taking off from the ground. She smiled and went on with her chores.

A few minutes later, she glanced out the window. Alonzo was nowhere to be seen. Mrs. Daniels ran out to the yard. Alonzo had vanished. She would never see her son alive again.

Neighbors searched the yard and the apartment building basement. Police interviewed the occupants of the entire building. Adjacent buildings were searched. It had happened in Salt Lake City. A youngster had apparently been carried away in broad daylight without being seen by anyone and without leaving a trace.

Thirteen months later, 11-year-old Kim Peterson told his parents that a man he had met at a skating rink had offered to purchase his skates. Kim wanted a new pair. This was his chance to add to the monies he had already saved.

On November 9, 1980, Kim informed his parents that he had been offered $35 for his old skates. He ran out of the house, shouting over his shoulder that he had an appointment to meet with the prospective purchaser on a street corner. When Kim failed to return home, his parents notified police.

Detectives interviewed everyone at the skating rink who could have seen Kim speaking to an older man. Several witnesses recalled seeing him. The man he was talking to was chubby, wore blue jeans and an army-type jacket. Most thought he was between 25 and 35 years of age.

Several witnesses agreed to undergo hypnosis in order to better describe the suspect. In this way, police learned that he was six feet tall, 200 pounds, with bushy eyebrows. That's as far as they got. The investigation wound down.

A year later, on October 20, 1981, four-year-old Danny Davis went shopping at a supermarket with his grandfather. The little boy was hardly out of his grandfather's sight, yet he vanished.

Store employees and customers frantically searched for the youngster. Police were summoned. They were successful in locating several customers who remembered seeing a little boy fitting Danny's description playing with a gumball machine. Ominously, they also recalled a male adult helping Danny work the machine.

That evening, as searchers roamed the desert and nearby hills, the temperature dropped to zero. It was imperative they locate the missing youngster, as he might die of exposure if left out all night. He was wearing only a t-shirt, thongs and a pair of light blue trousers.

Next day, police divers searched Big Cottonwood Creek. Every pond and ditch was combed without results. Posters throughout Utah displayed Danny's photo. The hunt for Danny Davis was the largest ever conducted in and around Salt Lake City up to that time.

While the investigation into Danny's disappearance yielded no useful clues, it made officials aware that all three youngsters had disappeared within two weeks of Hallowe'en in three consecutive years. As Hollowe'en of 1982 approached and passed, they breathed a sigh of relief. It was possible that the man who plucked boys out of their backyards, off street corners and out of supermarkets had relocated or even died.

Their relief did not last long. On June 22, 1983, Troy Ward, celebrating his sixth birthday, was abducted from the play area of Liberty Park. After an extensive search, the best the police could come up with was a witness who saw a boy matching Troy's description leaving the park with a young smiling man. The youngster and the man got along so well the witness thought the stranger was the little boy's father.

By now, slayings in neighboring states were being checked for similarities with the Salt Lake City crimes. No connection could be found between these crimes and the ones committed in and around Salt Lake City. The Hallowe'en theory was thrown out as a coincidence.

Graeme Cunningham, 13, was excited about going on a camping trip with a teenaged buddy and an older man, Roger Downs, 32, a highly-respected accountant. Two days before they were to leave on the trip to the Lake Tahoe area, Graeme disappeared.

Downs and Graeme's friend went on the camping trip. They appeared to be genuinely surprised when they returned to learn that Graeme had not been located. Police questioned Downs as to his relationship with the missing boy. Initially, Downs could offer no useful information, but gradually police detected discrepancies in his story. Little by little, he broke down. After a night of questioning, Roger Downs confessed to sexually attacking and murdering the five boys.

Next day, Downs led police to the gravesites of Alonzo Daniels, Danny Davis and Kim Peterson. Displaying great willingness to co-opperate, Downs next led police some 100 kilometres to Big Cottonwood Creek, where he pointed out the burial sites of Troy Ward and Graeme Cunningham.

Downs would only tell police that he had killed the boys because he was afraid they would tell their parents of his sexual advances.

A thorough check of the mild-mannered accountant's past revealed that his real name was Arthur Bishop. Bishop was born in Hinckley, a small town in Utah. In high school, he was an honor student, an Eagle Scout and a devout Mormon. He graduated with honors in accounting from Stevens Henager College.

Then, something went drastically wrong. In February 1978, Arthur was accused of embezzling more than $8,000 from a car dealership where he was employed. He pleaded guilty and was placed on five years' probation. Arthur promptly skipped and was excommunicated from the Mormon Church.

He roamed the country working at odd jobs and changing his name frequently. Using the name Roger Downs, he settled in Salt Lake City.

Arthur Bishop was charged with five counts of first degree murder. At his trial, the jury deliberated only five hours before finding him guilty of all five murders. Bishop has never displayed any remorse for his horrible crimes. In fact, during his taped confession, he said, "I'm glad they caught me, because I'd do it again."

Bishop was sentenced to death. In compliance with Utah law, he was given the choice of death by firing squad or lethal injection. He chose lethal injection.

As this is written, Arthur Bishop languishes on Death Row awaiting his execution.

IAN BRADY
MYRA HINDLEY

The story you are about to read involves two of the most reprehensible criminals who ever lived. The depths to which their depraved acts plummeted have not been equalled in modern times. If the retelling of this grisly true tale cautions just one parent to the dangers of allowing their children to accompany not only strange men, but strange women, then this effort will have been proven worthwhile.

At 12:40 p.m. on January 2, 1938, unwed Margaret Stewart gave birth to a son in Rotten Row Maternity Hospital, Glasgow, Scotland. For the first 12 years of his life foster parents brought up the lad as if he were their own child. Margaret, a waitress, visited her son Ian at every opportunity and contributed financially to his upbringing. In 1950, Margaret met Patrick Brady of Manchester. Recognizing her chance for happiness and escape from the slums of Glasgow, she married Patrick and moved to Manchester. Ian remained with his foster parents.

Ian was not your average child. There is evidence of his cruelty to animals while still in his preteens. He threw cats off five-storey buildings to prove that they didn't have nine lives. Once he crucified a frog and relished the sheer agony he caused the helpless creature. Between the ages of 12 and 15 he broke into several shops and houses, getting caught more often than not. Judges were lenient with the pale, lean lad who stood before them. Each time he was apprehended he was put on probation so that he could continue his schooling.

When Ian was 15, he left school and was promptly charged with nine counts of housebreaking. His foster parents gave up. They would have nothing more to do with the problem child. He was given one more chance by another lenient magistrate, and left Glasgow to live with his mother and stepfather in Manchester. He took his stepfather's last name, becoming Ian Brady.

Ian drank, couldn't keep a job and continued to break into houses. Apprehended again in the act, he finally met a magistrate who sentenced him to two years in Borstal. On June 9, 1958 Ian was released from prison, but nothing had changed. He sometimes worked in a Manchester fruit market, but still couldn't hold a steady job. In February 1959, Ian answered a newspaper ad for a clerical position. He got the job at Millards Merchandise Ltd., a chemical supply company in West Gorton, Manchester. The job paid £12 a week. Ian kept to himself, opened the firm's mail and filed orders. At night he read about Adolph Hitler and the Marquis de Sade.

Myra Hindley was born in 1942 on Eaton St., Gorton, in the slums of Manchester. When she was four, her mother gave birth to a second daughter, Maureen. As the result of the overcrowding at Eaton St., Myra moved in with her grandmother a block down the street. She seldom saw her paratrooper father. Although her IQ was slightly above average, she was not a particularly good student. Myra left school while in her teens and drifted from job to job. Finally she managed to secure a position as a shorthand typist. The job paid £8.10 a week. It was with Millwards in West Gorton. Much of her typing was for a lean, pale, rather eccentric young man who fascinated Myra. His name was Ian Brady.

We will never know what catalyst was at work in the offices of Millwards which allowed two children of the slums to meet, become infatuated with each other and ultimately to become monsters living in the guise of human beings. The pair became inseparable. Myra purchased a mini-van, and since Ian didn't drive, it was she who chauffeured the pair to and from work.

Throughout the years Myra remained friendly with her younger sister Maureen, who joined Millwards in 1963. Now that the sisters were employed under the same roof, Myra confided to Maureen that she was having an affair with Ian Brady. When Myra and her grandmother moved to Wardle Brook Ave. in Hattesley, Ian moved in with them. The elderly grandmother kept to herself and never interfered with the machinations of Myra and her live-in boyfriend.

Slowly Ian's fascination with Nazi Germany began to rub off on Myra. She became enthralled with Irma Grese, the Beast of Belsen, and tried to emulate her heroine. Evenings were spent experimenting with sexual perversions, drinking cheap wine, and wandering the countryside outside Manchester in the mini-van. On their days off, Ian would indulge in his hobby, photography. Myra was a willing model, posing in the nude in every conceivable position or stance which Ian suggested.

Mrs. Sheila Kilbride gave her 12-year-old son John a peck on the cheek before he scampered off with a friend to attend the movies. The two lads left the movie theatre at 5 p.m. and wandered over to Ashton Market to see if they could perform some odd jobs for the tradesmen. It was getting late. John's friend caught a bus home. He last saw John talking to a friendly blonde lady. The lady was Myra Hindley.

Little John Kilbride never returned home. Police were notified and a comprehensive search followed. Months were to pass without the police uncovering anything approaching a clue as to what happened to the missing boy.

Ten-year-old Lesley Downey was excited this Boxing Day of 1964. Her mother had reluctantly given her permission to attend a fair being held only 200 yards from her home. Lesley was stepping out with neighborhood children. It all seemed so harmless. By 5 pm., Mrs. Jean Downey became apprehensive when little Lesley failed to return home. She called on her neighbors and was startled to find out that the other children had been home for some time.

A mini-van parked ominously beside the fair grounds. Every so often the van circled the fair grounds, its occupants looking for a young girl. There's one! A little girl watched the bobbing painted heads of the wooden ponies on the merry go round. The mini-van came to an abrupt stop. A blonde woman approached the little girl and the pair began talking. It wasn't long before the blonde woman found out that the youngster had spent all her money. The blonde lady volunteered that she would be happy to pay for another ride and another after that. What 10-year-old child could resist such good fortune? Lesley Downey jumped on the wooden pony. Later she mentioned to the young lady that she'd better get home as her mother would begin to worry. The kind lady urged the child not to be concerned. She would personally give her a lift in her mini-van so she needn't be late after all. Lesley knew everything would be all right. Her mother had told her never to accept a ride with a strange man, but she had never said anything about a friendly, kind lady.

Lesley Downey jumped into the mini-van beside her friend Myra Hindley. In the shadows in the back seat, behind the unsuspecting child, lurked Ian Brady.

Lesley Downey was never seen again. A massive search was conducted by police which involved the questioning of 5,000 individuals and the distribution of 6,000 posters. Weeks turned into months, until gradually the investigation into the mystery of Lesley's disappearance wound down. Ten months after her ride in the mini-van her fate was to make headlines around the world.

When Myra's younger sister Maureen married David Smith, it seemed most natural for the two couples to become close friends. Especially so, since the Smiths moved into an apartment within walking distance of Myra and Ian. David Smith was not exactly lily white. He had been in several scrapes with the law and had an assault conviction on his record. David could never hold down a job for any period of time. He welcomed Ian's hospitality.

The two men were accustomed to staying up half the night drinking cheap wine, while Myra and Maureen went to bed. During one of these lengthy drinking bouts, Ian broached David with the idea that they rob a bank. He told David he had been planning such a caper for years. David seemed receptive, but Ian's scheme didn't progress beyond the planning stages.

The strange double life being led by Ian Brady and Myra Hindley erupted into violence and terror on the night of October 6, 1965. On that night, Myra's 77-year-old grandmother took a sleeping pill at 8:30 p.m. and retired for the night. Myra and Ian cruised the streets of Manchester in her mini-van. Myra parked the vehicle near Central Station while Ian took a stroll. He soon returned with 17-year-old Edward Evans. Edward was a homosexual who had gladly accepted an invitation to return to Ian's home for a drink.

Once back at Wardle Brook Ave., Ian and Edward engaged in conversation while Myra called on her brother-in-law, David Smith. She convinced David that Ian had some miniature bottles he wanted to give away. David was delighted to accompany Myra back to her home.

Myra and David lingered in the kitchen admiring the miniature bottles. Suddenly a blood-chilling scream ricocheted through the house. Myra screamed, "Dave, Dave, come and help Ian!" Smith ran from the kitchen into the living room and into hell.

The only light came from a television set. In its eerie glow David saw Edward Evans, whom he didn't know, lying half on the floor and half on a couch. Blood was cascading from Edward's head onto the floor. Ian Brady stood over the fallen youngster with a bloody hatchet in his hand. As David watched in terror, Ian brought the hatchet down on Edward's head time and time again. Edward tried to crawl away from his tormentor, but with each vicious blow his actions became weaker.

Ian interrupted his murderous frenzy to nonchalantly comment to no one in particular, "This one's taking a while to go." Then he attached an electric cord around his hapless victim's neck, and pulled until Edward Evans lay still in death.

Ian was soaked in blood. The room looked like a slaughterhouse. Myra's clothing had been splattered with blood as well. David Smith had been an audience of one to a murder which had been orchestrated just for him. Ian commented rather sheepishly, "It's the messiest one yet. Normally one blow is enough."

At Ian's urging Myra went about cleaning up the room. Ian then changed his clothing. Upstairs Myra's grandmother slept through it all. Ian solicited David's help in carrying the body upstairs to a bedroom. Myra then put on a pot of tea and while David inwardly shuddered, she and Ian gloated over their recent victim.

At about 3 o'clock in the morning David suggested that he should head home, and was surprised when his companions bade him goodnight and let him leave. For Smith the whole evening had been unreal. He felt he had lived through a nightmare.

David Smith ran all the way home. He was so terrified of Ian and Myra that he waited three hours before he dared to sneak out of the house in order to call the police.

When detectives arrived at 16 Wardle Brook Ave. they were let in by Myra. They had been told by Smith that the living room would be spotless. A search of the back bedroom revealed the horribly mutilated body of Edward Evans trussed up in a plastic bag. Taken to a police station, Ian confessed to murder and at every opportunity tried to implicate David Smith. Three bloodstained carpets and the murder weapon were carried away by the police from the murder house. Later, a post mortem revealed that Evans had been struck with 14 blows to the skull.

As police proceeded to interrogate Ian, and later Myra, it became obvious that neither of them had met Edward Evans before the night of the murder. What was their motive for luring the victim to their home to kill him? Was it possible, as it appeared to be, that the murderous pair had timed the first blow to coincide with David Smith's arrival so that he would be a witness to murder?

The house on Wardle Brook Ave. was practically dismantled in an attempt to discover further clues. The investigating officers were successful in their endeavors. They found Ian Brady's notes. On one page they came across the name John Kilbridge, the little boy who had been missing for almost two years. There was more. Police discovered that Ian had checked two suitcases at Manchester's Central Station. They were recovered and found to contain pornographic pictures of Myra, but more importantly there were weird photographs of the lonesome moors outside Manchester. Some of the photos showed Myra staring straight down at the moors, as if standing over a grave in mourning.

Police searched for and found the actual sites depicted in the photographs. They dug up the bodies of John Kilbride and little Lesley Downey.

The case was one of the most amazing murder cases ever uncovered. Christened the Murders on the Moors by the press, it received worldwide publicity. The trial took place at historic Chester Castle on April 19, 1966. Due to the nature of the evidence, it was felt that the two accused could very well be assassinated in the courtroom. When it came time for them to testify they were protected by four-inch thick bulletproof glass on three sides. The pornographic pictures, the photos of the gravesites of the two children, and Brady's diary left little doubt as to the guilt of the accused pair.

One piece of evidence was so horrifying that hardened homicide detectives left the courtroom when this particular evidence was presented. Myra and Ian had lured little Lesley Downey to their home and recorded on tape her agony as they sexually abused and tortured her to death. The tape, which also had Christmas carols as background music to the horror they were inflicting on a 10-year-old child, had been discovered intact by police.

The Moors jury took only two hours and 22 minutes to find Ian Brady guilty of three separate counts of murder. He received three life sentences, while Myra received two life sentences for the murder of Downey and Evans. She received a further seven years sentence for harboring Brady in the case of Kilbride.

Ironically, Ian Brady and Myra Hindley escaped the hangman's noose. A few months prior to their trial capital punishment had been abolished in England. They both remain in prison to this day.

TED BUNDY

The delays had come to an end. Theodore Robert Cowell Bundy had a date with Florida's electric chair.

In January 1989, Florida's governor, Bob Martinez, signed the official death warrant shortly after the U.S. Supreme Court turned down Bundy's final appeal. Sternly, the governor stated, "Bundy is one of the most notorious killers in our nation's history. He has used legal manoeuvring to dodge the electric chair for ten years."

Ted Bundy was brought up in Tacoma, Washington. There was nothing in his youth to indicate that the handsome charmer would become a notorious serial killer, known simply as "Ted" to the law enforcement agencies of four states.

He graduated from Wilson High School with a B average, attended the University of Puget Sound, switching to the University of Washington for his sophomore year. In 1972, Ted graduated and, for a short time, worked for the King County Law and Justice Planning Department. While thus employed, ironically, he wrote a pamphlet on rape.

Ted entered the University of Utah Law School. A few months later, young girls began to disappear without a trace. Lynda Ann Healy, 21, a University of Washington student, vanished from her apartment. On March 19, Donna Munsen, 19, a student at Evergreen State College, disappeared on her way to a music recital. A month later, Susan Racourt, 18, left Central State College at Ellenburg to take in a movie. She was never seen again. On May 6, Roberta Parks, 22, walked out of the Student Union building of Oregon State University and vanished.

Ted, who by now had quit law school, obtained employment with the Emergency Service in Olympia. Girls continued to disappear. On June 1, Brenda Ball, 22, vanished after leaving a bar with the express intention of going home. Georgann Hawkins, 18, left her sorority house at the University of Washington. She, too, was never heard of again. Slim, handsome Ted Bundy continued to counsel troubled individuals all that summer down at Emergency Service.

In August, Ted left his job to continue his law studies in Salt Lake City. Soon, girls in that area began to vanish. An old girlfriend of Ted's back in Seattle read about the rash killings in Utah. She was troubled. Witnesses claimed that a young man who called himself Ted was known to have attempted to pick up girls. He would approach them, wearing a plaster cast on one arm, and ask for assistance placing a small boat on top of his tan Volkswagen. The Ted she had known in Seattle drove a tan Volkswagen.

With many misgivings, she called police. After she told them of her suspicions, they decided to check out Ted Bundy at the University of Utah Law School. Their cursory check of Ted's records and application at the school indicated that the former girlfriend had either made a mistake or was one of those vindictive women who was seeking revenge. After all, this guy had a recommendation letter on file from no less a personage than Washington's Governor Don Evans.

On November 8, 1974, something happened to Ted that had never happened before. One of his victims escaped. Carol Da Ronch, 18, was approached by a young man who claimed to be a police officer. He told the girl that someone had been apprehended burglarizing her car and asked her to accompany him to the police station to identify the stolen goods. Carol got in the Volkswagen. She then asked the police officer to identify himself. Instead, the man pulled out a pair of handcuffs and a pistol. He threatened, "Be still or I'll blow your brains out!"

Carol didn't hesitate. She jumped from the car, stumbled and fell. Her assailant had also left the car and now stood over the fallen girl. Carol got up, scratching at her attacker's face as he attempted to control her. The terrified girl ran to the centre of the street and managed to hail a passing motorist. Her potential abductor raced to his Volkswagen and sped away.

Now that they had a surviving witness, police were anxious to show photos of suspects to the badly frightened girl. Carol failed to pick anyone who resembled her attacker. Inexplicably, she was not shown Ted Bundy's photograph.

Ted moved on to Colorado. Soon after, Julie Cunningham, 22, Denise Oliverson, 23, and Melanie Cooley, 21, vanished. At the Wildwood Inn near Aspen, a Michigan nurse, Caryn Campbell, 23, disappeared from the corridors of the inn. Her terribly mutilated nude body was found some ten miles away months later. A brochure from the Wildwood Inn would later be found in Ted's Volkswagen. Also, credit card purchases would indicate he had been in the area when all four women disappeared.

Police attempted to find Ted, now wanted for questioning, but it would be nine months before he would be taken into custody by a highway patrol officer whom Ted attempted to evade. Inside his car, Ted had little goodies, such as a crowbar, handcuffs, a nylon stocking and an ice pick.

Ted Bundy was arrested. Current photos were taken of him and, together with other photos, were shown to Carol Da Ronch. She pulled out Ted's photo without hesitation. "This is the man!" she shouted.

Ted Bundy, now a likely suspect in the murders of girls in Washington, Colorado and Utah, as well as in the kidnapping of Carol Da Ronch, was released on $15,000 bail.

Law enforcement agencies of three states were sure they were all looking for the same man, yet they didn't have any direct proof. This changed when the material vacuumed from the floor of Ted's van revealed pubic hair which matched that of Melissa Smith, the murdered daughter of Midvale, Utah's police chief. They also found hair which matched that of Carol Da Ronch and Caryn Campbell. Together with the Wildwood Inn pamphlet and credit card purchases from Colorado, police felt they had enough evidence to proceed with the prosecution of the Colorado killings.

Meanwhile, Ted was tried and found guilty of kidnapping Carol Da Ronch. He was also sentenced to 60 days in jail for evading a police officer. While in custody, he was charged with the murder of Caryn Campbell. At the time, Bundy stated, "I have never killed, never kidnapped, never designed to injure another human being. I am prepared to use every ounce of my strength to vindicate myself."

Charming Ted was now a prime suspect in a grand total of 32 cases involving missing and murdered women. Over the years several decomposed bodies were found and identified. Others have never been found.

Ted informed the court that he wished to represent himself in future court appearances. As a result, he was given access to the Glenwood Springs Library. One day, left alone to pore over law books, he jumped out a window to the pavement 20 feet below. Ted managed to steal a Cadillac, but was soon picked up and hustled back to jail.

Ted wasn't through escaping from jail. His second attempt was far more successful than the first. He managed to lose a great deal of weight in a short time. Now slimmer than usual, he squeezed up into the false ceiling in his cell and crawled to freedom.

In the following weeks, Ted travelled by car, bus and plane, making his way to Chicago. On New Year's Day, 1978, he took in the Rose Bowl game on TV in a bar in Ann Arbor, Michigan. His old school, the University of Washington, won the game.

A week later, the most wanted man in America made his way to Tallahassee, Florida, and took a room a few blocks from Florida State University under the name Chris Hagen.

It was killing time in Florida.

In the wee hours of January 15, Nita Jane Neary returned to her university dormitory after a date. A man, clutching a two-by-four piece of wood brushed past her on his way out. Nita rushed upstairs in time to see 21-year-old Karen Chandler, soaked with blood, stagger out of her room. Nita looked into her friend's room. She saw Cathy Kleiner lying on her bed with blood gushing from her head.

Soon, 40 coeds were milling about, ministering to their wounded friends. There was more. Margaret Bowman, 21, lay motionless in death. A maniac had crushed her skull and twisted a pair of panty hose around her neck. Lisa Levy, 20, had been sexually attacked and beaten to death. Her killer had bitten deeply into her breasts and buttocks.

Ted Bundy became unnerved at the police activity taking place so close to his rooming house. He left that very night, checking into a Holiday Inn in Lake City, about 100 miles down the road from Tallahassee. Next day, 12-year-old Kimberley Leach disappeared from her school. No one connected her disappearance with the slaughter which had taken place in Tallahassee.

Five days later, an alert Pensacola police officer picked up Ted in a stolen Volkswagen. He claimed to be Kenneth Misner, a Florida State student. He had 22 credit cards to prove it. Next day, the real Kenneth Misner called police to report his wallet and credit cards stolen.

When Ted's photo appeared in the paper, he was recognized in the rooming house back in Tallahassee as Chris Hagen. A fellow roomer had seen the man he knew as Chris enter the rooming house at 4 a.m. on the morning of the killings. Fingerprints identified the bogus Kenneth Misner and Chris Hagen as escaped convict Ted Bundy.

Florida authorities didn't want to release Ted to another state. They endeavored to build an airtight case against their man. They managed to do just that.

Dental technicians were given teeth mark impressions taken from Lisa Levy's body. They matched in every detail impressions taken from Ted's teeth. The Florida jury which heard the Bundy case took only six and a half hours to find him guilty. They recommended death in the electric chair.

In February 1980, Ted stood trial once more for murder, this time for the murder of 12-year-old Kimberley Leach. Once again, he was found guilty and sentenced to die.

For ten years, Ted danced around Florida's infernal machine. He had several dates with death, on occasion coming within days of being executed. The story of his life and his killing spree was dramatized in a made-for-television movie starring Mark Harmon.

At 7 a.m. on Tuesday, January 24, 1989, Ted Bundy was executed in Florida's electric chair.

DALE BURR

Back in 1983, Dale Burr's farm was considered one of the finest in Johnson County, Iowa. Every farmer around Lone Tree would be quick to tell you that Dale deserved everything he had acquired over the years. True enough, his father had given him a prosperous 160-acre spread as a wedding present when he married Emily Wacker, but Dale had worked hard and had expanded the farm to well over 500 acres.

Dale had helped his son John to acquire a 200-acre farm close to his own. The Burrs had two other children, Sheila and Julia. Sheila had married and moved to Arkansas, while Julia had become a teacher and had left the farm as well.

Dale Burr's farm was a rich productive unit, raising corn, beans and pork. His spread was valued at around $2 million, but that was academic. Dale was a purchaser of land, not a seller. He had been born into farm life. It had been good to generations of Burrs before him and it was good to him and his family.

What went wrong?

In one season, between 1983 and 1984, prices paid to farmers for their crops dropped drastically, in many cases almost a dollar a bushel. Such a drop can be disastrous to a farmer producing tens of thousands of bushels.

To expand their farms, large landholders had borrowed from local banks to finance their latest acquisitions. There was nothing wrong with this time proven method of expanding one's farm, but by the mid-1980s, two factors turned bank debt into a nightmare. Prices of crops fell and the value of land dropped appreciably.

Loans for seed money, which had been routine for years, became a humiliating experience for farmers. They were constantly being told that the amount of their loans was fast approaching the value of their collateral, which was usually their farms and the buildings on them.

Dale's son required a bank loan. He had used up all his credit, but his father had no difficulty borrowing the funds. Dale gave the nearby Hills Bank and Trust Co. a mortgage on a portion of his property. When his own cash flow wasn't enough to meet current expenses, he mortgaged more of his property at the Hills Bank.

Bank president John Hughes was a married man with two teenaged daughters. Mostly he was well liked in Hills and Lone Tree, but there was one thing. John Hughes was a stickler for collateral. He wanted his loans covered. There was no way his bank would go under because of the economic disaster that was sweeping the rural communities of the United States. He wasn't above foreclosing and selling off farmers' assets to repay bank loans. It was common knowledge that one sentimental banker who had loaned farmers money on their good word had committed suicide rather than foreclose on personal friends. That would never happen to John Hughes.

After Dale had exhausted his credit at government agencies and the bank, Hughes wrote him a scorching letter, warning him to curtail some of his farming methods and become more efficient. There would be no more bailouts for him or his son. The two men met on several occasions to discuss the problem, but nothing was finalized.

Dale didn't view his obligation as an honest debt which must be paid. He understood only one thing; he and his family before him had worked the soil for generations and now a banker was threatening to take it all away. There was more than money involved. There was humiliation and disgrace. At age 62, Dale Burr had difficulty raising enough money to purchase groceries. He borrowed $500 from his daughter

Julia. Then he acted.

On Monday, December 9, 1985, Dale dug his old model 31 Remington out of his basement and shot his wife of over 30 years directly through the heart. He sat down at the kitchen table and a wrote a note to his son: "John, I'm sorry, I just couldn't stand all the problems." It was signed 'Dad.'

Dale jumped into his 4X4 and headed for town. He drove directly to the Hills Bank, where he attempted to cash a $500 cheque. When assistant vice president Roger Reilly told him his account was overdrawn by $55, Dale gave Reilly $60 in cash and was given a receipt. He then chatted with a few other customers and left the bank.

Calmly, Dale drove down the street and purchased a box of shotgun shells. Once again he drove into the bank's parking lot. He loaded his Remington and shoved the weapon down the leg of his coveralls. Dale, who had once had a bank balance in the hundreds of thousands of dollars now had loans against his farm that he couldn't possibly repay. This same bank, which had once solicited his business, wouldn't honor his $500 cheque.

Dale limped towards President John Hughes office. He stood in the doorway, pulled his Remington from his coveralls, quickly aimed, fired, and blew off the left side of John Hughes' head. He moved a few feet to Roger Reilly's office, pointed the gun at Roger and said, "I'm going to get you too!" Roger could only reply, "Dale, please, you can't do this!"

Bank officer Dale Kretchmar, who had been talking to Roger when John Hughes had been shot, flung out his arms, striking the barrel of the Remington. Reilly dove under a desk. Dale stared at Kretchmar, who firmly thought he was about to be shot. Instead, the desperate man backed out of the office and walked out of the bank. He tossed his Remington onto the front seat of his 4X4 and drove away. Dale had one more score to settle.

Years earlier, in 1983, farmer Rich Goody and John Burr had had a dispute over a section of the Goody farm. Rich had sued John and had been awarded some $6,000, which

Dale had to pay. In Dale's eyes, the entire incident had been a demeaning experience. Now he sped in his pickup to the Goody farm. The two men met outdoors. Dale shot Rich fully in the face from a distance of 15 feet. The blast spun the man around. Another shot plowed into Rich's back, killing him instantly. Dale jumped into his vehicle and drove away.

Just then Deputy Sheriff David Henderson received word on his police radio that Dale Burr had shot John Hughes and was heading towards his general area. Henderson spotted the wanted man before the message was completed. He turned on his siren, but Dale continued on for another half mile before pulling over to the side of the road. Henderson parked a cautious 30 yards away.

Dale placed the butt of his Remington on the floor and positioned the barrel against his chest. He pulled the trigger, but the weapon slipped. The blast shattered some ribs and hit his left arm, but was not fatal. Desperately, he managed to eject the shell and reload the Remington. This time he was successful.

Other policemen joined Henderson. Dale Burr was long past the concerns of this world. In the space of one hour he had killed his wife, the president of a bank, a fellow farmer and himself.

RICHARD CHASE

Richard Chase was born in 1950, the second of two children, to a middle-class couple in Sacramento, California. As a teenager, he was a fair student and managed to graduate from Mira Loma High School. He tried college, but his grades deteriorated and he dropped out. Somewhat of a string bean, Richard didn't bother bathing and let his hair grow to his shoulders. He smoked marijuana daily.

At age 20, Richard moved out of his parents' home into an apartment with two roommates. His behavior was so erratic that his roommates asked him to leave. On one occasion he was reported to police for shooting a gun. In an unrelated incident, he was taken into custody after running down a street completely nude.

By the time he was in his mid-twenties, Richard would fight with anyone who disagreed with him. He visited various hospitals, complaining about a variety of symptoms. At this stage in his checkered career, the idea of steady employment was out of the question. Employers would take one look at the scraggly young man and say thanks, but no thanks. From time to time Richard admitted himself into psychiatric institutions, where he was diagnosed as schizophrenic, but not a danger to himself or others. On these occasions, he or his parents facilitated his discharge.

Over the years Richard displayed an abnormal interest in blood. He believed that drinking it would cure his various ailments. Sometimes he killed birds and drank their blood. He captured small dogs and carried them to his apartment, where they were put to death for their blood.

Four days after Christmas 1977, Richard decided to kill a human being. It would be an experiment just to see if he could accomplish the task. The blood drinking would come later.

Ambrose Griffin was a 51-year-old engineer, who lived on Robinson St. in a suburb of Sacramento. He didn't deserve to die, yet he was killed as he innocently walked from his home to his car. Someone drove by his house, took aim with a .22 calibre handgun and fired. Ambrose, a family man without an enemy in the world, fell dead on the driveway of his house.

Neighbors along Robinson St. were questioned. No one had noticed the killer or his vehicle. Richard Chase had killed for the first time.

On January 23, 1978, several individuals saw a skinny dirty man walking down Tioga Way. He stopped at 2360, the home of Teresa and David Wallin, and tried the front door. It was unlocked. Teresa had just arrived home loaded down with a bag of groceries. She spun around, dropped the groceries and faced the man pointing the semi-automatic .22 at her. There was no talk. Richard Chase aimed and fired. Teresa fell to the floor. Richard leaned over and fired a second shot into her skull. He dragged her into the bedroom, where he extensively mutilated her body.

David Wallin walked into his home and found his wife dead. Unlike the murder of Ambrose Griffin, this time the killer left a clue — a distinctive bloody shoe print on the floor. There were also several small bloody circles on the floor near the body, but the significance of these circles was not apparent at the time.

Four days after the Wallin murder, Richard Chase struck again. Thirty-eight year-old divorcee Evelyn Miroth was excited for her six-year-old son Jason. A good friend and neighbor on Merrywood Dr., Neone Grangaard, was planning to take Jason, along with her own children, into the nearby Sierra Nevada mountains to play in the snow. Evelyn was a bit disappointed at not being able to get away herself. She had promised to baby-sit 22-month-old David Ferreira that morning. David's mother, Karen, had dropped the baby off at Evelyn's home.

Evelyn's boyfriend, Danny Meredith, would be visiting her later that day. She would walk Jason over to Neone's house just across the street in a few minutes. The two neighbors could see each other's front doors from their own homes.

When a half an hour passed with no sign of Evelyn or Jason, Neone decided to go over to find out what was holding them up. No one answered the door. How inconsiderate of Evelyn to go out without cancelling her son's trip to snow country, Neone thought. She mentioned the slight to another neighbor, Nancy Turner. Nancy tried Evelyn's back door. It was open. She walked into the house and let out a scream that could be heard throughout the subdivision.

Danny Meredith was lying in the hall. He had been shot to death, as had little Jason Miroth. Evelyn's body was horribly mutilated. There were the telltale bloody circles on the carpet near the body. A police physician thought the circles had been made with human blood, possibly the overflow of a small pail or container.

Distinctive bloody shoe prints matched the prints found in the Wallin home. There was no doubt in investigators' minds that a madman was killing and mutilating individuals in a confined area of Sacramento. There was no connection between victims. The killer was choosing them at random.

Another ominous element entered the case when police learned that little David Ferreira was nowhere to be found. Obviously, the killer had taken the baby with him after he had killed the other three people in the house.

Over 50 detectives were actively engaged in following leads. It was routine police work which finally uncovered a clue to the killer's identity. Detectives questioned everyone who worked or lived in the area. One woman, Nancy Holden, told police that she had been approached in a shopping mall by a tall, dirty man whom she identified as an old high school classmate. She had barely recognized the man, who had acted so strangely, even though she had been out on one date with him as a teenager. His name was Rick Chase.

At the time, it wasn't much of a lead. There were hundreds of tall dirty men in California. When Chase's name was checked out through motor vehicles, it was learned that he lived at 2934 Watt Ave., only a few blocks from the scenes of the murders.

Chase was picked up and his apartment was searched. At the time of his arrest, he was carrying the .22 calibre semi-automatic which had taken so many lives. He was also in possession of Danny Meredith's wallet containing Meredith's credit cards. A pair of Chase's athletic shoes had made the bloody prints found in both the Wallin and Miroth homes.

The interior of Chase's apartment was spattered with blood. Dog bones were strewn about the filthy premises. As for Chase, he admitted to capturing dogs and drinking their blood, but despite the evidence against him, he denied killing anyone. He claimed he had no idea of the fate of little David Ferreira.

On March 24, 1978, less than a mile from Chase's apartment, a janitor at the Arcade Wesleyan Church peered into a cardboard box lying in a pile of garbage on the church grounds. David Ferreira's fate was no longer a mystery.

On January 2, 1979, Richard Chase stood trial on six counts of murder. He admitted from the witness stand that he had killed so that he could drink his victims' blood. He pleaded not guilty by reason of insanity in order to escape the death penalty, but was found guilty and sentenced to death in California's gas chamber.

Chase was lodged on Death Row in San Quentin Prison. The prison physician prescribed three daily 50 mg tablets of doxepin hydrochloride to combat depression. Richard Chase saved up his daily dose for three weeks. He consumed his entire supply at one time and successfully committed suicide.

ANDREI CHIKATILO

The world's most prolific serial killer, a Russian? Impossible! We tend to categorize these reprehensible monsters as American or British phenomena. Berkowitz, Bundy, Gacy, the Yorkshire Ripper, names indelibly carved in our memories. Yet there was one Russian who operated over a longer period of time and killed more of his fellow human beings than any of those infamous predators.

The little boy who grew up in the Ukrainian village of Yablochnoye lived through the ravages of the Second World War. Looking back at his earlier history, there is little to distinguish him from other little boys who were brought up in similar circumstances.

Andrei Chikatilo developed into a big, strong teenager. He did excellent work in school, joined the Communist party and looked forward to a higher education. There was one disturbing physical defect which bothered the young student. He couldn't perform with members of the opposite sex. He tried; he wanted to, but he physically couldn't do the trick. The few teenage girls who participated in Andrei's immature attempts at lovemaking ridiculed their awkward partner. It was humiliating.

Andrei entered a technical college and graduated as a communications engineer. After a short period of time spent in the work force, he was drafted into the army, where he served three uneventful years. In 1960, at age 24, Andrei returned to his home village of Yablochnoye, but the rural Ukrainian village was not for him. He gravitated to a town about 20 miles removed from Rostov, where he found a job as a telephone engineer.

Because of his inability to perform sexually, Andrei tended to avoid women and developed into somewhat of an introvert. His only sister, Tatyana, was concerned. She introduced him to her friend, Fayina. The pair hit it off and in 1963, they married. Their honeymoon was less than a roaring success. Fayina was patient with her inept husband, but it took a week before the marriage was consummated. In the months to follow, the sex act between Andrei and Fayina became a clumsy obligation rather than an act of love. The couple managed to have two children, a boy and a girl. Andrei doted on them both. In his spare time, he attended Rostov University, obtaining a degree in philology and literature in 1971.

With degree in hand, Andrei changed careers, accepting a position as a teacher in the town of Novoshakhtinsk, about a two-hour train ride from Rostov. It was while teaching that he got into trouble for the first time. In 1973, he was accused of fondling a 15-year-old pupil. When the girl screamed, Andrei experienced a degree of pleasure. He was lectured about his behavior and was asked to resign when a second incident occurred.

Andrei was hired to teach at another school in Shakhti. The Chikatilo family moved into a comfortable four-room apartment. No one was aware that the new teacher purposely rode on crowded trains so that he could rub up against young girls and boys. The urges were getting stronger. Andrei made preparations for what was to follow. He rented a dilapidated one-room hovel at 26 Mezhevoi Perevlok on the edge of town.

Andrei roamed the city searching for a likely candidate to participate in his sexual fantasies. He found partners in destitute prostitutes who would sell their bodies for a slug of vodka and something to eat. Unlike his wife, they would do anything he wanted. He liked it best when they screamed in agony and offered resistance.

On December 22, 1978, Andrei picked up nine-year-old Lena Zakotnova. To the little girl, he looked like a kindly grandfather. She consented to visit his one-room hovel. No one saw the pair walk down the dark lane and enter number 26. Lena became the monster's first murder victim. Later he would explain that inflicting pain was no longer enough to satisfy him. He stabbed Lena time and time again, after which he strangled her to death. Andrei carried her body to the River Grushevka and threw it in. Two days later, Lena Zakotnova's body was found a short distance downstream.

Andrei was caught up in the murder investigation. Neighbors had seen him take several girls into his shack. His record at his old school was exposed. As luck would have it, at this time 25-year-old Aleksandr Kravchenko, who had committed a similar crime years earlier and had spent six years in prison, lived a few doors down the lane from Andrei. Kravchenko was questioned extensively and eventually confessed to Lena's murder. At his trial, he claimed to have been beaten by police and recanted his confession. He was tried, found guilty and sentenced to 15 years hard labor. The state appealed the light sentence. They succeeded in having Kravchenko sentenced to death. Years later, in 1984, he was executed by a firing squad.

In March 1981, Andrei was dismissed from his teaching position, but soon was hired as a supply clerk for a large industrial company. The job entailed travel procuring supplies, enabling him to roam far afield in search of victims.

Seventeen-year-old Larisa Tkachenko became Andrei's second victim in September 1981. He met her at a bus stop and lured her to a wooded area near railway tracks, where he pounced on the hapless girl, beat her about the body and strangled her to death. The second murder was easier than the first. Andrei Chikatilo, university graduate, husband and father, was now a sex-starved killing machine. His life revolved around killing. At home, Fayina knew nothing of her husband's strange behavior. He made sure never to return home immediately after a killing. Those he raped, mutilated and strangled in his rented room were disposed of elsewhere. He had plenty of time to wash up the large amounts of blood involved. Andrei liked the sight of blood.

In 1982 he killed a total of seven individuals, among them little children, mature women and young boys. He travelled great distances and often committed his murders hundreds of miles from his home base. Despite the variety of his victims and the widespread locations of the crimes, a pattern eventually emerged. Around 1983 police realized that a number of the murders committed in wooded areas near remote railway stations all bore distinctive mutilations. There were many stab wounds concentrated near the eyes of the victims.

During a two-month period in 1984, Andrei stabbed and strangled 10 people. Once, on a seven-day trip to Tashkent, he killed two women. No one ever suspected the supply clerk who lived and worked hundreds of miles from the scenes of the crimes.

It was easy for Andrei to lure his prey off the train leading into Rostov. Sometimes their bodies were found within days. Sometimes they weren't found until months of hot weather had reduced their bodies into nothing more than skeletons.

Finally, several police agencies combined forces and acknowledged that they had a serial killer of monstrous proportions on their hands. They elicited the aid of the Criminal Biology Dept. of the Russian Ministry of Health, which was given all the physical evidence available. It was ascertained that the killer's semen found on several victims was type AB.

On September 14, 1984, an alert plainclothes police officer grew suspicious of a man who had been attempting to pick up women for hours. Upon being questioned, the man claimed he simply liked talking to members of the opposite sex. When the bag he was carrying was checked, it was found to contain knives and a rope. Still, no crime had been committed. The officer took the man's name and wrote out a routine report for his superior. The man was none other than Andrei Chikatilo.

Major Gennady Bondarenko, head of the Rostov police, had Andrei brought in for further questioning. He had a record of molesting children when he had taught school. A footprint found near one of the victims had been made by the same size shoe as that worn by Andrei.

A blood test indicated that Andrei's blood was type A. Because sperm found on the clothing of several victims was type AB, authorities were convinced that they had the wrong man. It is believed by many that the Russians botched the testing. At any rate, Andrei was absolved of involvement in any of the murders. Secretly, he was amazed that the police had failed to nail him.

Detectives conducting the massive investigation had compiled index cards on over 25,000 individuals. Out of this large number, card number nine was devoted to Andrei Chikatilo. It noted that he was absolved of any complicity in the serial killings because he had the wrong blood type. The murders and mutilations continued.

In November 1990, hundreds of plainclothes police officers travelled on the trains around Rostov. Others were staked out at small railway stations. The blanket manhunt paid off. Sgt. Igor Rybakov spotted a man with a blood-stained cheek leaving a lonely wooded area near a remote station where a body had been found some time earlier. He questioned the man, scrutinized his identification, but had no reason to detain him. Later, Rybakov had second thoughts and filed a report on the incident.

A few days passed before the report was deemed important enough to have the area thoroughly searched. About 50 yards from where the first body had been found, another was discovered, covered with leaves. That did it. Andrei was taken into custody.

In time, Andrei confessed to 52 murders, the most recorded by any serial killer in history. He described in detail his urge to inflict pain and death on his victims. He also confessed to cannibalism and necrophilia. The lengthy trial, which held Russia spellbound, featured the accused, head shaven, confined to a cage for his own protection.

Andrei Chikatilo was found guilty of 52 counts of murder and was sentenced to death. President Boris Yeltsin rejected clemency. On February 14, 1994, the Rostov Ripper was put to death.

DEAN CORLL

Arnold and Mary Corll were both 23 years old when their first son, Dean, was born on Christmas Eve, 1939. The Corlls almost immediately started to disagree on the way the child should be brought up. Arnold was a strict disciplinarian who thought that young Dean should be taught to obey his parents, almost before he learned to walk. This proved to be a bone of contention and when Arnold was drafted into the air force and stationed in Memphis, Tennessee, it became apparent that the marriage had a limited lifespan. Sure enough an amicable divorce took place and the couple separated, but not before another child, Stephen, was born.

Mary, who still loved Arnold, sold her comfortable little home, bought a trailer and headed for Memphis, where she put Dean in school. She and Arnold took up where they had left off, fighting and arguing, and eventually, despite bickering, they decided to give marriage another try. When Arnold received his discharge from the air force, Mary, Arnold and the two children headed for Houston, Texas. At first they lived in a trailer, but later they bought a house. Their attempts to salvage their marriage proved futile, and they agreed to their second amicable divorce. Mary and her two sons moved again, this time to an apartment.

Dean and Stephen were again enrolled in a strange school, and it was here that doctors discovered that Dean suffered from a congenital heart defect. Dean had his first taste of being different from other boys. While they played energetic games he watched from the sidelines. While they ran, he walked.

In 1953, when Dean was an impressionable 14-year-old, his mother married a salesman named West. The entire family moved to Vidor, Texas, where Dean attended Vidor High School. Because of his heart trouble, he took up music and played the trombone as a member of the school band. Dean was an average trombone player, an average student and was so inconspicuous that many of his teachers don't remember him.

In his spare time he helped his mother sell pecans from her garage. When he graduated from high school in 1958, he saved his money and bought a car. His mother started to manufacture pecan candies and he worked for her for two years, delivering candies to stores which had placed orders.

In 1962, Mary West had a flourishing little candy business going at 721 East 6 1/2 Street. She had set up a kitchen and turned the garage into a candy store, and Dean's workload grew steadily as the family business prospered.

In 1964, Dean was drafted into the army and sent to Fort Polk, Louisiana. He was later transferred to Fort Hood in Texas, but received a hardship discharge on July 11, 1965, as he was needed at home to keep the candy factory going. By this time the factory was relocated at 505 West 22nd Street, and the West family moved to an apartment at 1845 Airport Blvd., with the exception of Dean, who lived by himself in an apartment a block away at 444 West 21st St.

Across the street from the Corll Candy Company was the Helms Elementary School, and quite naturally the children were constantly dropping into the store section of the candy factory. Dean built a games room at the back of the factory and installed a pool table for the use of his customers. At the time the family thought the room was an astute business move, but in hindsight Dean's motives appear more sinister. The nature of his mother's business was enough to attract young boys, and the poolroom made the bait doubly allur- ing. If Dean had homosexual tendencies at this period in his life, he managed, by accident or design, to place himself in an ideal position to indulge his sexual appetite.

Dean's mother went through another divorce, and then

met and married a seaman, who took an immediate dislike to Dean and his habit of entertaining young boys in the candy factory. The marriage only lasted a matter of months, ending in divorce in 1968. Then the Corll family started to break up. Mrs. Corll dissolved the business and moved to Manitou Springs, where she set up another thriving candy factory, Stephen took a job as a machinist in Houston, and Dean went to work for the Houston Lighting Power Company as an electrician.

By 1969, it is certain that Dean Corll was a confirmed homosexual who regularly enticed young boys to his residence at 2020 Lamar St. No physical harm was done to the youngsters, and either fear or shame prevented them from ever talking about their experience. One youngster, 14-year-old David Brooks, came under Corll's spell so completely that he dropped out of high school in order to spend all his time with his older friend. Brooks was to state their relationship started with Corll paying him for sexual favors. Brooks was a tall, slender, good-looking boy, with long hair falling to his shoulders. His parents were divorced, and he spent time with each parent, travelling from Houston to Beaumont.

In 1970, David Brooks introduced Dean to Wayne Henley. A relationship grew between Wayne and Dean, until gradually the boy fell completely under the spell of the older man's dominant personality. Wayne was a carbon coy of Brooks in appearance — lean, good-looking, with long hair. The three of them, all the products of broken homes, were inseparable. The two younger boys were so subservient to Corll that they would carry out his every desire without question.

The world heard for the first time of Dean Corll, David Brooks and Wayne Henley on Wednesday, August 8, 1973. The police received a telephone call reporting a shooting at 2020 Lamar St. When they arrived at the scene they were stopped by three youths, two boys and a girl, standing in front of a white frame house. Wayne Henley gave his name to the police and handed them a .22-calibre pistol. The gun held six spent shells. Then Henley introduced five-foot-two-inch Rhonda Louise Williams, a 15-year-old with the knowing

look of someone twice her age. She hung on Henley's arm
while he told the officers that the other youth's name was
Tim Kerley.

The three teenagers told of shooting a man named Corll,
and were hustled into a patrol car. As the officers entered the
hall of 2020 Lamar St., they could see the naked body of
Dean Corll spread out on the floor. Tiny holes dotted the
dead man's back, and his legs were entangled in telephone
wire. The police went out to a bedroom, where they carefully opened the door and stood amazed at the strange paraphernalia which lay before them. The floor was covered with
beige carpeting, which in turn was covered by a sheet of
clear plastic. The room contained a long pine board with
holes in each corner. These holes had chains running
through them, and at each corner of the board was fastened
a pair of handcuffs. There was also a long knife on the floor.

Detective Sergeant Dave Mullican, a huge, 220-pound,
six-foot-two career cop, had investigated many homicides
and he knew instinctively that he was now involved in something beyond a routine killing.

An examination of the body showed that Corll had been
shot six times, the full capacity of the .22-calibre pistol which
Henley had turned over to the police. He had been shot
once in the shoulder, once in the head, and four times in the
back. The board found in the bedroom measured two-and-a-
half feet wide by eight-feet long, obviously designed to
accommodate a human being. A total of eight sets of handcuffs and a gas mask were found in the house. In the garage
attached to the house, the police found traces of dehydrated
lime on the floor.

Henley told the story of what went on at 2020 Lamar on
the night Dean Corll met his death. It all started when Corll
asked Henley to a party at his house. Henley had brought
Kerley, and the three men sat around smoking pot and drinking beer, when Henley thought it would be a good idea to
bring his girlfriend Rhonda Williams over to the party. He
called Rhonda, who managed to sneak out of her home to
meet them. The two boys picked her up in Kerley's

Volkswagen and drove back to the house. Corll was furious that they had brought a girl to the party, but was soon pacified. The three youngsters started inhaling the fumes from acrylic paint sprayed in a bag. All the while Corll smoked pot and drank beer, the three youngsters "bagged" the fumes. Eventually, they passed out.

When Henley came around, he found that Corll had handcuffed him. He looked about the room and saw that Rhonda and Kerley were both handcuffed and had masking tape over their mouths. Corll was acting like a madman, waving a knife and brandishing a pistol. When Kerley and Rhonda regained consciousness he threatened to torture them all and then kill them. Henley realized that somehow he had to reason with Dean, for he was the only one who could talk. He started to get on Corll's good side by promising him that he would assist him in torturing Kerley. Slowly he gained Corll's confidence, convincing him that he would help him to kill his two friends. Corll and he devised a further plan; Corll would assault Kerley and Henley would rape Rhonda, after which they would kill them both. On this understanding, Corll unlocked Henley's handcuffs.

With a great deal of difficulty Corll proceeded to handcuff his two captives to the board. He then undressed the pair and started to assault Kerley, who despite being handcuffed, tried to fight him off. In the meantime, Henley tried to have intercourse with Rhonda, but found that he couldn't.

While all this was going on Henley noticed a pistol on a small table, the one piece of furniture in the room. On the pretence of going to the bathroom, he managed to leave the room. When he returned he picked up the pistol and pointed it at Corll, who was still fighting with the desperate Kerley. The moment Corll saw the gun, he rushed Henley, who started pressing the trigger and didn't stop until all six bullets were discharged. Corll fell to the floor and died instantly. Henley unlocked Kerley's and Rhonda's handcuffs. The three got dressed and called the police. Not wanting to stay with the dead man, they waited outside for the police to arrive.

Had Henley stopped talking it is in the realm of possibility that the police would have wound up the case. It was a weird sex dope killing, but Henley's story had a ring of truth to it, and was corroborated by all the physical evidence.

But Henley didn't stop. For some reason he thought the police didn't believe him and he figured the only way out of his dilemma was to paint Corll as a sex-crazed monster. He requested another interview with the police, and this time he added that Corll had once boasted that he had killed some boys. He remembered the names Cobble and Jones, and thought Dean had mentioned that he had buried them in a boathouse. Detectives checked the names, and sure enough, Charles Cobble, 17, and Marty Jones, 18, who had lived together, had disappeared on July 27, about two weeks prior to the shooting of Corll. The backgrounds of these two boys had already been checked, and had been found to be normal in every way. They were achieving good marks at school and both got along well with their parents. They had disappeared without any warning and no trace of them had been found since they were reported missing.

Henley told the police he thought he could direct them to the boathouse. The police took him up on his offer and equipped with shovels and ropes, they proceeded out of the city. The handcuffed Henley directed them to a field adjoining Silver Bell Street, where there stood a long corrugated steel structure. "That's the boathouse," said Henley. Inside were 20 stalls, measuring 12 feet wide and 30 feet deep. Each stall had six-foot-wide double doors, which were securely locked. Henley pointed out Stall 11 as Dean's, and volunteered that the owner of the boathouse lived just a minute or so away.

The police explained their mission to Mrs. Mayme Meynier, the owner of Southwest Boat Storage. She confirmed that Stall 11 had been rented to Dean Corll, but stated that only he had the key. The police broke the lock and entered. The first thing that came into sight was a bicycle leaning against the righthand wall. As their eyes became accustomed to the semi-darkness they discovered two bags of dehydrated lime and a plastic bag containing a pair of new red shoes and other clothing. The police cleaned out the stall and commenced digging. Only six inches below the surface their shovels struck something harder than earth. The heat inside the corrugated boathouse was intense, and the men soon became soaked in perspiration, except Henley, who sat handcuffed on the ground beside the patrol car.

The men were now being hampered by the fading early evening light, but they carried on, gently parting the earth with their hands. Finally the object of their efforts became all too visible; the body of a young boy wrapped in a clear plastic sheet. The body was removed from the hole with great care and placed outside the boathouse. The men returned to their distasteful task. A second corpse, which had been buried for a longer period of time, was uncovered and removed from the boathouse.

By this time, the unmistakable stench of death was permeating the entire area surrounding the boathouse. The police installed fans and lights to aid the diggers, who were now reinforced by eight trusties from a nearby jail. The entire floor of the stall was being excavated in six-inch levels. As the night wore on, the fans whirred and the lights cast strange shadows on the eerie scene. The diggers found a third body, then a fourth, then a fifth, and a sixth. Some were recent victims, wrapped in clear plastic, while others had been in the earth longer and were decomposed beyond recognition. By the time the diggers stopped at 1 a.m., two further bodies had been dragged from the boathouse.

By now the case was receiving nationwide and even worldwide attention. On Thursday morning, August 9, 1973, newspapers, radio broadcasts and early morning television news carried the sensational story of the eight bodies found in the boathouse. One ghostly presence held sway over the eerie events. That presence belonged to Dean Corll. His name was on everyone's lips, but he was dead and it was left to others to explain his strange impulses and passions.

Wayne Henley told of an association with Corll which went back several years. It all started when Dean offered him $200 to procure young boys. Henley said he did nothing about the offer for a full year, but then, when he badly needed money, he took Corll up on the proposition. And so it began; sometimes he would just pick up a lad who was hitchhiking, and on one pretence or another deliver him to Corll. Dean was a sadistic homosexual, who would often use the boys, then kill them in front of Henley. Henley claimed that although he had been present, he had never taken part in torturing or killing anyone.

Typical of the many stories Henley told of picking up boys for Dean was the one about the youngster who was reported missing only six days before Dean himself was killed. Fourteen-year-old James Stanton Dreymala was riding his bike when Henley and Corll, who were parked in Corll's van, called him over. Dean told the boy he could have some empty Coke bottles he had found in his van and take them in the store to get the deposit, which he could keep for himself. When James came out of the store he strolled over to the van and thanked Dean. Corll then told the boy to throw his bicycle into the van, explaining that he had more bottles at home. James jumped at the chance to earn some extra money, and after putting his bike in the van, he clambered in beside Henley and Corll. They drove out to 2020 Lamar St. where Corll assaulted the boy, tortured him, and then strangled him to death. It was his bicycle which was found in the boathouse. Henley kept up his nonstop stories of horror, but the strange case was to take another bizarre twist.

A Mr. Brooks arrived at the Houston police station with his son, David, who gave the police a statement about his relationship with Henley and Corll. He implicated Henley far more than Henley had admitted, but predictably stated emphatically that he himself was only a witness to all the unnatural sex acts and murders. When Henley was told that David Brooks was making a formal statement he immediately said, "That's good, now I can tell the whole story."

Henley told of meeting Brooks, who in turn had lured him to Corll. He now described in detail how he had actively participated in killing some of the boys and he offered the startling information that there were a lot more bodies than those found at the boathouse. Henley was blossoming in the glare of publicity, and once he started he didn't want to stop. He said one burial site was near Lake Sam Rayburn in San Augustine County and another was on High Island Beach in Jefferson County.

Hardened detectives winced; they believed the boy and thought they would find more bodies at these locations. How was it possible for a man and two youngsters to kill in wholesale lots and remain undetected? Henley explained that Corll moved a lot so that any suspicious action would be an isolated case and not one of a series of incidents that might be reported to the police. His van was ideal for transporting bodies. It could be backed up to a door, so that no one could see what was being put in or taken out. There were a lot of hitchhikers who didn't hesitate to accept a ride and were susceptible to being invited to a party. Dean had developed these parties to a fine art, and always had some beer and grass available for the youngsters. Nothing untoward happened at many parties; sometimes they were over early and the boys left with a promise that they would be asked to the next one. Some of them felt secure because they knew either Henley or Brooks personally.

Brooks and Henley both felt that Corll was growing more demanding in his desire for young boys, and was in fact going mad. As matters now stood, Henley admitted to active participation in the murders, but Brooks claimed he was only a bystander.

Digging at the boathouse continued the next day, and more bodies were uncovered. Four more bodies were lifted from Stall 11 before the diggers broke for lunch. In the afternoon and early evening five bodies were brought to the surface, making an unbelievable total of seventeen excavated from the boathouse in two days. The diggers then hit solid rock, and the authorities knew that here at least their work was done.

The ever co-operative Henley led police to where he and Dean had buried more boys on the shores of Lake Sam Rayburn. He even gave the police the name of one of the youngsters before they started digging. Sure enough, only a few minutes later the body of a young boy was uncovered. He pointed to another site, where he said Corll and Brooks had buried another boy. In a matter of minutes another body was uncovered. In all, four bodies were removed from the shores of the lake, making a total of 21 victims.

Brooks and Henley then directed the police to High Island where six additional bodies were found, bringing the final total to 27. The two boys couldn't remember any more names or grave sites, so the search was stopped. At the outset they had estimated that there had been between 20 and 30 victims. No one will ever know for sure if 27 is the correct total.

Tim Kerley and Rhonda Louise Williams, the two youngsters who witnessed the shooting of Dean Corll, were released. Wayne Henley was charged with the murder of eight boys, and David Brooks was charged with two. Both received lengthy prison sentences designed to keep them behind bars for the rest of their lives. The authorities ruled that Henley's killing of Corll was an act of self-defence, and Henley was not charged with Corll's murder.

At the height of the investigation, a small 15-minute service was held at Pasadena's Grand View Memorial Park. About 35 friends and the immediate family of the deceased wept as the Reverend Robert D. Joiner of the Sunset United Methodist Church said a few kind words. The flag of the United States draped the casket. Just before it was lowered into the ground, the flag was presented to Dean Corll's father.

JEFFREY DAHMER

During the day he worked at the Ambrosia Chocolate Co. in Milwaukee. At night he killed people and cut up their bodies.

Jeffrey Dahmer had always been a bit different. As a kid in Akron, Ohio, he loved to dissect insects and small animals. When his middle-class parents divorced in 1978, Jeffrey was attending Ohio State University. He dropped out after only one semester. That same year, 18-year-old Jeffrey committed his first murder.

Stephen Hicks had hitchhiked to a rock music concert 30 miles from his home in Coventry, Ohio. Then he simply disappeared off the face of the earth. His parents offered a reward to anyone who could lead them to their son, but no one came forward with information. Stephen, one day a typical teenager, next day had ceased to exist.

It would be 13 years before his parents would learn that Jeffrey Dahmer had given their son a lift after the concert. The boys drove to Jeffrey's house for a few beers, but when Stephen attempted to leave, Jeffrey struck him over the head with a barbell and proceeded to strangle his unwary companion. Jeffrey had nothing against Stephen. He just didn't want him to leave.

Jeffrey dragged the body outdoors into a crawl space between the ground and the floor of the house. He cut the body into pieces and poured acid over the parts. It took a few weeks before he was able to remove excess flesh from the bones, which were then crushed with a sledgehammer. Once the bones were in tiny pieces, they were scattered over his backyard.

Out of sight, out of mind. Jeffrey joined the U.S. Army and served overseas in Germany for three years before being discharged for excessive drinking. In 1982, he moved in with his grandmother in West Allis, a suburb of Milwaukee.

For the next few years, Jeffrey drank heavily and was in and out of trouble with the law. He was given suspended sentences for his sex-related crimes. Once he lowered his trousers in a crowd. On another occasion, he was accused of masturbating in public.

Almost 10 years had passed since the murder of Stephen Hicks. That strange urge which he had managed to suppress for so long again had to be satisfied. It was 14-year-old James Doxtator's misfortune to cross Jeffrey Dahmer's path. Doxtator was accustomed to selling his body to wierdos for a price. Jeffrey picked him up with the promise that he would pay well if the boy would pose for nude pictures. Doxtator was drugged, strangled and dismembered. Acid was applied to his body, which was eventually pulverized with a sledge-hammer.

Jeffrey Dahmer frequented gay bars where men were susceptible to being picked up. Richard Guerrero was one such man. He disappeared after falling into the deadly grasp of the man with the unnatural compulsion to kill and mutilate.

It became increasingly difficult and inconvenient to bring men to his grandmother's home. Jeffrey moved into the Oxford apartments at 808 N. 24th St. in Milwaukee. Later he would move into apartment 213, an address which would one day be flashed around the world.

Not everyone lured to Jeffrey's apartment was murdered. A few boys sensed that drugs had been placed in their beer or coffee and raced out of the apartment. One boy, a Laotian named Sinthasomphone, pressed charges. As a result, Jeffrey found himself convicted of sexual assault. He received a five-year jail sentence, but was allowed out on day parole so that he could continue working at his job at the chocolate factory.

Ten months later, he was given full parole.

The killings continued. Anthony Sears, Ray Smith, Edward Smith, Ernest Miller and David Thomas all were reported missing in the 18-month period between March 1989 and September 1990. Jeffrey would later claim that he had had sex with these men before strangling them.

By now, Jeffrey Dahmer had developed an extraordinary trait, one which places him in a unique category among serial killers who keep trophies of their kills. While trophy collecting is common amongst serial killers, most keep items such as a glove or wallet. Jeffrey kept heads and entire limbs. Anthony Sears' skull was painted and stored in a refrigerator. Other heads, limbs and organs were kept as mementos of sex and murder.

Months passed. Neighbors complained of the odor emanating from the Dahmer apartment. Jeffrey satisfied them with plausible excuses and promises that he would remedy the situation. No one took any concrete action. The killing spree went on unabated. Curtis Straughter, 18; Errol Lindsey, 19; and Tony Hughes, 31, all ended up as victims of the human monster who retained portions of their bodies as trophies.

Konerak Sinthasomphone, 14, coincidentally the younger brother of the boy responsible for Dahmer's earlier imprisonment for sexual assault, was a student at Pulaski High School. He was picked up by Jeffrey Dahmer and enticed into unit 213 at the Oxford apartments. Konerak was given a beer laced with a knockout drop. He fell unconscious and was subjected to a sexual attack. Noticing that he was out of beer, Jeffrey left to pick up a six-pack. While he was gone, Konerak regained consciousness and staggered, bleeding and naked, out of the apartment and down into the street, where he was spotted by Dahmer.

Others also witnessed the scene and called the police. Three patrolmen, John Balcerzak, Joe Gabrish, and Richard Porubcan were soon at the scene of the incident. All three officers were experienced members of the Milwaukee Police Force. Throughout their careers they have received several citations for heroism and acting beyond the call of duty.

Jeffrey had to talk fast. He assured the officers his gay lover was a drunken adult and that there was really nothing amiss. The officers accompanied Jeffrey to his apartment, unaware that the body of Tony Hughes lay decaying in the bedroom at the time of their visit.

Jeffrey showed the officers Polaroid pictures of Konerak posing in a skimpy bathing suit. The officers assumed they had been called to a domestic dispute between two consenting males. They were tragically wrong. After they left, Jeffrey strangled Konerak Sinthasomphone to death.

All three officers would later be suspended with pay for their actions that night. The three policemen maintained that there appeared to be a loving relationship between the two participants and that there were none of the usual warning signs that anything was drastically wrong.

The brief brush with the law didn't discourage Jeffrey. On June 30, 1991, Matt Turner was murdered in the apartment. Jeremiah Weinberger, Oliver Lacy, and Joseph Bradehoft met the same fate. All four heads were later found in the refrigerator.

On July 22, 1991, police officers Robert Rauth and Rolf Mueller were in their patrol car when they were flagged down by Tracy Edwards. Edwards wanted the cops to get him out of the handcuffs he was wearing. He told the officers a wild story of a man who had threatened to cut out his heart and eat it. The officers had the frightened man lead them to Jeffrey Dahmer's apartment.

The first thing to hit the officers was the vile odor of the apartment. They questioned Jeffrey and radioed headquarters to do a routine check on their suspect. Word came back that Dahmer had a felony conviction against him. The officers looked around the filthy apartment. One of them opened the refrigerator door and within hours the world was privy to the secret life of Jeffrey Dahmer.

Once in custody, Dahmer admitted to having committed 17 murders in all and to having practised cannibalism.

In February 1992, he was found guilty of 15 murders and

was sentenced to 15 consecutive life sentences. He is eligible for parole in 936 years.

LAURIE DANN

Winnetka, Illinois, was a good place to live, a good place to bring up a family. The pleasant Chicago suburb of 14,000 was a safe haven, relatively free of the violence which has reached epidemic proportions in major U.S. cities. That is, until May 20, 1988, when Laurie Dann went berserk.

It wasn't supposed to happen that way. Born Laurie Wasserman, the daughter of an affluent accountant, she was a graduate of exclusive New Trier East High School. She went on to the University of Arizona before returning to Chicago.

In 1980, Laurie dated Russell Dann, whom she married two years later. For awhile she seemed content to be the suburban housewife ensconced in her quarter of a million dollar home, but the marriage gradually deteriorated. In 1984, the Danns divorced and Laurie returned to her parents' home.

The signs were there if only someone had paid attention. Laurie commenced to behave in an irrational manner.

Her ex-husband, Russell Dann, was stabbed while he slept in bed. The wound was serious and Russell was hospitalized. Later, he revealed that Laurie had admitted stabbing him. Russell realized that his ex-wife was unstable and didn't press the matter. Besides, there was no definite proof that Laurie had committed the crime.

A short time later, Laurie, for no apparent reason, began phoning an Arizona University grad whom she had dated while attending university. The old acquaintance, who was now a medical doctor, was amazed at the string of calls.

When Laurie threatened his wife and children, he contacted his lawyers, who wrote to her parents, advising them of the unnatural series of phone calls. Questioned by local authorities, Laurie swore she was pregnant by the doctor, whom she had not seen for over five years.

At any time during this period of irrational behavior, someone could have suggested professional help for the mature woman who was obviously deranged. But things don't always work out that way. In hindsight, Laurie should have received treatment. As events unfolded over the years, she was thought of as a harmless oddball.

In 1987, Laurie advertised herself as a competent baby-sitter. Those who hired her recommended her to friends. Occasionally, there were incidents, such as the time one couple found that their sofa had been slashed after Laurie had been baby-sitting for them. Laurie swore she had no knowledge of the damage, which was reported to the police. They felt that Laurie may have had a hand in the vandalism, but had no proof.

Now caught up in a veritable frenzy of strange behavior, Laurie moved out of her parents' home and took an apartment on the Northwestern University campus. Almost immediately, there were complaints of raw meat being left to spoil in various locations in the apartment building. University officials asked Laurie to move.

Meanwhile Laurie had gained a measure of notoriety as a baby-sitter. There were complaints of theft of food and damage of property. She became known to the police as a very troubled individual. Her father paid for any damage attributed to her. She wrote threatening missives to her ex-husband's parents. The Danns implored the Wassermans to have Laurie institutionalized. Again, with the benefit of hindsight, we can see the avenue which should have been taken. Looking at events as they occurred, who can blame a parent for not wanting to institutionalize a daughter? One must remember that despite her strange behavior, Laurie could turn on the charm when the occasion arose.

Laurie moved to Madison, Wisconsin, and became a part-time student at the University of Wisconsin, where she lived in a dormitory. She was considered a loony by the other students. Laurie rode the elevators up and down for hours. Sometimes she showed up in the dining room in her pyjamas and slippers.

In March 1988, Laurie was apprehended while shoplifting. After spending the night in jail, she was sentenced to perform community service. Within weeks of being sentenced, she set fire to the rooms of two fellow students.

By April, Laurie, who was now well-known to the local police, may have been considered something more than a troubled oddball to the authorities. Known by the FBI to have purchased three pistols years earlier, they thought it advisable to pay her a visit. They were too late.

On May 14, Laurie slashed a fellow student's clothing. Because the semester was over the next day, most students had left their living quarters. Laurie was found in a storage bin in the basement of the school. Police were summoned. Next day, the FBI dropped by to question Laurie. She was gone.

On May 19, Laurie Dann showed up at the home of Padraig and Marian Rushe. The Rushes had previously used Laurie as a baby-sitter and never suspected her of any wrongdoing. When Laurie offered to take two of the five Rushe children to a fair the following day, the Rushes consented.

On May 20, the evil machinations at work in Laurie's brain predicated that she rise at 7 a.m. It would be an eventful day.

Laurie delivered packages of fruit juice to eight suburban homes. All contained arsenic. At two other homes, she left plates of Rice Krispies on the doorstep. Both contained arsenic. At 9 a.m., Laurie picked up Patrick Rushe, 8 and his little brother, Carl, 4. She gave the two boys cartons of milk, but the milk didn't taste good and the youngsters only took a sip before placing them on the seat of the car. Fortunately, there were no casualties as a result of Laurie's poison attempts.

Laurie drove to Ravinia School and set fire to a plastic bag filled with gasoline, which she placed near the school. Returning the two Rushe children to their home, Laurie bid a cheerful goodbye to Mrs. Rushe, who was busy in the laundry room. As soon as Laurie left, the laundry room stairs burst into flames. Marian Rushe miraculously tore out an entire window frame and, together with her two children, managed to escape the fire.

Laurie Dann, armed with a .22-calibre Beretta, a .357 Magnum and a .32-calibre Smith and Wesson revolver, drove to Hubbard Woods School. She walked into the boys' washroom and shot the first little boy to enter the room. Robert Trossman, six, took the full force of the .357 Magnum in the chest and stomach. Laurie tossed the gun to the floor beside the form of her first victim. Unbelievably, Robert survived.

Laurie entered a classroom and gave an order to teacher Amy Moses. Ms. Moses refused to respond. Laurie pulled out two pistols. Amy Moses couldn't quite comprehend the situation. She found herself in a hand-to-hand struggle with a mysterious woman who had two guns. Laurie broke loose and opened fire on a group of children. Lindsay Fisher, eight; Peter Munro, eight; Kathryn Miller, seven; and Mark Teborek, eight, were wounded. Little Nicholas Corwin, eight, took the time to push a friend out of Laurie's line of fire. The friend escaped unscathed, but Nicholas was shot through the heart and died instantly.

Laurie dashed out of the school, jumped into her Toyota and roared down a dead-end street. She hit a tree. Deserting her car, she ran into the home of Ruth and Raymond Andrews. The Andrews were talking to their son Philip, 20, a student at the University of Illinois. Wielding two pistols, Laurie hurriedly explained that she had just been raped. The Andrews were unable to comprehend the entire situation, but all three realized that something terribly wrong had just taken place. They cajoled Laurie into calling her parents. She told her parents the police were closing in on her, as indeed they were.

By gestures, Philip Andrews conveyed the message to his

parents to leave the room while Laurie was still on the phone. Once his parents were safe, Philip made a desperate grab for the .22 calibre Beretta. Laurie shot him in the chest. Philip staggered outside before collapsing. Although seriously wounded, he survived.

Meanwhile, a SWAT team surrounded the Andrews' home. It wasn't until seven that evening that they stormed the house. In an upstairs bedroom, they found the body of Laurie Dann. Earlier in the day, she had placed the .32 calibre Smith and Wesson in her mouth, pulled the trigger and ended her troubled life.

No one knows why the pent-up evil that filled Laurie's mind exploded in a classroom on a quiet day in May in a quiet suburb of Chicago. There is no reasonable explanation, except for the terrible mental illness that drove her to murder and suicide.

ALBERT DE SALVO

The Hillside Strangler kept the city of Los Angeles in a reign of terror. Wayne Williams, who murdered young children in Atlanta, Georgia, terrorized that city. But nothing before or since has ever held a city in the grip of fear quite like the Boston Strangler did back in 1962.

From June 1962, to January 1964, the citizens of Boston and its suburbs talked of little else but the weird, sexually motivated murders of women ranging in age from 19 to 85.

The sale of locks escalated rapidly. Some apartments resembled armed camps, yet a cunning, deranged man talked his way into hundred of apartments to molest, rape and, in 13 instances, kill innocent women.

On the evening of June 14, 1962, Juris Slesers, 25, a research engineer at M.I.T., climbed the stairs to his mother's third floor apartment at 77 Gainsborough St. The 55-year-old Anna Slesers had been looking forward to her son's visit. She had prepared his favorite dishes for dinner.

Anna didn't answer Juris' knock. Inside the apartment, she lay on the floor, dead. Juris broke down the door to the apartment and found his mother's body. It was not a pleasant sight. Anna lay on her back. Her robe appeared to be open on purpose, displaying her nudity. She had been strangled with her bathrobe cord, which had been knotted around her neck and tied in a bow.

The house had been ransacked, indicating to police that the killer may have been robbing the apartment when Anna, who was preparing to take a bath, heard something, opened the bathroom door and was attacked. There was water in the bathtub. Anna had not been raped, but had been sexually molested. The door to her apartment had not been forced. Would Anna greet a stranger in her bathrobe?

No one knew it at the time, but the Boston Strangler, as he was soon to become known, had murdered for the first time.

Two weeks later, on June 30, the temperature in Boston hit 90 degrees F. Nina Nichols, 68, was on the phone speaking to her sister when the buzzer to her apartment sounded. She told her sister, "Excuse me, Marguerite, there's my buzzer. I'll call you right back." Nina Nichols never called back. She answered the door and became the Boston Strangler's second victim. The building janitor eventually opened the door with a passkey and found her body.

Nina Nichols had been strangled with her own nylon stocking, which had been grotesquely knotted into a bow around her neck. Her underclothing had been pulled up to her waist, exposing her nude body. Although her apartment had been ransacked, no money, jewelry or other valuables appeared to be missing.

That same night of June 30, Helen Blake, 65, was strangled to death. When neighbors couldn't contact her, they called police. Helen was found on her bed, face down, nude except for her pyjama top. She had been strangled with her nylon stockings and brassiere, which had been tied around her neck in the familiar bow. She had been sexually assaulted.

Now the rash of murders were attributed to one man, dubbed the Boston Strangler. Each murder was stranger than the last. The victims were unknown to each other. Although their apartments had been ransacked, nothing appeared to be missing. Why were the victims exposed and made to look ridiculous in death? Who was this man who seemed to be able to talk any woman into opening the door of her apartment? Who was the Boston Strangler? No one knew. The murders continued.

Ida Irga, 75, was strangled on August 19. Next day, Jane

Sullivan, 67, met her death at the hands of the Strangler. That winter, on December 5, Sophia Clark, 20, was murdered. Over three weeks later, Patricia Bissette, 23, was killed in the Strangler's unique way.

It should be noted that another murder, at first not thought to be the work of the Boston Strangler, but later attributed to him, took place during the summer of 1962. Eighty-five-year-old Mary Mullen died of a heart attack in the Strangler's arms before he had a chance to strangle her.

The series of weird murders were the main topic of conversation in the greater Boston area. Delivery men had a difficult time performing their duties. Parcels were left outside doors. Men walked their dates to their front doors and waited until their companions had securely locked themselves in.

The killings continued. March 9, 1963, Mary Brown, 69; May 6, 1963, Beverley Samans, 23; September 8, 1963, Evelyn Corbin, 58; November 23, 1963, Joann Graff, 23; January 4, 1964, Mary Sullivan, 19. In all, 13 innocent victims fell to the madness that was the Boston Strangler. Who was he?

Albert De Salvo was born in Chelsea, a suburb of Boston. His father, who was a wife-beater, taught little Albert the art of shoplifting when the lad was five years old. Albert was in and out of trouble during his early years. At 16, he joined the army, where he served for over eight years. During a five-year stint in Germany, he married. At the conclusion of his army service, he returned with his bride, Irmgard, to live near Boston. They had two children, a boy and a girl.

In 1961, Albert achieved some degree of infamy posing as the Measuring Man. He would knock on an apartment door, first making sure that the lady of the house was home alone. Flashing his boyish grin, he would explain that he was recruiting models for a project where they could earn $40 an hour. To add credibility to his patter, he would produce a measuring tape, explaining that nudity was not involved. The modelling was for evening gowns.

If the lady of the house refused, Albert would bow and move along. If she consented, he measured her from every conceivable angle. He would then shake hands, with a promise that a woman from his agency would be in contact.

No crime was actually committed. No woman from the agency showed up. However, on one occasion, Albert was spotted dashing through an alleyway by an alert police officer. Once in custody, he admitted to being the Measuring Man. He explained that he meant no harm. It just gave him a thrill to talk to and measure women. Albert was sentenced to 18 months for attempted breaking and entering. He was paroled from the Middlesex County House of Correction in April 1962, after serving 11 months.

Another weirdo was out on the streets. Albert now became the Green Man, as well as the Boston Strangler. Dressed up in a green uniform, he gained entrance to the apartments of even the most careful women. Once inside, he molested and raped his victims, after apologizing for the intrusion. Many women didn't report the Green Man's crimes, so we will never know how many women the Green Man raped. Police estimate over 300. Albert was later to say between 600 and 1000. We do know that he often raped four women on the same day.

One victim gave such a detailed description of her attacker's face that an artist's sketch was matched to a photograph of the old Measuring Man. The similarities were startling. Albert De Dalvo was picked up and questioned. Under urging by his wife, he confessed to being the Green Man. He had committed scores of crimes, which were never attributed to him, sometimes ranging into Connecticut, New Hampshire and Rhode Island. At no time did Albert De Salvo admit that simultaneously to being the Green Man, he was operating and killing as the Boston Strangler.

While awaiting trial, Albert began to act in an irrational manner, often talking to his wife and police officers in his cell in the middle of the night. After a sanity hearing, he was incarcerated in the Bridgewater State Hospital until deemed fit to stand trial.

In Bridgewater, Albert became friends with two-time killer, George Nassar, an unusual inmate who had an IQ of 150. Albert bragged incessantly to Nassar about his successes with women while posing as the Measuring Man and the Green Man. Initially, Nassar paid little attention, but when Albert claimed to be the Boston Strangler, he listened more closely. He soon came to believe that Albert was telling the truth. Nassar contacted his lawyer, F. Lee Bailey, considered one of the finest defence lawyers in the country.

Bailey took on Albert's case. He listened to his story, which was full of details only the authentic Boston Strangler could know. There was no doubt about it. Albert De Salvo was the Boston Strangler.

Albert was deemed competent to stand trial. He was found guilty of assault and sex crimes committed as the Green Man. As a result, he was sentenced to life imprisonment, but never stood trial for the 13 murders he committed as the Boston Strangler.

In 1967, Albert again made headlines when he escaped from Bridgewater. Newspapers, radio and television blared out the warning that the Boston Strangler was at large. Albert listened to the hunt on his transistor radio before walking into a clothing store and giving himself up to a clerk.

On November 26, 1973, Albert De Salvo was stabbed to death by a fellow inmate in prison.

MARK ESSEX

Mark Essex was raised in a fine home by fine parents in the fine Midwest town of Emporia, Kansas. From the time he joined the U.S. Navy in 1969, until January 1973, something turned Mark Essex into a raging killer.

While in the navy, Mark completed a three-month dental assistant's course. The 21-year-old black man with the solid background let it be known that he intended to become a dentist.

But the navy held many surprises for Mark. He was unaccustomed to racial prejudice and was ill-equipped to cope with the petty indignities passed out by the white servicemen. Mark soon discovered that blacks were given the distasteful duties. The whites treated the black servicemen as inferiors.

In 1970, Mark couldn't stand the discrimination and abusive behavior any longer. He left the navy without leave and returned to Emporia. The young man who returned to his parents was a bitter individual. The world outside his sheltered Midwest existence was not what he imagined. With a minister's help, his parents managed to talk Mark into returning to the navy after he had brooded at home for a month.

Court-martialled, he was confined to the naval base for one month and sentenced to forfeit $90 pay each month for the next two months. Mark's court-martial trial dwelt on two salient issues, namely Mark's above-average ability at his dental work and the amount of racial abuse he had encountered in the service. However, the punishment devastated Mark and reinforced his now deep-rooted belief that all whites were the black man's natural enemy.

Discharged from the navy, Mark once more returned to his home town, where he stayed with his parents until 1972. He then took several trips to New York, before moving on to New Orleans. While in New York, Mark picked up a .44-magnum carbine and a .38-calibre Colt revolver. In New Orleans, he took a vending machine repair course.

Mark was somewhat a lone brooder until November 16, 1972. That was the day a university demonstration in Baton Rouge culminated in two black students being shot by police. The Baton Rouge incident firmly committed Mark to a course of action from which there was no return. He wrote his parents, affirming his commitment to the cause of the black man in America. Mark even decorated the walls of his apartment with racial slogans.

On New Year's Eve of 1972, Mark secreted himself across the street from the New Orleans police department's Central Lockup and opened fire with his Ruger .44-magnum semi-automatic carbine. One shot struck police cadet Al Harrell, 19, in the chest, killing him. Ironically, Harrell was one of the few black cadets attached to the New Orleans police force. The same bullet exited Harrell's body and hit Lt. Horace Perez in the ankle. In a matter of minutes, scores of police were looking for the mysterious sniper, but the madman had disappeared.

A few blocks away from the Central Lockup building, two policemen were checking out an alarm that had sounded in the offices of a factory building. Unknown to the police, Mark Essex lurked in one of the offices. A shot rang out, and Officer Edwin Hosli slumped to the floor. Two months later he would die of his wounds.

Thirty-five police officers surrounded the factory. Shots ricocheted off the walls, but once again, the sniper made good his escape. This time police found bloodstains, indicating that their quarry had been wounded.

Police followed the sniper. It wasn't that difficult. He left a trail of bullets, as if inviting police to follow. The trail led to the First New St. Mark Baptist Church. However, not wanting to have another shootout that night, the police retreated from the area. Once more, the sniper had eluded capture.

A week passed. On January 7, Mark walked into a grocery store managed by Joe Perniciaro and shot him in the chest. Mark ran from the store and commandeered a car idling at a stop sign. He then drove to Howard Johnson's Hotel in downtown New Orleans.

Mark proceeded up an outside staircase to the 18th floor of the hotel before he could gain entrance. Lugging his rifle with him, he briskly walked by three black hotel employees. He reassured them with the comment, "Don't worry, I'm not going to hurt you black people. I want the whites."

Dr. Robert Steagall had the bad luck to cross Mark's path. Mark shot him the chest and arm. Betty Steagall knelt to comfort her husband. As she did so, Mark shot her in the head. He then entered the Steagalls' room and set fire to the curtains.

Mark made his way down to the 11th floor, where he met bellman Donald Roberts and office manager Frank Schneider. The two men took one look and ran for their lives. Bullets slammed into the walls. One struck Frank Schneider in the head, killing him instantly.

The sniper shot at anyone he met. General manager Walter Collins, accompanied by janitor Lucino Llovett, went looking for the sniper. They found him on the 10th floor. Collins was shot in the back.

Meanwhile, as the slaughter progressed, someone called police, who arrived along with the fire department. A ladder was raised outside the building. Lt. Tim Ursin was climbing the ladder when Mark spotted him. Ursin was shot in his left arm. The wound was severe enough to necessitate the later amputation of the arm.

One can imagine the chaos the shooting caused in a large hotel. Guests screamed and ran for their lives. Occasionally, police would shoot at a moving object on an upper floor. The number of police mounted until well over 600 surrounded the building. Mark kept moving, setting fires in rooms as he spread havoc throughout the hotel. Firemen, attempting to battle the flames, feared for their lives; not only from the sniper but from the indiscriminate police gunfire.

Several men were wounded by the sniper. Patrolman Charles Arnold opened a window of a building directly across the street from the hotel. As he did so, a bullet smashed into his face. Robert Beamish, a hotel guest, was shot in the stomach. Officer Kenneth Solis was shot in the shoulder. When Sgt. Emanuel Palmisano came to Solis' aid, he was shot in the back. Patrolman Paul Persigo wasn't so lucky. He was shot dead by the sniper.

The strange scenario unfolding in New Orleans took on an unreal aura. Armed civilians joined the large crowd that stared up at the smouldering top floors of Howard Johnson's. Many shouted encouragement to the sniper.

Finally, the police advanced upward in the hotel, but not without paying a price. Deputy Superintendent Louis Sirgo was shot dead on the 16th floor. The sniper retreated to the roof. The first policeman to gain the roof was Officer Larry Arthur. He was shot in the abdomen, while the gunman shouted, "Free Africa! Come on up, pigs!"

Tear gas was fired to the rooftop without effect. To taunt police, Mark shouted, "I'm still here, pigs!"

A helicopter was brought in to stamp out the sniper. Unbelievably, Mark's fire drove off the first few passes. An armored helicopter carrying two Marine sharpshooters and three police officers was then used. The sharpshooters poured bullets into the roof. Several volleys almost killed police officers who were hiding in stairwells and behind abutments. Nine policemen were wounded by their colleagues' fire.

Darkness descended on New Orleans. The armored helicopter, with its sharpshooters, made pass after pass at the lone sniper. A bullet wounded Mark, who then came out from cover and attacked the helicopter, firing from the hip. Bullets poured into Mark's body — from the helicopter, from the roof, from the stairwells.

In all, over 200 bullet holes were found in the unrecognizable mass that was once Mark Essex. In his wake, he left nine dead and 10 wounded. Mark Essex's body was returned to Emporia, Kansas, where he was buried in an unmarked grave.

LARRY EYLER

By the summer of 1983, police were certain that a serial killer was operating in the greater Chicago area and across the border in Indiana. The bodies of young men between the ages of 16 and 28 were turning up in epidemic proportions.

On May 9, 1983, Dan McNeive, a 21-year-old hustler, was found stabbed to death in a field in Henderson County, Indiana. The many stab wounds on his body were typical of the injuries found on the dozen victims discovered during the previous year. Dan frequented gay bars and had often been seen in the company of gay men. Most of the victims were homosexuals and were well known in the gay communities of Chicago and Indianapolis.

A task force was formed to take over the investigations already underway. This force spread out, checking gay bars in several localities within 150 miles of Lake Michigan. In this way, the name Larry Eyler first came to the attention of police. An anonymous phone call suggested him as a suspect because he had been in some trouble five years earlier.

At that time, Larry worked in a liquor store and frequented gay bars. In 1978, he had picked up a hitchhiker in Terre Haute, had driven him to a field outside town and had threatened the man with a knife. Larry's captive was handcuffed and stabbed repeatedly. Despite the handcuffs and his serious wounds, the injured man was able to roll off the back of Larry's pickup truck and escape. He spent several days in the intensive care unit of a local hospital and was fortunate to survive the attack.

After posting bond of $10,000, Larry was released from custody. When his trial date approached, his lawyer offered the victim $2,500 to cover his medical expenses and wages lost because of his hospitalization. The young man accepted the cash and agreed not to press charges. Larry, who had been planning to plead guilty to aggravated assault, changed his plea to innocent. The case was dismissed. Larry paid $43 in court costs.

The task force investigation brought many suspects into their net, but Larry Eyler's name always rose to the surface. Although he lived in Terre Haute, he roamed the Indiana/Illinois border where most of the bodies were recovered. The victims had usually been stabbed. Many had indentations around their wrists, leading investigators to believe they had been handcuffed before being murdered. The bodies were found in woods and fields near highways. Larry continually travelled these roads and it was well known in the gay community that he was deeply involved in bondage. Despite the fact that police were keeping an eye on Larry, bodies continued to show up, all bearing the tell-tale multiple stabbings.

On September 30, 1983, task force detectives staked out a gay bar on North Clark St. in Chicago. Inside, Larry Eyler was having a midday beer. He came out and drove away in his 1982 Ford pickup. Detectives followed. Larry cruised at a snail's pace, obviously looking for a male companion. When fog settled on the seamy north side, the detectives lost their quarry. They did, however, report to task force headquarters that their prime suspect was in Chicago and apparently was on the prowl.

Meanwhile, Larry had picked up a drifter. As soon as the man was in the vehicle Larry propositioned him. He wanted to tie the man up and would pay him $100 for his trouble. Larry promised that the fun and games wouldn't hurt. Finally, the drifter agreed to the proposition. Larry parked the truck and the two men walked the short distance into a field. The drifter didn't like the proximity to the road and suggested they find a more secluded spot. Larry agreed.

The two men were walking back to the truck when State Trooper Kenneth Buehrie just happened to pull up. He thought the circumstances were suspicious and decided to question the two men, as well as to radio for a vehicle registration check. He was informed that Larry Eyler was a prime suspect in a serial murder investigation.

Larry was taken into custody and detained in a cell while police searched his truck. The soles of Larry's shoes corresponded with footprints made at the scene of one of the murders. A bloodstained hunting knife, some rope and a key for unlocking handcuffs were found in the truck. Despite the grave suspicion that they had the right man in custody, police doubted that they could hold him based on the evidence. Larry admitted to his bondage fetish and informed his interrogators that he had cut his finger on his hunting knife weeks earlier. The drifter told police that he had gone willingly with Larry. After being held for 12 hours, Larry Eyler was released.

Next day, Larry's home in Terre Haute was searched. Telephone records revealed that he had called a male lover in Chicago before each one of the serial killer's victims was murdered. While in Chicago, Larry lived with this lover.

When the body of Ralph Calise was found, authorities felt that there was enough cumulative evidence to arrest Larry Eyler and charge him with Calise's murder. Larry hired respected lawyer David Shipper to defend him on the murder charge. There was far more at stake than a single murder. Police were certain they were dealing with a monster who had killed 19 times with seeming immunity from prosecution.

At a pretrial hearing held in January 1984, defence lawyer Shipper tore the initial police investigation to shreds. Larry had been held in custody for over 12 hours without being charged with any crime. Police had searched his truck without obtaining a warrant. Although Larry had cooperated fully with police, he had been handcuffed. No one had advised him of his rights.

The presiding judge decided that the search and treatment Larry received was illegal, making most of the subsequent evidence against him inadmissable. The court didn't get to hear about the bag of rope in Larry's truck, nor did they hear about the bloody knife. The judge reduced bail from $1 million to $10,000. Larry's family deposited the required 10% and Larry walked out of court practically a free man. True, the decision to reduce bail would be appealed, but that could be 18 months down the road. Larry's friends and relatives rejoiced. The families of many victims wept openly in court.

A friend fixed Larry up with an apartment at 1628 West Sherwin Ave. in Chicago. To one and all he announced that he was beginning a new life. However, he continued his love trysts with his regular lover and often picked up transients.

On August 21, 1984, the janitor of Larry's apartment building thought several plastic bags of garbage were unusually heavy. On his way to tossing them into a dumpster, he decided to open one. Inside he discovered the dismembered body of 15-year-old male prostitute Daniel Bridges. The garbage belonged to none other than Larry Eyler.

Police were called. They immediately recognized the name. Had a suspected serial killer become so brazen that he had killed in his own apartment and had attempted to dispose of the body behind his own building?

A search of Larry's apartment revealed that it had been freshly painted. Despite the new paint job, bloodstains were found, which proved to be the same blood type as the victim's. In addition, Larry had been seen lugging the garbage bags outdoors.

In October 1986, the entire despicable life led by Larry Eyler was paraded before a jury. The evidence led to no other conclusion but guilt. Larry was sentenced to death for the murder of Daniel Bridges. Many believe that he was responsible for a total of 21 victims.

Larry offered to plead guilty to all 21 murders in exchange for a life sentence. His offer was rejected. In March 1994, Larry Eyler died of AIDS in a Pontiac, Illinois prison.

JOHN WAYNE GACY

John Wayne Gacy would grow up to be the manager of a chain of southern fried chicken stores, a successful shoe-store manager, a respected member of the Junior Chamber of Commerce, a performing clown, a precinct captain in the Democratic Party, and the owner of his own prosperous contracting business. He also was to become the most prolific mass murderer in the history of the United States.

John's formative years hold no clue to his future bizarre behavior. Gregarious, fun-loving John Gacy was an average student who took a job as a shoe salesman after graduating from Northwestern Business College in Chicago.

In 1964, when he was 22, he was so highly regarded by the shoe firm that he was transferred to Springfield, Illinois, where he was made manager of the company's retail outlet. A few months later he was dating and eventually married co-worker Marlynn Myers.

John, who always had a weight problem, tipped the scales at approximately 220 pounds and stood only five-feet, eight-inches tall. His sparkling personality more than made up for his chunky appearance. He joined the Junior Chamber of Commerce, where he was one of the hardest working and most popular members of the local chapter.

When his father-in-law offered him a job in Waterloo, Iowa, working for his chain of southern fried chicken franchise stores, John jumped at the opportunity. Soon he was effectively running the chain, often working sixteen hours a day. John joined the Jaycees and quickly became a valuable member of the organization. He was named chaplain as well as chairman of the group's prayer breakfast. Marlynn gave birth to two healthy children, a son John and a daughter Elaine.

In the spring of 1968 the veil of respectability which shielded John Gacy's world began to crumble. A local boy claimed that while he was working for John in one of the food outlets, he had accompanied the older man to his home. Mrs. Gacy and the children were not in.

After providing his visitor with a few drinks, John suggested oral sex. When the boy refused, John threatened him with a knife and fastened him to a bed with chains. Gacy proceeded to choke the young lad until he was almost unconscious, abruptly releasing him and allowing him to leave the house.

A second boy told much the same story. His experience culminated with being forced to perform unnatural sex acts. John was arrested, and after much plea bargaining, was charged with committing sodomy. Understandably, at this time his wife left him.

John was sentenced to ten years imprisonment at the Iowa State Reformatory for men at Anamosa. Anamosa boasted one of the first Jaycee chapters formed in an American prison. John threw himself into chapter work with the same vigor he had employed at Waterloo. As a result he became president of the organization. Eighteen months after entering prison, John was paroled.

Still under thirty, John returned to Chicago. For a while he lived with his mother, having gained employment as a cook in a nearby restaurant. Four months after his release, with his mother's help, John purchased his own home at 8213 West Summerdale Avenue in suburban Norwood Park.

On February 12, 1971, a short time after moving into his own home, John was charged with disorderly conduct by Chicago police. A teenaged admitted homosexual claimed that John picked him up, drove him to his home, and attempted to force him to perform unnatural sex acts. When his accuser failed to show up in court, the charges against

John were dropped.

No one has ever been able to explain why the Iowa Board of Parole was not made aware that Gacy had been charged with a sex crime in another state. Still on parole on the sodomy charge, Gacy's activities certainly would have been curtailed had a routine check been carried out. Unfortunately, the board was never informed. One month later Gacy was officially discharged from parole.

On the surface it appeared that Gacy was rebuilding his life. He met Carole Hoff, the divorced mother of two little girls, who would soon become the second Mrs. Gacy. He made friends with his neighbors. Everyone liked big John Gacy.

What no one knew, and could not possibly conceive, was the horrible fact that the most prolific mass murderer in U.S. history was already killing boys and burying them under the crawlspace of his home. It is believed that the first murder took place on the night of January 3, 1972. The killings were to last for the next seven years.

After John and Carole became husband and wife, she and her two children were to remain in the death house for the next four years. Carole was completely unaware that John could only gain sexual gratification by killing. She was well aware that her husband was forever doing carpentry jobs around the house, making additions to this, enlarging that. Many men do the same thing. She never gave it a second thought.

Around this time a strange musty odor became noticeable in the Gacy household. John claimed it was a broken sewer tile. The old tile was replaced, but the odor didn't abate until John closed off the vents leading from the crawlspace.

Meanwhile, John was a considerate husband to Carole and a good father to her two children. Around the neighborhood he gained something of a reputation as a party giver. A couple of times a year he would throw a big barbecue. It wasn't uncommon for these feasts to be attended by more than a hundred friends and neighbors. John loved to dress up as a clown and entertain the neighborhood children.

Gacy left his job as a cook and opened his own business, P.D.M. Contractors, Inc. It was successful from the beginning. John hired experienced older men for skilled tasks, but drew his manual labor from young boys who were willing to work for low wages. His construction company expanded rapidly, and soon John was bidding on and obtaining contracts worth up to $100,000. He purchased a Cadillac and became active in the Democratic Party.

All the while renovations were taking place at the Gacy home. John built a storage shed at the end of the garage. It was customary to see young boys coming and going. Everyone knew John hired them for his construction company.

Carole became disenchanted with her marriage. Her husband spent all his time either working at his business or working for the Democrats. He seemed to prefer the company of young boys to hers. She filed for divorce and left her husband on March 2, 1976.

For seven years boys and young men had been picked up by Gacy off the streets or were befriended when they applied for employment with his construction company. He gratified his strange sexual desires before killing them and burying them on his own property.

Robert Piest was a conscientious high-school student who worked in a drugstore on a part-time basis. At 8:00 p.m., when his mother called at Nissons Pharmacy in Des Plaines to pick up her son on the evening of December 11, 1978, Robert asked her to wait in the store for a few moments. He had to talk to a man named John Gacy about a contracting job which paid quite a bit better than his present job at the drugstore. Gacy was waiting in his pickup truck in the parking lot. Robert left the store, telling his mother that he would be back in a few moments. He never returned.

Mrs. Piest searched the parking lot. She questioned Robert's friends. No one could help her. Finally she called the police. Next day detectives were extensively questioning John Gacy about the missing boy. Gacy denied having any knowledge about the disappearance. When detectives were informed of Gacy's criminal record, they obtained a warrant to search his home.

Rows of bodies, some little more than skeletons, were found buried in the crawlspace of the house. Others were found buried under the recreation room, while still others were buried in the garage. In all, twenty-nine bodies were removed from Gacy's property. Four other victims had been thrown in nearby rivers.

Gacy's murder trial concluded on March 13, 1980, when he was convicted of murdering thirty-three young men and boys, more than any other person in U.S. history.

In May 1994, John Wayne Gacy was executed by lethal injection in Statesville Penitentiary near Joliet, Illinois.

GERALD GALLEGO

They told little nine-year-old Gerald Gallego that his father had died in a car accident. They lied.

Gerald was a bad little boy. By the time he was 13 he displayed an abnormal tendency toward sadism and sex. A few months after his thirteenth birthday, he was incarcerated by the California Youth Authority for having sex with a six-year-old girl.

Gerald went on to spend most of his formative years behind bars. He married seven different women between prison sentences, often without benefit of divorce. We need only concern ourselves with his seventh wife, Charlene, who strangely relished her husband's wild lifestyle. Unlike Gerald, Charlene came from a secure, loving family, who were well respected in the Sacramento, California area. For reasons only she understands, she fell in love and married Gerald Gallego.

Charlene was 24, Gerald 32, when the pair graduated from child molesting, rape, and robbery to wanton serial killing.

On September 11, 1978, Rhonda Scheffler, 17 and Kippi Vaught, 16 set out in the Schefflers' family car for a shopping mall in Sacramento. The girls never returned home. Two days later their bodies were found about 15 miles outside the city. They had been beaten with a tire iron and shot in the head with a .25 calibre pistol. Both had been sexually abused.

Nine months later, on April 24, 1980, Stacy Redican and

Karen Chipman-Twiggs vanished from another Sacramento shopping mall. Their decomposed bodies were found in July by picnickers 75 miles north of Reno. They had been beaten about the head with sufficient force to crush their skulls.

Linda Aquilar, 21, was five months pregnant when she disappeared while hitchhiking from Port Orford, Oregon. Her body was recovered from a shallow grave a few miles south of Gold Beach. She had been bound hand and foot with nylon rope. An autopsy revealed that death had been caused by vicious blows to the head with an iron object. She had been buried while still alive.

In hindsight, we are connecting the murders, but at the time separate investigations were being conducted in all three cases. They were not considered to be related. The crimes took place in different locales and the victims were from vastly different backgrounds. One victim was pregnant and was apparently picked up by her killer while hitchhiking. The others were abducted from shopping malls.

Waitress Virginia Mochel walked out of the Sacramento bar where she worked into the parking lot toward her car. While walking those few yards, she disappeared. Virginia's body was found three months later just outside Sacramento. Her arms were securely tied behind her back.

Customers at the bar were questioned. Many remembered that Virginia had spoken to a man and woman several times while they drank. The man, who said he was a bartender, was outgoing and loud, while his companion was docile and spoke very little. That's about all the police had to go on. The killings didn't stop.

Mary Beth Sowers and her fiancé, Craig Miller, attended California State University in Sacramento. They were a popular young couple who had every reason to look forward to a happy and prosperous future. Craig had been named Man of the Year at the university for 1979.

Mary Beth and Craig attended the Sigma Phi Epsilon Founders Day dinner at the Carousel, a well-known Sacramento restaurant. Mary Beth was resplendent in a formal gown. Craig was decked out in a tuxedo.

Arm in arm, they left the restaurant at midnight. Out of the darkness, a woman lurched toward them. Too late, they saw she was pointing a handgun in their direction. The woman ordered them into a parked 1977 Olds. An adult male occupied the front passenger seat.

The woman with the gun jumped into the driver's seat and sped away, but not before a friend of the students witnessed the abduction. He had gone over to investigate and had received a slap from the woman before she jumped into the vehicle. The alert friend jotted down the licence number and phoned police. The number was fed into the police computer. A few minutes later they had the name of the registered owner — Charlene Gallego.

The car containing the two abducted students pulled onto a secluded road in El Dorado County. Craig was ordered from the vehicle and told to lie face down on the road. The man, now equipped with a handgun, fired three shots into the back of the hapless student's head.

Mary Beth Sowers cowered in horror while her fiancé was murdered in cold blood. She was then driven to a Sacramento apartment where she was raped.

The man's companion waited outside the bedroom door. Mary Beth was taken from the apartment and driven a few miles outside the city, where she too was shot three times in the head.

The day after these murders, Charlene Gallego was questioned by police. She told them very little other than that she was drunk the night before and couldn't remember anything that had happened. The police had no idea they were involved in a murder investigation. They only knew they had a report that two students had left a fraternity dinner under suspicious circumstances. As far as they were concerned, it could be nothing more than university student hijinks.

Later that same day, when Craig's body was found, police raced back to Charlene's apartment. She and the Olds were long gone. A few inquiries revealed that Charlene's husband was one Gerald Gallego, a man with a long police record, including many sex crimes.

Charlene contacted friends, attempting to have them wire money to her. Police were notified and were waiting for the Gallegos in a Western Union office in Omaha, Nebraska. Returned to California, both initially pleaded not guilty to charges of murder and abduction. A few weeks after they were taken into custody, the body of Mary Beth Sowers was found in a little-used field.

Charlene, who was seven months pregnant at the time of her arrest, gave birth to a boy while in jail. The baby Gerald Jr., was given to relatives to raise.

Months passed. Charlene was removed from the dominating personality of her husband. Slowly she revealed the details of the killing spree. At the same time, she plea-bargained for her life. She would receive a prison sentence of 16 years and eight months for the murders of Craig Miller and Mary Beth Sowers and another concurrent sentence of 16 years and eight months in the deaths of Stacy Redican and Karen Chipman-Twiggs in Nevada. She would be immune from prosecution on all other charges. In return she would tell all she knew about her husband's involvement in the killings.

Charlene told plenty. Sometimes she had been used as a lure to entice girls into their car. Other times she used a gun. The motive for the crimes had been Gerald's perverted sexual desire. In all cases he had his way with the victims while Charlene watched or waited until he was satisfied. The victims were then killed.

In the summer of 1982, Gerald Gallego stood trial for the murder of Craig Miller and Mary Beth Sowers. The trial lasted three and a half months. Gallego was found guilty and sentenced to die in California's gas chamber.

Because of California's reluctance to execute its killers, it was decided that Gerald should stand trial in Nevada for the murders committed there. It was felt that there was a better chance that Nevada would carry out his execution. Once again, he was tried, found guilty and sentenced to death. He is presently awaiting execution on Death Row in Nevada State Prison in Carson City. Charlene is serving her time next door in Nevada Women's Correctional Centre. There is no contact allowed between husband and wife.

Why was nine-year-old Gerald Gallego told that his father had died in a car accident so many years ago? Ironically Gerald Sr. was a 28-year-old convict when his son was nine. After gaining his release from San Quentin, he killed a man who was booking him into jail. After making his way to Mississippi, he was recaptured. Gerald Sr. tossed lye in a guard's face and stomped the blinded officer to death.

In 1955, the senior Gallego was the first man executed in Mississippi's new gas chamber. Should his son eventually be executed, it will be the first time a father and a son have been tried, found guilty and executed for multiple murder.

BELLE GUNNESS

Belle Paulsen's father was a magician who travelled the length and breadth of Norway with his magic act. Belle was born in 1859 and grew up to be a slim, well-behaved child who became adept at tightrope walking, delighting her father's audiences with daring stunts on the taut wire. When her father retired from the transient life of a magician and bought a farm, Belle found the change from being a performer to the solitude of rural life unbearably boring. Now an impetuous teenager, she decided to emigrate to the United States.

After she arrived in the U.S., Belle, a shapely 24-year-old, met Mads Sorensen, a Swede, who courted her and won her hand in marriage. The couple settled in Chicago, Illinois, and the marriage commenced to bear fruit in the form of two offspring, Lucy and Myrtle. Two years after the marriage, Mads had a heart attack and died. There was a small group of friends and relatives in the close-knit Scandinavian community who never for a moment thought that it was a heart attack that had put an end to Mads. They whispered that he had been poisoned, and they fingered the widow as the administrator of the deadly potion. But even though Belle collected $8,500 in insurance money and sold Sorensen's home for $5,000, nothing came of the distasteful rumors.

The now well-heeled Belle and her two children moved to Austin, Illinois, where they purchased a new home. One cold night the house mysteriously caught fire, and while the insurance company suspected that the fire wasn't accidental, there was no proof of any monkey business and they paid off.

Belle moved back to Chicago in the grip of an obsession. She had somehow acquired a ravenous appetite, and ate to such an extent that she started to gain weight rapidly. She became fatter and fatter, until the scales tipped 200 lbs. This five-foot, seven-inch dumpling was no longer recognizable as the slender Norwegian girl who had married Mads Sorensen. Her face had been plain to begin with, but now it became bloated and ugly. In Chicago, she purchased a candy store, which soon burned to the ground. Again with some misgivings, the insurance company paid off. We can imagine Belle, relaxing with a box of chocolates, figuring that the greatest prerequisite for success in the world of commerce was to have a quick hand with a match.

With the proceeds of her fires she purchased a 48-acre farm about a mile from La Porte, Indiana, and quite by chance had an unexpected addition to her family. Antone Olson had recently lost his wife, and felt ill-equipped to take care of his daughter Jennie. Belle, who had known the Olsons for years in Chicago, was only too happy to take Jenny in, and as she put it, "treat her like one of my own."

Belle soon ballooned to a substantial 230 lbs. She worked her farm and gained a sort of local fame by butchering her own farm animals, particularly hogs, and selling the meat in the nearby town of La Porte. In April 1902, she met Peter Gunness, who, like Belle, was Norwegian. We don't know where Peter came from, but he settled in on the farm and appears to have been well liked by his neighbors and people who came in contact with him in La Porte.

The neighbors had only a short time to make any judgment about Peter, for only seven months after he married Belle, disaster struck. It came in the form of a sausage grinder, and it struck poor Peter square on the head, killing him instantly. The grinder sat on a high shelf and, as luck, or whatever, would have it, Peter picked a spot directly under the grinder to rest his weary bones. Coincidentally enough, the grinder chose this opportune moment to totter and fall, striking Peter a fatal blow to the head.

During his short but noteworthy appearance upon the stage with Belle, the unlucky Norwegian managed to accomplish three things. He changed Belle's name from Belle Brynhilde Paulsetter Sorensen to Belle Gunness, for which he earns our gratitude. He was also thoughtful enough to insure his life for $4,000, which Belle reluctantly allowed to be pressed into her chubby hands. And he wasn't fully acclimatized to his new surroundings in the grave when Belle discovered that she was heavy laden with child, as they used to say. "Son of a bitch," Belle hissed between her teeth when she discovered the dirty trick he had pulled on her from the grave. The object of her dilemma popped into the world in 1903, and was named Phillip for no particular reason.

After the birth of her son, Belle settled down to farming, and occasionally hired a transient hand to help her. Most stayed for a short time and moved on. There was something strange and sinister about working for the quiet, puffing butterball, who could not only pitch hay with the best of men, but who also seemed to take a delight in butchering her own hogs. Rough and tough as these men were, Belle's actions didn't appear natural to them.

Belle worked hard, but a chubby nymphomaniac needs a man around the house. Like so many men and women in similar circumstances, Belle gravitated to advertising in matrimonial journals. This direct approach had produced many good husbands and wives, so we cannot completely condemn the practice of selecting a partner by mail order. But it would be as well to warn the lovesick advertiser that a certain risk is involved in communicating with a total stranger. Belle reduced the risk factor, but unfortunately her male partners weren't quite as cautious. She refined the ads and eliminated a lot of riffraff with her no-nonsense approach.

For example: "Comely widow who owns a large farm in one of the finest districts in La Porte County, Indiana, desires to make acquaintance of a gentleman equally well provided, with view of joining fortunes. No replies by letter considered unless sender is willing to follow answer with personal visit.

No triflers please."

The number of men attracted to ads of this nature is uncertain. For one thing, we will never know how many men showed up at the widow's doorstep, took one look at Belle's 230 lbs., and said thanks, but no thanks. Conversely, we have no way of knowing how many prospective suitors didn't measure up to Belle's standards. She obviously preferred men of Scandinavian extraction who had accumulated some cold, hard cash.

In answer to one of her ads, a Norwegian named John Moo arrived from Minnesota in 1906. John must be placed in the missing, presumed dead category, for he was seen and met by neighbors as the bridegroom apparent, and just as suddenly as he appeared on the scene, he vanished. During the inquiries that followed, not a trace of him could be found, and Belle claimed she had no idea where he went when he left the farm.

Another native of Norway, George Anderson, travelled from a small village in Missouri to meet Belle. By now she had developed a line that could charm the birds out of the trees. Mr. Anderson had taken the precaution of not bringing his nest-egg with him, but admitted later to being completely captivated by his hostess. She wined and dined him in the grand manner. Visions of the good life on the farm danced before his eyes, giving a rosy tinge to her obvious shortcomings. One night at the farmhouse, Anderson was startled out of a deep sleep. There, towering over him by candlelight, was the huge form of Mrs. Gunness with a strange, wild look in her eyes. As he awoke she ran from the room, and Anderson, scared half out of his wits, made the wisest move of his life. He got out of bed, put on his pants, ran all the way to the station in La Porte, and went back to Missouri on the next train.

Not quite as fortunate was Bud Budsberg, another native of Norway, who arrived at Belle's door in 1907. Mr. Budsberg had travelled from Iola, Wisconsin, with $2,000 in his poke. Despite extensive inquiries conducted by relatives back in Wisconsin, Bud was never heard from again. He simply crossed Belle's threshold and disappeared.

Nothing seemed very permanent on the Gunness farm. But there was one exception; Belle had finally found a hired hand who didn't move on like the rest. He was a French Canadian named Ray Lamphere, who was not only willing to tolerate Belle as an employer, but actually fell in love with her. Ray, who had the personality of a born follower, was of average height and had a handlebar moustache and bulging eyes that made him look as if he was always afraid of something, as well he might have been. It is pretty certain that Belle kept Ray around the farm for a variety of reasons, not the least of which was instant sex. Her other gentlemen friends had developed the annoying habit of disappearing, but steady, if not heady, Ray was always available. Jealous though he was of the other men who were continually coming to the farm, Ray was secure in the knowledge that he would outlast them all.

At about this time neighbors noticed that a large eight-foot-high fence had been put up around the farmhouse. The shutters on the windows were closed for weeks on end, and it was well-known that the basement was equipped as a slaughterhouse for Belle's hogs. She had a large table down there, as well as a pulley system for raising the carcasses of slaughtered animals. Along one wall hung a top-quality set of butchers' knives and cleavers.

The parade of suitors continued. Andrew K. Helgelein arrived from Aberdeen, South Dakota, with $3,000 in a bulging wallet. This gentleman differed from those who had come before in that he got under Ray Lamphere's skin. For some reason, Ray, who had become accustomed to seeing his beloved being courted by other men, couldn't take it when Helgelein and Belle were together. Ray and Belle argued bitterly about this, and Ray packed up his belongings and left the farm in a tantrum.

He went to La Porte and started gossiping about his former lover and employer. Nothing serious, mind you, but enough so that when word of his loose tongue got back to Belle she had him arrested and tried to have him judged insane and committed to an institution. A sanity hearing actually took place, and Lamphere was declared sane. He made up with Belle, and returned to the farm. He commenced to pick another fight; this time Belle had him arrested for trespassing. Lamphere was found guilty of this offence and paid a fine.

Still in La Porte, the French Canadian continued to badmouth Belle, even mentioning to a farmer, Bill Slater, "Helgelein won't bother me no more. She fixed him for keeps."

By coincidence Helgelein had disappeared the day before this conversation took place. Then something happened that was even more vexing than Ray Lamphere shooting off his mouth in town. For the first time in all her years on the farm, Belle was the recipient of a serious threat, in the form of inquiring letters from Mr. Asle Helgelein of Mansfield, South Dakota, who was the brother of the missing Andrew. Belle met his pointed questions with the claim that Andrew had gone back to Norway, to which Asle replied, "Rubbish."

With the heat definitely on, Belle hitched up the team, drove into La Porte and paid a visit to her lawyer, M.E. Leliter. On April 27, 1908, Belle asked the lawyer to draw up her will, leaving her estate to her three children, with the proviso that should she outlive her children, the money would go to a Norwegian orphanage in Chicago. She said the reason for this sudden urge to put her affairs in order was because Ray Lamphere was threatening to kill her and burn down her farmhouse. She told Leliter that she was in mortal fear of the insanely jealous Lamphere. The whole thing took a matter of minutes, and was drawn up and signed before she left the lawyer's office.

That very night the new hired hand, Joe Maxon, said goodnight to the family and went to bed. In the middle of the night, he was awakened by the loud crackling of a fire. Shaking the cobwebs from his mind, he rose slowly, then realized that the entire house was engulfed in flames. He shouted at the top of his lungs to wake Belle and the children, then staggered toward the window, and jumped from the second storey, wearing only his underwear.

The next morning, as the charred rubble cooled, the remains of Belle's three children, Lucy, Myrtle, and Phillip, together with the headless body of a woman, were found in the cellar, having fallen through the floor.

Because of the veiled threats made by Lamphere, and the well-known feud that existed between him and Mrs. Gunness, he immediately came under suspicion. A youngster swore he had not only seen Lamphere near the farmhouse on the night of the fire, but had actually spoken to him. Ray was arrested, and Belle's lawyer came forward and told of her accusations against the accused man. In due course, Lamphere was charged with the murder of Belle Gunness.

Neighbors who had known Belle for years were asked to identify the headless corpse. At the time of the fire Belle was estimated to weight 280 lbs. - not an easy figure to mistake. All her neighbors said the burnt corpse was too short and far too light to be Mrs. Gunness. This rather startling development threw an entirely new light on the macabre affair. For starters, who was the burned, headless corpse? If the corpse wasn't Mrs. Gunness then where was she? To further confuse an already confusing situation, Mr. Antone Olson heard about the fire and rushed down to the farm to find his Jennie. She too was nowhere to be found, although neighbors said that some time previously Belle had mentioned that she had gone to California to continue her schooling.

The authorities searched everywhere for the missing head, but try as they might, they couldn't find it. Then Mr. Asle Helgelein showed up, looking for his brother. He didn't even know there had been a fire, but he had a deep suspicion that his brother had met with foul play at the hands of the woman he had come to Indiana to marry. Asle noticed that the Gunness' yard was uneven, and that patches of earth in the yard were of different colors. Maxon, the hired hand, volunteered that there had been slight depressions in the ground, and Mrs. Gunness had told him to bring earth from an adjoining field to even it off. Asle wasn't taking any offhanded answers, and urged the police to dig in these areas. The very first hole they dug uncovered the corpse of Andrew Helgelein, whose brother had the unfortunate experience of staring down at it as it was unearthed. He positively identified the body, and the digging started in earnest.

The next hole produced the body of Jennie Olson, who hadn't gone to California at all. Three more bodies were uncovered before darkness fell on the eerie scene and the diggers had to stop for the night. The next day, May 4, 1908, four more bodies were dug out of the farmyard, and on the third day another body was uncovered. The bodies were in various stages of decomposition, and some were never to be identified. Others were positively identified as John Moo, and Bud Budsberg. Over and above these complete corpses police uncovered bits and pieces of other bodies that had no matching parts, leading them to believe that many more suitors had been put to death on the farm. With the discovery of these parts of human bodies, the police had to consider Belle's private abattoir in the basement. The implication was obvious - had Belle been butchering more than hogs?

Gossip comes a narrow second to farming as the principal occupation in the Hoosier State, and the murder farm was soon on everyone's lips. Crops lay unattended as men gathered to discuss the case, with the more curious driving out to the farm to peer at the now excavated farmyard. All the while they talked, exchanging information, telling stories, until one bit of gossip became so prominent that it took on the status of a distinct possibility.

The night the house burned, Belle had been seen heading for her farm in her buggy with a stout lady. Joe Maxon, who was in the house that night, said that he didn't see any stout lady, but added that it would have been possible for a woman to be in the house without his knowledge. The local speculation was that Belle had somehow arranged to bring a strange woman out to the farm, kill and decapitate her, set the house on fire, and take off, thinking that everyone would believe she had perished in the fire. She had come up with a stout lady, but she couldn't quite duplicate her own massive poundage.

By now the weird case was on the front page of every newspaper in the U.S. and, because of its doubtful aspects, it gave rise to theory and speculation. Everyone had a story to tell about Belle or one of the victims. Dr. Ira P. Norton read about the case and volunteered the information that he had once done dental work for Belle, and could identify his own work if the authorities could produce it. This appeared to be a hopeless task, as the police felt that a fire hot enough to destroy a head would certainly melt gold caps and change porcelain beyond recognition. The doctor explained that this was not so, and that if his dental work could be found, it would be easy to identify. The police looked at the rubble of the burned farmhouse and realized they had a mammoth task before them.

Into a case already loaded down with strange and interesting characters came the most colorful of all, Louis Schultz. He had heard about the missing old dental work in the rubble of the fire. Louis was an experienced gold miner just back from the Yukon, and told the police that if they would build him a sluice box, he would sluice the entire farmhouse and if there was any gold in the rubble he would find it, using the same methods he had used in the Yukon.

The scheme seemed practical enough. In due course the sluice box was set up in the farmyard with running water piped over from the barn, and Louis set to work.

The sluice box manned by Louis in the yard received almost as much publicity as the crimes themselves. Crowds poured out to the farm to take in the spectacle of a sourdough mining gold on an Indiana farm. They cheered Louis on, and rising to the occasion, he waved and joked with the crowd. Christened Klondike Louis by the press, he was always good for a colorful quote, and because of him and the eeriness of the scene, on a good day the crowd surrounding the farm swelled to 5,000. You could even place a friendly wager as to whether or not Louis would strike gold.

Then it happened. After four days on the job, and after washing tons of mud and debris through his sluice box, Schultz came up with a bridgework containing two lower bicuspids capped with gold and four porcelain teeth. Louis was proclaimed a hero, and the teeth were rushed to Dr. Norton for examination. He positively identified the work as his own, and the teeth as belonging to Belle Gunness.

This lent considerable weight to the assumption that Belle's head had been completely burned by the fire and only dental work had survived. Ray Lamphere stood trial for Belle's murder. The evidence against him was strong; he had argued bitterly with Belle and had been seen near the house on the night of the fire. There was just one thing - the jury didn't believe that Mrs. Gunness was dead. Lamphere was acquitted, but was tried for arson and convicted. After hearing all the evidence, the jurors came to the conclusion that Belle was alive but that Lamphere had burned down the farmhouse. Lamphere was suffering from tuberculosis, and died in Michigan City Prison in December 1909.

Before he died, he told two different versions of his life with Belle and particularly what happened on the night the house burned down. The first version was told to a friend in prison who came forward after Ray's death. Ray told him that the whole thing was a setup - Belle did not die in the fire. She had advertised for a housekeeper and had culled the applicants, trying to find one as large as herself. With pressure mounting from Andrew Helgelein, she had to settle for the stoutest woman she could find, but one still far short of her massive structure. After drugging her, Belle cut off her head, and Ray and Belle buried it in quicklime in the nearby swamp. Belle had dressed the stranger in some of her own clothing to further aid in the identification; then she had killed her three children, leaving Ray to light the fire. Ray claimed that he never actually killed anyone himself, but had aided Belle in any way she asked in getting rid of the bodies. She had killed her own children because they knew too much of the strange goings on. He said there had been 28 more murders committed on the farm that were never uncovered. Belle butchered the bodies in her basement, feeding the small parts to the hogs and burying the larger pieces in quicklime in the swamp.

Upon hearing the story of the hogs' unorthodox eating

habits, the man who purchased them in La Porte was reported to have remarked: "They were still the best damn hogs in the county."

Lamphere said that Belle had sneaked up behind Mr. Gunness and split open his head with an axe. She then placed his body under the shelf that held the sausage grinder and dropped it on his head. A little girl in La Porte remembered a conversation she had with Belle's daughter Myrtle who told her, "Mama brained Papa with an axe. Don't tell a soul."

Lamphere died shortly after telling his friend these details about the crime. After he had passed away, Reverend E.A. Schnell, the prison minister, told of Lamphere's confession of his part in the crimes. This version differs in many details from that given to his friend. Lamphere told the minister that on the night of the fire he had chloroformed the three Gunness children and set fire to the house. He said he was completely captivated by Belle and would comply with anything she desired. But whatever the major variations, the two stories were the same in one important detail - he swore that Belle had not died in the fire.

Readers can pick their own version of what took place that last night on the farm, but whichever they choose they must consider Belle's bridgework found in the debris of the burned-out farmhouse. Is it within the realm of possibility that Belle, operating in a mad frenzy, with her three children dead beside her, could have taken a pair of pliers and torn the permanent bridgework from her own mouth? Dentists have recorded instances where lumberjacks and others working in isolation have suffered from terrible toothaches and have pulled out several of their own teeth. A 280-lb. woman who had disposed of a possible 42 human beings might not find the act as appalling as it appears to us.

Belle Gunness has not been seen or heard of since the night of April 27, 1908, when her house burned to the ground.

JOHN GEORGE HAIGH

John George Haigh was born in Stanford, Lincolnshire, on July 24, 1909. It was a difficult time for the family; John Sr. was an electrical engineer and had been out of work for several months. Being deeply religious (the family belonged to an austere sect known as the Plymouth Brethren) they were too proud to ask for help from friend or neighbor.

Their affairs took a turn for the better when Haigh Sr. obtained employment at the Lofthouse Colliery. He was to stay in their employ for the next 25 years, but the new job necessitated a move to Outwood, a small village near the city of Wakefield. Here they moved into a comfortable house that came with the job.

The Haighs have come under close scrutiny in hindsight, but nothing detrimental can be conjured up about them. John and Emily were a deeply religious couple, and no doubt the severity of their beliefs sometimes spilled over into the upbringing of their only son. Young George was brought up to respect authority in the puritanical atmosphere of their home. His parents were kind and loving to a point, but at the same time they were harsh and stern when it came to the qualities they and the Brethren deemed sacred. Qualities such as punctuality and obedience were deeply instilled in the young lad, and most probably he chafed at the bit under the strict rules.

When he became a teenager he mastered the organ and piano. His voice was better than average, and soon he was singing in the choir in Wakefield cathedral. The proud and pious Haighs delighted in listening to their John sing - a bizarre picture of domestic bliss in view of the grim events that were to befall the family in later years.

For the moment, time passed pleasantly enough for the respectable Haighs and their respectable son. In his last year at school, John won a prize for studies in divinity. He became very interested in automobiles and at the age of 18 got his first job as junior salesman at Appleyards, a car dealership in Wakefield. This position lasted about a year.

Something of a loner, Haigh had no close friends or social life. He was a strange fellow, but no worse than many blokes struggling to make a living. He was of average height, had a full crop of black hair, was always neatly dressed, and generally made a good impression on those he met.

For the next two years John moved from job to job and showed a distinct lack of interest in bettering himself. Then, when he was 21, he and a partner started a business, a combination advertising agency and real estate firm in Leeds. For a short while it prospered, but then the tiny company fell on hard times. In order to keep the business going, John tried to obtain funds under false pretences. He glibly misrepresented some buildings he was trying to sell, and obtained advances based on his misleading claims. The police picked him up, but because it was a first offence the charges were dismissed.

He then joined a combination car rental and insurance company, again based in Leeds, and again did very well at the outset. In fact, he was remembered as the ace of the staff. Then the bombshell fell. John was making up and signing fraudulent contracts, and had been doing so since joining the company. He had actually started up a dealership to perpetrate his frauds. He would sell a non-existent vehicle from his garage, and send the hire purchase contract to the company he represented. They in turn would send Haigh's garage a cheque, and of course Haigh would receive his commission from the company for bringing in the business. He had to keep meticulous records in order to make sure that all his fraudulent contracts were being paid each month, as it obviously wouldn't do to have someone trying to contact one of the false names and addresses which appeared on the contracts. One wonders if Haigh's penchant for forgery wasn't practice for bigger and better things that were to follow.

When his frauds were uncovered, his father made arrangements to pay the company the money that was missing and keep his son out of jail.

Haigh moved to Leeds, where he met, wooed and married Beatrice Hamer. He hadn't known the 21-year-old Beatrice very long and the wedding was not a gala affair, as John's parents didn't approve of the union and the bride's parents were not thrilled with John. The young couple exchanged vows, without benefit of parents at a registry office on July 6, 1934.

Fifteen months later John was again charged with fraud. Unbelievably, he had managed to secure employment with a branch of the same company from which he had previously been fired. He even used the fraudulent contract scheme again. This time he received 15 months in prison. While he was serving this sentence his wife gave birth to their baby. John was never to live with his wife again, nor was he ever to lay eyes on his child; he abandoned them without a thought for their welfare. He received three months off for good behavior, and was out after serving one year. His parents, who by now were feeling the disgrace of their son's petty crimes, still stood behind their only offspring. He swore that he was turning over a new leaf and, like parents everywhere, they believed him.

Haigh's father introduced him to a man who owned a dry cleaning plant in Leeds. John told the truth about his past, and because of his sincerity, got the job. As always, things went well at first and John soon became assistant manager. Then, following his previous pattern, he was found to be promising people jobs for small cash considerations. He was fired on the spot, and moved on to bigger and better things in London.

He got a job as manager of an amusement park in Tooting. For twelve months he worked diligently for the owner, William McSwan, and his son, Donald. Then Haigh got that old urge to take another short cut. He left the McSwans and somehow or other hit upon a novel get-rich-quick scheme.

He would find the name of a legitimate lawyer in one town, and set up a law office in another, using the legitimate lawyer's name. He would then write to a selected list of clients that he was winding up an estate. This fictional estate would have some stocks that would be offered at slightly less than the current market price. For a small deposit Haigh would hold the stock for the proposed buyer. After he had accumulated enough cheques, and just before his clients started to demand delivery of the stocks, Haigh would close shop and set up in another town under another name.

On November 24, 1937, the authorities caught up with him. This time he got four years in Dartmoor. He received time off for good behavior and was released in 1940. In the summer of '41, he sold some furniture that didn't belong to him, for which indiscretion he received 21 months in Lincoln Prison. Upon being released in 1943, John moved to Crawley, where, with the help of forged references and educational documents, he got a job with a light engineering firm owned by a Mr. Stevens.

Stevens was so taken with Haigh that he invited him to stay with his family, and John was quick to accept his offer. The Stevenses had two daughters. The younger of the two was usually underfoot, but Barbara was another story. She was an attractive young girl, and she and John became good friends. Barbara, like Haigh, loved good music, and the two of them spent many pleasant evenings discussing various compositions and composers. Sometimes Haigh played the piano while the entire family sat around and listened attentively.

John left the Stevens home and employ after six months, had some personal cards printed that read "J.G. Haigh, B.Sc., Technical Liaison Officer, Union Group Engineering," and started a light engineering firm on his own in London. At first he did rather well, and in 1944 he moved to Onslow Court Hotel in South Kensington. He had devised another get-rich-quick scheme, and this time it included murder.

One day, John bumped into young Donald McSwan on the street, and the two men struck up a conversation about the good old days when they had worked together in the amusement part in Tooting. Donald was a pleasant enough lad, somewhat taller and more extroverted than Haigh. In the course of making small talk with Haigh, he mentioned that he had sold his share of the amusement park and had invested his money in some property. No doubt Haigh's interest in his old friend blossomed with this information, and they got along so well that Donald invited John over to his home to have a meal with his elderly parents. Haigh accepted this invitation, and the McSwans were genuinely happy to see him again.

Donald and Haigh became chums. They would meet every so often for a meal or just to pass the time of day. There is no doubt that the friendship was being cultivated by Haigh for his own devious purposes and, on September 9, 1944, these purposes became clear enough. Haigh invited Donald over to his workshop at 70 Gloucester Road, sneaked up behind his chum and hit him over the head with a piece of pipe. He later claimed that it was only then that he thought of the perplexing problem of getting rid of the body. The idea of submerging it in sulphuric acid came to him the next morning. He had been using the acid to scale metal, and it was "mere coincidence" that two carboys of acid were at hand.

The next morning Haigh placed the body in a drum. He then had the rather difficult task of taking sulphuric acid out of a carboy and transferring it, with the aid of a pail, into the drum containing the body. It was a tough job, and several times the burning fumes were too much for him and he had to go out for fresh air. Slowly but surely the drum filled with sulphuric acid, completely immersing the body. Haigh was sure that he was removing both the body and all traces of the murder. What he didn't know is that certain parts of the human body, as well as foreign materials, take varying lengths of time to disintegrate. Gallstones may take a very long time to disappear completely, and human fat will remain for years. Haigh was later to refer to this fat as sludge, and it was this sludge that proved beyond a doubt that a human being had been disintegrated in his workshop.

Haigh left his gruesome deposit and travelled to Scotland. Here he forged a letter to the older McSwans in their son's handwriting, saying that he had skipped to Scotland in order to avoid being called into the service. Donald had mentioned his reluctance to enter the armed serves before, so the old couple had no reason to be suspicious.

Then Haigh came back to his workshop in Crawley and poured the now dissolved Donald down the drain. With commendable patience, he waited 20 months before he invited the elderly McSwans to 79 Gloucester Road, on a warm July day, and killed them both with vicious blows to the head.

Conscientious monster that he was, he had now outfitted himself with the tools of murder. He wore a mackintosh when he struck the fatal blows, in order to keep the blood off his clothes. He had also outfitted the workshop with a stirrup pump to transfer the sulphuric acid from the carboy into the drum. With two bodies on his hands, he now had two drums to fill, and had taken the precaution of wearing a gas mask to protect himself against the fumes.

Having disposed of their mortal remains, he equipped himself with forged power of attorney documents and ingeniously went about liquidating and transferring all the McSwans' assets to himself. They had two properties, a bank account, and some stocks.

When questioned about the missing couple, he would quickly produce personal letters in the McSwan's handwriting. These letters gave plausible excuses for their absence and assured anyone who inquired that they were fine. In order to make legal contracts, Haigh would produce the necessary forged documents demonstrating that his dear friends had empowered him to make transactions in their names. No one became suspicious. The McSwans were an unobtrusive lot who had never harmed anyone. It was just their bad luck that they crossed the path of our friend, John George. Haigh realized about £4,000 from the deaths of the three McSwans, and went home for Christmas, satisfied and now prosperous, to his mother and father.

Throughout all his activities Haigh was writing and seeing his old girlfriend, Barbara Stevens. He treated her with the utmost respect, and at no time was he anything but a perfect gentleman to her. A deep and lasting friendship developed between them. He confided many of his innermost thoughts to her, and a strong attachment grew between the couple. Dashing John was the greatest thing that had ever happened to Barbara. The well-groomed, mature charmer was very different from the awkward local lads her own age. They took in symphonies and plays, and had intellectual conversations on a variety of topics. This rather weird relationship got to the stage of discussing marriage, but of course we know that Haigh was already legally married.

Not once did Barbara ever suspect that her boyfriend was anything other than he seemed.

At this stage of his career, John had money in his pocket, a pretty girlfriend, and had successfully murdered three innocent people.

At about this time he decided to give up his shop at 79 Gloucester Road, the scene of his three murders, and take up a new location on Leopold Road in Crawley. He told the company he rented the premises from that he planned to conduct several experiments there.

In September 1947, Haigh answered an advertisement offering a house for sale at 22 Ladbroke Square, London. The home belonged to Dr. Archibald Henderson and his wife, Rose. Haigh didn't buy the house, but soon became a close friend of the handsome and wealthy Hendersons. For six months he cultivated their friendship and stored away all the personal bits and pieces of information he could. When he knew enough about the Hendersons, it would be time to kill them.

Haigh picked his spot. He waited until they were on vacation. Then one day he dropped in on them at the

Metropole Hotel in Brighton, and suggested that the doctor might care to visit his "factory" in Crawley. It wasn't much of a drive, so the doctor accepted. As soon as they entered the storeroom, Haigh shot Dr. Henderson in the head from behind. His now familiar, macabre procedure was set into motion. The stirrup pump transferred the sulphuric acid from the carboy into the drum, and Haigh scurried about the small building in his gas mask, much like a busy chef overseeing a gourmet feast.

He then rushed back to Brighton and told Mrs. Henderson that her husband had suddenly been taken ill. On this pretext she accompanied him back to Crawley. Once in the storeroom he shot her in the back of the head and proceeded to dispose of her body in the same manner as that of her husband. Haigh had taken the liberty of stripping both bodies of a substantial amount of jewelry before placing them in the sulphuric acid, and he later sold the jewelry for £300.

A few days after these murders, on February 16, Haigh showed up at the Metropole Hotel in Brighton. He had a letter, apparently signed by Dr. Henderson, instructing the hotel to give him the Henderson's baggage. Haigh had studied the doctor's handwriting and forged the letter.

Mrs. Henderson's brother soon contacted Haigh regarding the whereabouts of his sister and brother-in-law. Haigh told him the couple had had a very serious disagreement in Brighton and had decided to go away by themselves to work out their marital difficulties. To facilitate their rush to privacy, Haigh told Mrs. Henderson's brother, he had loaned the couple £2500. He added that, if they didn't return in sixty days, the Hendersons were to give him their car and home. He showed the brother a document to this effect, apparently signed by the doctor.

The brother didn't like this story one bit, and insinuated that if he didn't hear from his sister soon, he would go to the police. Haigh dashed off a forged letter from Rose to her brother. Cunning devil that he was, he had learned and stored away very personal family matters. He even copied her style of writing. This letter substantiated Haigh's story, and set Rose Henderson's family at ease for the time being at least.

Haigh followed up with postcards and telegrams, and set up a fictitious situation that was extremely believable. Finally, he forged a 15-page letter from Rose to her brother, post-marked Glasgow, Scotland. In the letter, Rose explained that due to personal financial problems, she and the doctor were going to South Africa. The letter carefully stated that the brother should settle the £2,500 debt to their friend, John Haigh, and take his advice in clearing up all money matters.

Scotland Yard maintains that this letter, in the exact style and handwriting of Rose Henderson, is one of the most brilliant forgeries they have every encountered.

Rose Henderson's family now considered Haigh a dear friend who had done many favors for the doctor. It is estimated from Haigh's bank statements that he realized over £7,000 from the Henderson murders, but within a year he had blown the money on high living, and was looking around for more people to kill.

The Onslow Court Hotel caters mainly to elderly ladies who have been left considerable incomes. Most of the ladies are there on a more or less permanent basis. They pass the time sitting on wicker chairs, sipping tea and recalling days gone by. John Haigh, a permanent resident himself, was popular with his more senior associates of the opposite sex. In fact, one might say that many of them doted on him.

Mrs. Durand-Deacon was typical of the residents at the Onslow Court. Grey-haired and matronly, she could have been typecast for the part. She and John Haigh sat at adjoining tables at breakfast and often passed the time of day. Sometimes Mrs. Durand-Deacon expressed an interest in Haigh's engineering business. In fact, Mrs. Durand-Deacon had the bright idea that she wanted to manufacture artificial fingernails. Haigh, who had the patience of Job and would wait until his victims almost begged to become entwined in his net, expressed keen interest in this. He thought it might be a good idea if she were to accompany him one day to his factory in Crawley.

On February 18, Haigh was having lunch at the Onslow Court when Mrs. Durand-Deacon suggested that it would be as good a day as any to visit the factory in Crawley. Haigh thought the day was just perfect. Mrs. Durand-Deacon told her good friend Mrs. Lane that she had an appointment with Haigh later that afternoon.

Haigh left the hotel heading for Leopold Road, carrying a hatbox, which, unknown to the occupants of the hotel, contained a revolver. He entered his workshop with Mrs. Durand-Deacon. Two sides of the main room had workbenches running the length of the walls, and three carboys of sulphuric acid took up much of the available space. By five-thirty that same afternoon Haigh had gone through the preliminary portion of his macabre routine. He had donned his mackintosh, shot Mrs. Deacon, and placed her body securely in the empty drum. Then, exhibiting a quirk that most normal people have difficulty comprehending, John Haigh got hungry. He slipped over to Ye Olde Ancient Prior's Restaurant in the square in Crawley and had poached eggs on toast and tea. This brief respite is well documented, as he chatted with the owner of the restaurant.

Then, back to work. He donned rubber gloves and gas mask, started up the stirrup pump, poured in the sulphuric acid, and poor Mrs. Deacon was well on her way to disintegration in the drum.

Haigh was back in London by ten o'clock that night. When Mrs. Durand-Deacon didn't show up for dinner, her friend Mrs. Lane was mildly alarmed. When her friend didn't show up for breakfast, she approached Haigh for an explanation. He had a story ready. He told Mrs. Lane that he had an appointment to meet Mrs. Durand-Deacon in front of a store, but she didn't show up. He waited for her for over an hour, then decided that she must have been delayed or changed her mind, and went on without her.

He left the worried Mrs. Lane and went to Crawley to check on the disintegration of Mrs. Deacon and pay a visit to his girlfriend Barbara Stevens. Both Barbara and her mother

116

were to state later that on this particular visit John looked ill and had a hoarse voice. The hoarseness of the voice we can attribute to too many acid fumes, and the peaked condition could be laid at the doorstep of the inquisitive and annoying Mrs. Lane back at the Onslow Court Hotel.

Haigh should have known better. Surely one of the first rules in the mass murderers' handbook should be never, never mess with little grey-haired ladies. If either the victim or a friend of the victim's falls into this category, the entire operation is invariably ruined. Ladies of this ilk simply tend to spoil everything.

But let's get back to it. For the first time, one of his victims was missed by someone who didn't accept his glib explanations. The next morning was Sunday, and Haigh knew he would have to face the troublesome Mrs. Lane at breakfast. He decided to be aggressive, and was the first to inquire as to the whereabouts of Mrs. Durand-Deacon. He suggested they go and report the missing woman to the police. Haigh offered a lift in his car, and Mrs. Lane accepted.

The police took a routine report from Mrs. Lane, and a woman sergeant was dispatched to the hotel to question all the guests, including Haigh, who had been one of the last residents to see the missing woman. The policewoman came away from the hotel with a nagging suspicion about this glib Haigh fellow. It bothered her so much she emphasized her suspicions in her report to her superior, Division Detective Inspector Shelley Symes. His first move was to check Haigh's record, and of course, he uncovered his lengthy criminal past. Inspector Symes decided to pay him a visit. On Monday Symes interviewed Haigh and was given substantially the same story as his sergeant had received. He obtained a picture of the missing woman and circulated it to the press.

The next day, Tuesday, Haigh checked the drum in Crawley, and discovered that the body had completely dissolved. He poured the liquid sludge out into the yard. On Wednesday Haigh was again questioned by the police. Again he gave the same story.

By Saturday, the police had located Haigh's landlord and

decided to break the lock of the "factory" door. Inside they found a revolver and ammunition. They also found documents belonging to Mr. and Mrs. McSwan and their son, Donald. Further documents were found belonging to a Doctor Henderson and his wife, Rose. They also found a dry cleaning receipt for a Persian lamb coat. Mrs. Durand-Deacon was last seen wearing such a coat. When it was retrieved from the cleaners, the detectives found that there was a patch on the sleeve. Inspector Symes searched Mrs. Durand-Deacon's room at the Onslow Court Hotel, and inside a sewing basket he found the same material that was used to patch the coat. Because of the publicity the case was receiving in the press, a jeweler came forward with jewelry sold to him by Haigh. Mrs. Durand-Deacon's sister identified it as belonging to the missing woman.

The police picked up Haigh outside his hotel and took him to Chelsea Police Station. Inspector Symes produced the fur coat and jewelry, and asked Haigh for an explanation. Haigh was starting to give a cock-and-bull story to his adversary when Symes was called out of the office. Left alone with Detective Inspector Webb, for some reason Haigh started to talk. The conversation bears repeating here. Remember, at this point no one actually knew a murder had taken place.

Haigh said, "Well, if I told you the truth, you would not believe me; it sounds too fantastic. Mrs. Durand-Deacon no longer exists. She has disappeared completely and no trace of her can ever be found again."

"What has happened to her?" asked Webb.

"I have destroyed her with acid. You'll find the sludge which remains at Leopold Road. I did the same with the Hendersons, and the McSwans. Every trace has gone. How can you prove murder if there is no body?"

Webb got Symes back in the office, and in front of Haigh told him what had transpired. Haigh interjected, "That's perfectly true, and it's a very long story and will take hours to tell."

Haigh spewed forth every detail of how he killed not only Mrs. Durand-Deacon, but the McSwans and the

118

Hendersons. These former murders were unknown to the police. He elaborated on his diabolic behavior by adding the fact that he had made a tiny incision in each victim's throat. From this incision, he claimed, he extracted and drank a glass of blood.

The authorities converged on Haigh's factory once more. Now they knew what they were looking for, and they found all the paraphernalia of murder. On the ground outside the workshop there was a greasy area where the drums of sludge had been emptied. After a minute examination of the yard (it was all actually lifted up and taken to Scotland Yard) some gallstones and a plastic denture were found. The denture was identified as belonging to Mrs. Durand-Deacon by her dentist. She had also suffered from gallstones. Tiny particles of eroded bones were also found.

There was no doubt about it. Haigh was what he claimed to be - a monster. Realizing that his one chance to live was to appear insane, he maintained that he had killed for a glass of blood and not for material gain. Due to the rather large sums of money he diverted to himself, this reason proved hard to swallow. When questioned by psychiatrists he told about dreaming of Christ with open wounds bleeding into his mouth, and claimed that in this way he acquired the uncontrollable urge to drink blood. No one believed the blood theory. It was obvious that Haigh was trying to feign madness.

While awaiting trial he received a letter every day from his mother. Barbara Stevens wrote to him and visited him often. She was the one exception in his life - the only one he had ever treated decently. In his way, Haigh seemed to be genuinely fond of her. She in turn shared his affection, and remained loyal to him until the last.

On July 18, 1949, Haigh stood trial for murder of Mrs. Durand-Deacon. Huge crowds gathered outside the courthouse to catch a glimpse of the mass murderer. He pleaded not guilty. The defence tried to prove him insane, and the prosecution tried to prove him sane. The jurors obviously believed the prosecution. They took exactly 15 minutes to find him guilty.

Facing death by hanging, Haigh took great pains to bequeath his clothing to Madame Tussaud's Chamber of Horrors. There were certain stipulations. Vain to the end, he insisted that his wax image be kept in perfect condition, hair combed and pants pressed.

He was executed on August 10, 1949.

H.H. HOLMES

Herman Webster Mudgett was born in 1860 to a respected family in the tiny New England community of Gilmanton where his father had been postmaster for over twenty-five years. Though young Herman early showed a vicious streak — neighbors of the Mudgetts were to recall seeing him setting a cat on fire — he had many redeeming features, not the least of which was his keen intelligence.

His teachers remembered him as a bright, alert scholar. After his graduation with honors from Gilmanton Academy, he eloped with a farmer's daughter from the nearby village of London, and paid his tuition at the University of Vermont, at Burlington, from a small inheritance his wife had just received. He transferred to the University of Michigan at Ann Arbor, where his wife gave birth to a son.

Mudgett started his criminal activities while still at university. He and another student concocted a scheme whereby Mudgett took out an insurance policy on his friend's life in the amount of $12,500. The friend promptly disappeared, leaving the way clear for Mudgett to steal a corpse from the dissecting room of the university, positively identify it as his missing friend, and collect the insurance. Shortly after the successful completion of this scheme, he qualified as a doctor of medicine and abandoned his wife and infant son. Mrs. Mudgett returned to Gilmanton, never to lay eyes on her husband again.

The doctor, now a tall, good-looking 24-year-old with all

the qualifications to be a legitmate success, struck out on his own. With his fashionable walrus moustache and his luminous brown eyes, he was a distinguished-looking gentleman. And when he was decked out in his bowler hat, tweed suit and shiny shoes, Herman held more than a little attraction for the opposite sex.

For six years he wandered through Minnesota and New York, making a dishonest dollar wherever he could. The fact that he could have made a fine living at his own profession apparently didn't enter his mind. Records show that in St. Paul he was appointed receiver of a bankrupt store. He filled the store with merchandise purchased on credit, sold off the stock at cost price or less, and took off with the proceeds.

In 1885, he reappeared in Wilmette, a suburb of Chicago, as an inventor, using the name Henry H. Holmes for the first time. He met a dark-haired beauty named Myrtle Z. Belknap, who was not only a looker, but also had a father who was one of the wealthiest residents of Wilmette. Holmes married her without going through the annoying formalities of a divorce from his first wife. He succeeded in getting enough money out of Myrtle's daddy to build a house, and then started forging Mr. Belknap's name on cheques. Though the family was furious, they decided to sidestep a scandal and not to prosecute the scoundrel, for he still held a fascination for his wife, who stood beside him no matter what sort of scrapes he managed to get into.

Next, Holmes answered an advertisement in the local newspaper requiring a chemist for a store owned by a Mrs. Holden on the corner of 63rd Street and Wallace, in Englewood, another suburb of Chicago. Mrs. Holden, who had been recently widowed, was thrilled to have such a highly qualified and handsome man apply for the position, and gave him the job without any qualms whatsoever. Almost at once she became disillusioned with her new employee and confided to close friends that she suspected him of theft from her store. Early in 1890, Mrs. Holden suddenly disappeared without mentioning anything to friends, except to Holmes, who claimed she had told him she was taking a long holiday in California. Then he soothed her acquaintances by telling them that she had sold the store to him and was staying on the west coast. It seems that no one was interested enough in Mrs. Holden to delve deeper into her disappearance, and she was never seen again.

In the meantime, with his knowledge of medicine, Holmes was making the business prosper. He had a few sidelines, such as his own patent medicines which he sold at enormous profits, and things were going so well that by 1892 he figured there was nothing further to be gained from the Belknap family, so he left his wife and moved into rooms above his store. Then he commenced the construction of a monstrous building directly across the street. It was three storeys high, measured 50 by 162 feet and contained more than 90 rooms. On the main floor Holmes opened a jewelry store, restaurant and drugstore. The false turrets gave the whole structure a somewhat medieval appearance, and the ugly pile soon came to be known as Holmes' Castle.

Ostensibly Holmes built the structure to accommodate the huge crowds which were expected for the Chicago World's Fair in 1893, and the third floor of the castle was divided into apartments for this purpose; but the second floor had winding staircases, connecting hallways, trapdoors, and asbestos-lined rooms, some of them equipped with gas jets. Holmes had his own comfortable quarters on the second floor; inside his closet were valves that controlled the flow of gas to the various rooms. From his bedroom Holmes could gas a victim, turn a switch that controlled a trapdoor and plunge the body down a chute to the basement. The basement was equipped with a dissecting table, medical instruments, a crematorium, a huge vat of corrosive acid and two further vats of quicklime.

Into this veritable murder castle came Mr. Icilius Conner, his wife Julia, his sister Gertie, and his eight-year-old daughter Pearl. Conner was a jeweler by trade and was looking for ways to get into business. Holmes obliged by making a part of his drugstore available to him for the sale of jewelry, and by hiring Julia as his personal bookkeeper. The Conners were an extremely handsome family, particularly Julia, and it wasn't long before the cunning doctor had alienated her from her husband, and she had in effect become his mistress. Holmes let it leak to Conner that his wife had been sharing his bed, and Conner left Chicago in disgust. Mrs. Conner and her daughter Pearl were to live with Holmes for the next two years. During these two years, Holmes took a trip to Texas, where he stayed for over six months, engaging in his usual activities of thieving and swindling before returning to Chicago.

In 1893, the doctor received a visit from an acquaintance he had met during his stay down south. Her name was Minnie Williams, and her greatest claim to fame was the fact that she and her sister Nannie jointly owned property valued at $50,000 in Fort Worth, Texas. She was a welcome guest to the castle, and it wasn't long before she was Holmes' mistress. Coinciding with her coronation as queen of the castle, Julia Conner and her daughter disappeared.

Holmes and his new flame lived together for a full year, and it was during this year that more visitors started to enter the death castle than were seen to leave it. It is difficult to believe that Minnie could have lived there at this time without having some guilty knowledge of what was going on. Holmes was easier to figure; if ever there was a born criminal it was Henry H. Holmes. He was motivated by lust and greed, not necessarily in that order, and seems never to have even considered leading an honest life.

The list of his known victims is a long one. Years earlier, while serving a three-month jail sentence in St. Louis, Holmes had met fellow inmates Benjamin F. Pietzel, a small time con artist, and a rather well-known train robber, Marion Hedgepeth. Pietzel was soon to be released to join his wife and five children, but Hedgepeth was awaiting transfer to a penitentiary and a lengthy sentence. Pietzel now showed up in Chicago and looked up his friend Holmes. He kept telling Holmes about a beautiful young girl he had met in Dwight, Illinois. Her name was Emeline Cigrand, and she had made a lasting impression on Pietzel, who told Holmes she was the most beautiful girl he had ever seen. Finally, at Pietzel's urging, Holmes corresponded with the girl and offered her a job at a salary far above the average. She couldn't resist the temptation, came to Chicago, entered the castle, and was never seen again. Her boyfriend, Robert E. Phelps, inquired about her at the castle, was invited in, and never left. Holmes was later to confess to Emeline's death, describing in detail how he kept her in a soundproof room for the sole purpose of having sexual relations with her. He claimed he didn't want to kill her, but Minnie got jealous and he had to do it. The boyfriend, Holmes said, was just too nosy to live.

Nannie Williams, Minnie's sister, came to visit. Holmes made love to her, got her to sign over half the property in Fort Worth, and killed her, in that order. He told friends of Minnie's that her sister had returned to Texas.

Now we enter the even stranger period in the saga of Henry H. Holmes. In the fall of 1893, he left his friend Ben Pietzel in charge of his various businesses and took a trip with Minnie to Denver. Using the alias of Howard, he married a Georgianna Yoke of Richmond, Indiana, without Minnie's knowledge. He spent many weeks in Denver living alternately with the two women, neither of whom knew of the other's existence. Even after Georgianna returned to Indiana, Holmes visited her on many occasions during the next two years and seemed to have become quite attached to her. She lived to testify at his trial and was the only person to speak highly of him.

Before Christmas 1893, Minnie made the same mistake as her sister Nannie; she signed away her half of the Fort Worth property and promptly disappeared. Later Holmes was to show the police where to find her skeleton and her sister's, in the cellar of the castle.

How was Holmes able to build a structure that was obviously custom-designed for murder? Firstly, he personally supervised the entire construction, from the cellar to the top floor. Then he kept the same crew of workmen for only a few days before he discharged them. A new crew would start, often entirely unaware of what had transpired before they appeared on the job. In this way, no one saw the master plan or knew that the cumulative effect of their labors was a bona fide murder castle.

When he had been in jail with Pietzel and Hedgepeth years earlier, Holmes told them that he had figured out a foolproof way of defrauding an insurance company. He said he needed a really smart lawyer to pull it off. Hedgepeth gave Holmes the name of his lawyer, Jeptha D. Howe of St. Louis, and received in return a promise of $500 after the scheme was successfully completed. Holmes kept this plan under wraps for a few years, and then took it out of mothballs in the early summer of 1894.

The scheme was the same one that Holmes had used so successfully in university. Pietzel was to have his wife take out insurance on his life, and then he was to drop out of sight, while Holmes was to come up with a corpse which would be identified as that of Pietzel. Mrs. Pietzel would collect the insurance and the partners would divide the spoils. Everyone agreed that the plan had some merit. Pietzel took out a policy amounting to $10,000. Then he went to Philadelphia and set up a shop as a patent attorney, using the name B.F. Perry. Within a month his body was found on the floor of his office, badly burned, particularly around the face. The police investigating the accident found a broken bottle of benzine on the office floor.

The preliminary assumption was that an explosion had taken place, causing the accident. Then an autopsy was performed and the death was found to have been caused by chloroform. Jeptha D. Howe reappeared on the scene and informed the authorities that the dead man was Ben Pietzel, and as Mrs. Pietzel's attorney, he was representing her in asking for any insurance money that was due his client. Pietzel's good friend Holmes arrived and also identified the body. The insurance money was paid off to Mrs. Pietzel; it was later dividied up, with Howe getting $2,500, Mrs. Pietzel $500, and Holmes receiving the balance.

Holmes, the arch-criminal, had really murdered his friend Pietzel. The corpse was no stranger to him, but he managed to deceive Howe and Mrs. Pietzel, who throughout the con thought that Pietzel was in hiding. Howe returned to St. Louis assuming that the scheme was a complete success and that Mrs. Pietzel would be joining Mr. Pietzel in a few months and that everyone would be happy. He visited his client Hedgepeth in prison and mentioned how well the scheme had worked. Hedgepeth was furious, as he had been promised $500 by Holmes and never received a cent. Hedgepeth called the warden and told the whole story. The warden called the insurance company, who in turn called in the Pinkerton Detective Agency to investigate the case. When Hedgepeth told the story he naturally repeated it as he had heard it from Howe; that it was a stranger's body that was found on the office floor, not Pietzel's. It didn't take long for the Pinkertons to realize that there was more than simple fraud involved, and they called in the police.

By this time Holmes had fled, and he proved to be an elusive quarry. He had talked Mrs. Pietzel into meeting him in Detroit. She took two of her children with her, while Holmes took the other three, Alice, Nellie and Howard. He told her they would all meet with Mr. Pietzel in Detroit in two weeks' time. Holmes arrived before the allotted time and placed the three Pietzel children in a boarding house while he scampered to Richmond, Indiana, returning with the lady who really thought she was his wife, Georgianna Yoke.

Holmes set up three different groups while in Detroit. One consisted of the three Pietzel children, another consisted of Mrs. Pietzel and the other two children, while a third contingent was made up solely of Georgianna. Holmes would join any of the three groups, who at no time knew of the others' presence in the city.

Finally he took all three households on the road, and it is a measure of his cunning that he managed to stay ahead of the police for two months. They finally caught up with Holmes in Boston on November 17, 1894. The other two detachments were accounted for when gullible Georgianna, who was innocent of any wrongdoing, was located by the police in Indiana where Holmes had stashed her, and Mrs. Pietzel and her two children were discovered living in

Burlington, Vermont, waiting for the reunion with her husband that was never to come.

Only Nellie, Howard, and Alice Pietzel, the three children who were travelling with Holmes, could not be found by the police, and Holmes steadfastly refused to give them any information concerning the three children.

The interior of Holmes' murder castle was now exposed, and the police realized they were dealing with one of the most hideous monsters who ever lived. The search was on for the three children; the trail led from Detroit to Toronto to Cincinnati to Indianapolis, throughout the midwest and back into Canada. Finally, at 16 Vincent Street in Toronto, the authorities found a house that had been rented to a man with two little girls.

The police found out that the man had borrowed a spade to dig a hole, supposedly to store potatoes. They were able to find the neighbor whose spade had been used, and he loaned the same spade to the police. The police dug up the same hole, and in it they found the pathetic bodies of Nellie and Alice Pietzel. In an upstairs bedroom of the house they found a trunk with a rubber tube leading from it to a gas outlet. Diabolical Holmes had enticed the girls to enter the trunk and had asphyxiated them. The discovery now accounted for all the family, except Howard.

While questioning neighbors in the area of 16 Vincent Street, the police found one who had talked to the two girls. This neighbor remembered the girls had mentioned their little brother lived in Indianapolis. The investigation moved to Indianapolis, where 900 houses were searched, and finally, in the suburb of Irvington, police found the house in which Holmes had lived for a week. It has been vacant since Holmes left, and the charred remains of Howard Pietzel's body were found in a stove in the kitchen.

Holmes made a full confession while in jail, but as it is sprinkled with proven lies, it does not give an accurate account of his atrocities. While it seems that he operated basically for gain, when his castle was dismantled it was discovered that he had a rack which he used to try to stretch people, believing that he could make them permanently taller.

Holme's trial for the murder of Ben Pietzel began on October 28, 1895. It was one of the most widely publicized trials of the last century. Every detail was reported in the press, for nothing quite like it had ever been perpetrated in the U.S. before. The jury was out for two and a half hours, but later a member of the jury was to state that the verdict was decided in one minute with a show of hands. They stayed out because it was a capital case, but no one wavered from their unanimous one-minute verdict.

While his appeals were being heard, Holmes embraced the Roman Catholic Church. All of his appeals failed, and on May 7, 1896, accompanied by two priests, Holmes mounted the scaffold at Moyanensing Prison. He made a short speech to the assembled onlookers, but saved his last words for the gentleman who adjusted the noose around his neck.

"Make it quick," he said.

H.H. Holmes, one of the most notorious murderers who ever lived, would have been 36 had he lived nine more days.

CARL ISAACS

The good folks of Seminole County, Georgia, gathered around the tombstones in the graveyard and prayed for the Alday family.

It has been over 21 years since animals, in the guise of human beings, killed six members of the old respected Georgia family. No one has yet paid the supreme penalty for the massacre, although the leader of the gang of killers, Carl Isaacs, says that if he is ever released from prison he will kill again.

After an adolescence marked with criminal activity, Carl found himself confined to Yoke Crest Inc., a minimum security institution for youthful offenders in Harrisburg, Pennsylvania.

A short time earlier, he and his younger brother were in a minor car accident. A woman, 58-year-old Anne Merrill Elder, had given them a lift to the closest service station. She identified Carl as the youth who had burglarized her neighborhood.

Carl couldn't get the thought of Mrs. Elder out of his mind. On January 14, 1973, after a stay of only one week, he walked away from the institution. It didn't take long for him to wreak his revenge. Within days he had stolen a car and had found Mrs. Elder's home. He lay in wait for her and shot her dead. Eleven days after the senseless murder, Carl was apprehended in his hometown of Baltimore while burglarizing a house.

Carl was surprised that he was wanted only for burglary.

The police didn't think a 19-year-old punk could have any connection to the murder of Mrs. Elder. Carl pleaded guilty to the robbery charges and was sentenced to four years imprisonment in the Maryland State Penitentiary.

In the spring of the same year, Carl was successful in obtaining a transfer to a minimum security institution, Poplar Hill. He had heard that his half-brother, 26-year-old Wayne Coleman, was serving time there. No sooner were the boys reunited than they were planning to escape. It required little effort. Together with Wayne's friend, George Dungee, they crawled through a bathroom window to freedom.

Robbing and collecting firearms as they travelled, the three escapees made their way to Baltimore, where they picked up Carl's 15-year-old brother, Billy. The four stole a 1965 Buick and headed for McConnellsburg, Pa. Carl called the foursome the Isaacs Gang and compared himself to John Dilinger and Billy the Kid.

The gang had car trouble in the country east of Baltimore. They stole a truck parked in a farmyard, but two miles down the road the truck chugged to a stop. It was high school student Richard Miller's misfortune to witness the theft. He watched as the four strangers made off with his neighbor's truck. Richard decided to follow the thieves in his new Chevy. He worked part time in a service station and knew very well that Lawrence Schoolby's truck wouldn't go far. When the truck stopped, so did Richard.

He approached the truck and stood transfixed when he saw two weapons pointed directly at his head. Richard Miller was driven to a wooded area where Wayne Coleman shot him dead.

The gang, now firmly committed to theft and murder as a way of existing, continued on their aimless journey. They drove to Seminole County, Georgia, where their lives were to become entwined with those of the Alday family.

If ever two groups of individuals were diametrically opposite, it was the Isaacs gang and the hard-working, well-respected Aldays. The family name is one of the oldest in that part of Georgia. All 7,500 citizens either worked or played with some member of the well-liked clan.

Ned Alday, 62, left most of the farm labor to his sons. He and his wife, Ernestine, led a contented life on their 525-acre spread. True, it wasn't an exciting life, but it was one of enjoyment in one's family. The Aldays had nine children, five daughters and four sons. Three of the boys worked on the farm. Jimmy, 25 and unmarried, lived in the farmhouse with his parents. Shuggie, 32, and his wife Barbara, 27, lived in a house trailer parked in the farmyard. Jerry, 35, and his wife Mary, 26, had another trailer parked about a half mile away. The fourth son, Norman, was in the U.S. Army, stationed in Munich, Germany.

On May 14, 1973, the Isaacs gang was down to its last 15¢. The looting of a house trailer netted $2, good enough for a six pack of beer. An isolated farmhouse yielded over $100. It seemed so easy. Out here in the Georgia countryside, most farmers didn't even lock their doors. Carl figured the Isaacs gang had easy pickings among the yokels.

Jerry Alday rose early. He joined his brother, Jimmy, and together they went to work in the fields. Jerry's wife, Mary, jumped into her 1970 Chevy Impala and headed for her job at the Dept. of Family and Children's Services. The Aldays' trailer was vacant. Mary didn't even bother to lock the door.

Carl Isaacs spotted the Aldays' empty trailer. It looked like child's play. Still driving Richard Miller's Chevy, they parked in the driveway. Within minutes the gang was looting the trailer.

Jerry Alday and his father, Ned had occasion to drive past the trailer during the course of their farm work. They noticed the green Chevy with Pennsylvania plates parked nearby and decided to investigate. They were spotted by the armed men inside.

The four men pointed weapons and led father and son into the trailer. The farmers where stripped of rings and watches. Then the gang members discussed who was going to have the pleasure of the kill. George Dungee actually begged, "Can I have one?" Despite his plea, it was Carl Isaacs who escorted Jerry Alday into a bedroom, forced him to lie on a bed and emptied his pistol into the side of the helpless man's head. Wayne Coleman shot Ned Alday dead with a .380 automatic. Carl Isaacs laughed uncontrollably as each man was murdered.

The noise of the shots had hardly subsided when Billy Isaacs sighted a truck pulling up to the trailer. Shuggie and his uncle Aubrey had seen the green Chevy and the family jeep parked beside the trailer. They told jokes to each other as they drove up to take a look.

The laughter stopped when the two men found themselves staring into the barrels of Billy's and Carl's handguns. Once inside, the captives were stripped of all valuables. Carl and Wayne then had a short discussion over who should do the killing. It was decided that Carl would kill Aubrey Alday. The young, gun wielding bandit led his older captive to a bedroom where he shot him dead. Meanwhile, Billy and Wayne forced Shuggie Alday into another room. He, too was shot dead.

Four members of the Alday clan lay dead in the trailer, but the slaughter wasn't over. Mary Alday drove up to her trailer after a day's work at the office. The terrified woman was held captive as still another Alday drove up to the trailer on a tractor. It was Jimmy, the youngest of the Alday boys. He opened the door of his brother's trailer to stare directly into the barrel of a gun. Once inside, Jimmy was made to lie on a sofa. Carl shot him in the head.

Mary Alday was sodomized, raped and driven a few miles into woods, where she too was shot in the head. George Dungee did the killing. It was his turn.

The Isaacs gang abandoned Richard Miller's car and drove away in Mary Alday's Chevy. That night, the bodies of the six Aldays were discovered. The citizens of Seminole County were stunned at the extent of the tragedy. Who were the madmen who descended from nowhere to mercilessly kill six of their own?

The Isaacs gang was soon identified from fingerprints found on Richard Miller's car. Their pictures appeared on television screens across the nation. In the meantime, they were making a desperate attempt to reach Baltimore, where George and Billy thought they might find refuge. But it was not to be. West Virginia State Patrol officers spotted the fugitives. All four were taken into custody when they made a wild dash to escape by foot.

Returned to Donalsonville, Georgia, the accused killers stood trial. Billy turned state's evidence and was not prosecuted for any of the murders. In exchange for his testimony he was charged only with armed robbery. For this crime he received a 40-year prison sentence. A year later he was returned to Pennyslvania and stood trial for the murder of Richard Miller. Found guilty, he was sentenced to 100 years imprisonment.

While the other killers were spending time in the Donalsonville jail, friends of the Alday family asked surviving members if they would approve of a lynching. The Aldays refused, expressing the opinion that there had been enough killing.

Carl Isaacs, Wayne Coleman and George Dungee were found guilty of six counts of murder and were sentenced to death. The men were transferred to Georgia State Prison to await their execution. Innumerable appeals followed.

Twelve years after the massacre, the U.S. Court of Appeals ruled that the accused could not have received a fair trial in Donalsonville. Despite the fact that the men had confessed, the court threw out the initial guilty verdict.

The men who killed the Aldays, although convicted and sentenced so many years ago, still languish in prison while their case again goes through the courts.

REVEREND JIM JONES

Who can forget the horrific photographs of the more than 900 corpses decomposing in the intense heat of the Guyana jungle?

The man behind the horror story that was soon to make headlines around the world was Reverend Jim Jones.

Jones was born in Lynn, Indiana in 1931, the son of an army veteran who was an enthusiastic member of the Ku Klux Klan.

In 1951, the 20-year-old Jones enrolled at Butler University, a school operated by the Disciples of Christ, and attended on and off for the next 10 years. But in 1953, Jones founded his own interdenominational Christian Assembly of God Church. By 1960 his People's Temple, located in Los Angeles, was a bona fide congregation of the Disciples of Christ, which had a membership of almost a million and a half, mostly living in the Midwest.

From 1961 to 1963, Jones performed missionary work in Brazil, organizing orphanages. There is evidence that he visited Guyana while in South America and, quite possibly, it was during this period that the seeds of his own colony in the jungle took root in his mind.

Upon his return from Brazil, Jones displayed a degree of entrepreneurial acumen by forming two non-profit organizations with headquarters in Indianapolis. The Wings of Deliverance was organized to spread the word of God, while the Jim-Lu-Mar Corp. was formed to purchase every money-making venture available. The latter company's elongated name was made up of his own first name as well as that of his mother, Lynette, and wife, Marceline.

During the '60s, Jones operated out of Ukiah, a small town about 160 km north of San Francisco. His headquarters, known simply as the People's Church, became a money-making machine. The strategically-located church afforded Jones and his followers the opportunity to swoop down on weekends to San Francisco and Los Angeles to spread the word, win followers and raise cash.

Sometimes the groups would return to headquarters richer by as much as $40,000. Members of the congregation turned over their social security cheques to Jones. As the flock grew, so did the routine amount of cash flowing into the church's coffers. Many members, completely enraptured with the charismatic Jones, turned over their entire life savings.

Jones wasn't above slick hucksterism. Photographs of "The Father," as he was now called by his followers, were considered to have healing powers. These bogus medical aids fetched a pretty penny, as did other religious artifacts.

In 1971, Jones purchased a former synagogue and moved the centre of his operations to San Francisco. The People's Temple held its opening service with much fanfare. Scores of gospel singers raised their voices in praise of the Lord. Angela Davis spoke. The People's Temple appeared to be a model of what God-fearing folks could achieve. It boasted a day-care, a carpentry shop and facilities to feed hundreds of the poor each day.

Soon the devoted congregation and its dynamic leader were being lauded by the media as a fine example of an efficiently operated and pure charity. Jones's photograph, depicting him handing over sizable cheques to worthwhile causes, often appeared in the press. His now 8,000-member church also became politically powerful.

In 1973, Jones dispatched 20 members of the People's Temple to Guyana, with the express purpose of finding a site for an agricultural mission. A year later, Father Jones leased 27,000 acres in the jungle near the town of Port Kaituma from the government of Guyana. The commune was called Jonestown after its founder.

As the colony was populated, glowing reports were received by relatives back in the States. Crops were flourishing, housing was more than adequate, and, above all, the individual freedom that the disciples enjoyed was lauded by all. The minister of foreign affairs for Guyana reported on Jonestown, "Peace and love in action."

In the '70s Jones was given numerous honors, including the annual Martin Luther King Jr. Humanitarian Award in 1977.

But there were some ominous rumblings. A few members dropped out of the congregation. Others sued, claiming they were brainwashed, beaten and stripped of their wealth. A handful of journalists made their way to Jonestown. Their stories were far from complimentary. They told of poor living conditions and disillusioned members. After their reports appeared in California papers, many of these journalists were threatened. The Guyanese government investigated and reported, "Not one confirmation of any allegation of mistreatment."

California congressman Leo Ryan, 53, was serving his fourth term when he became interested in the Jonestown commune. He decided to look into the matter.

This was not Ryan's first excursion into a high-profile investigation. It was he who strongly and successfully petitioned for the release from prison of his constituent Patty Hearst.

Ryan's entourage, including aides, lawyers, a Guyanese government official, newspaper reporters and a TV crew from NBC, landed at the closest airstrip, Port Kaituma. Only Ryan and four members of his party were allowed to proceed immediately to Jonestown. The rest followed four hours later.

Initial impressions of the commune were favorable. Food appeared to be plentiful. The Ryan group clapped to gospel music as they finished a pleasant meal. Members of the congregation conversed with Congressman Ryan. They told him they were experiencing the happiest years of their lives.

Throughout the informal introduction to Jonestown, benevolent Father Jim Jones presided, volunteering his views when asked.

Only Ryan and the four original party members were allowed to spend the night at the commune. The rest were transported back to Port Kaituma in a dump truck. Next morning they returned to Jonestown and were escorted around the compound by Marceline Jones.

Questioned by the reporters, Jones vehemently denied the allegations by former members of his flock of poor treatment. During the questioning, word drifted down to Jones and his interrogators that several members of the commune wanted to leave with Congressman Ryan and his group. Jones flew into a rage. Tension mounted. But no one prevented the dissident members from leaving.

As Ryan talked to the disturbed Jones, a member of the commune pulled a knife and attempted to stab the congressman. While he was being disarmed, the attacker was wounded.

Finally, Ryan, his entourage of officials, newsmen and defectors, boarded the dump truck for the return trip to the airstrip at Port Kaituma. Later, newsmen were to state that at this point they believed that Jones was an unstable character but they were under the impression that he was sincere in his desire to do good for his fellow man. True, there were some flaws to Jonestown but that was to be expected. Sixteen homesick dissidents out of 900 members was not out of the ordinary. No one seemed to be there against their will, no one appeared to be mistreated.

We can only guess at the state of mind of Jim Jones. Unstable, paranoid Jones believed the adverse publicity generated by the stories the newsmen would file would spell the ruin of his colony in the jungle. He also believed that the dissidents who joined Ryan and his group were only the beginning of a wave of dissension that would sweep Jonestown. He determined to force the world to sit up and take notice.

Two small planes landed at the Port Kaituma airstrip to take the visitors home. The dump truck that had originally carried the Ryan group to the landing strip pulled up with a tractor and flatbed. The truck parked but the tractor towing the flatbed drove up between the two aircraft. Suddenly, the men on the tractor and flatbed opened fire. Airplane tires were punctured. Jonestown defector Patricia Parks lay dead. Also killed in the rain of gunfire were San Francisco *Examiner* photographer Greg Robinson, NBC cameraman Bob Brown, NBC correspondent Don Harris and Congressman Leo Ryan. Others were wounded, some seriously.

While the Guyanese police looked on from a distance, one of the defectors pointed out that Larry Layton, posing as a defector, had opened fire on his fellow commune brothers.

Back in Jonestown, an unbelievable scenario was taking place. Cyanide was mixed with Kool-Aid and quickly distributed to members of the commune. Mothers forced the liquid down their children's mouths. No one refused to take the poison. Black and white, young and old, people who had fled the ghettos and streets of America for the jungles of Guyana, were committing mass suicide. They had followed their charismatic leader, who had promised them a better life. Instead, he led them to death. All 913 died.

On December 2, 1986, 41-year-old Larry Layton was convicted of conspiring to murder a U.S. congressman. He was sentenced to life imprisonment, the only person ever tried for the incident that took a total of 918 lives.

JOHN JOUBERT

It is a fact of life that there are predators out there stalking and killing innocent citizens. When they are apprehended, we are amazed that they do not look like monsters. The Ted Bundys and Jeffrey Dahmers of the world have the appearance of the average man on the street. This is the story of one such monster in disguise.

John Joubert was the product of a broken home. He and his sister were raised by their mother. John was a smallish boy who kept to himself during his school years. His main activity centred around the Boy Scout movement, which he would later say gave him a feeling of belonging.

As a teenager in Portland, Maine, John, who had never had a girlfriend, began to experience deep urges to hurt defenseless strangers. He fantasized as to how it would feel to actually attack someone. The urges grew stronger, until John decided to act out his fantasy in real life.

In the winter of 1979, he stopped an eight-year-old boy on the street and clutched him by the throat. The little boy struggled and broke free. John let him go. It had been an exhilarating experience, but he considered it a failure. He would try again. A month later, he stopped another eight-year-old — a girl this time. John struck up a conversation with the youngster but, for reasons unknown even to himself, he let her go without even initiating an attack. John was disappointed at not following through.

John rode past nine-year-old Sarah Canty on his bicycle. As she bent over, he thrust a pencil into her back. Sarah ran into her home crying. The pencil had not penetrated more than a quarter of an inch into her back and her wound soon healed. Although she described the boy on the 10-speed bike to the police, the culprit was never found.

It amazed John that his attacks had been accomplished with such ease. The youngsters were so vulnerable. They stopped and talked to him without question. It also occurred to John that if he was careful, he might never be apprehended. To his way of thinking, the police were incompetent stupid oafs. Next time he would use a knife.

On March 24, 1980, nine-year-old Michael Witham sloshed through the snow on his way home. John struck up a conversation with the little boy. As the youngster looked away, John slashed his throat. Michael was able to run home as blood poured from his neck. The wound would take 12 stitches to close.

John had discovered a new thrill. His crime was featured in the newspapers and on the radio. Commentators wondered what kind of person would slash a little boy's throat. For the first time John realized that the notoriety of his crime brought with it the danger of being caught. It bothered him. Two years would pass before he felt compelled to attack again.

After John finished high school, he tried his hand at college. It didn't work out. At age 18, he found himself at loose ends, wondering what to do with the rest of his life. Sometimes the urge to attack would come over him. On Aug. 22, 1982, he prowled the streets on his 10-speed bike, looking for a victim. He found one in 11-year-old Ricky Stetson, all 60 pounds of him. Ricky was jogging when John rode up on his bike. Next morning, his body was found by a passerby. Ricky had been stabbed in the chest and bitten about his calves.

John Joubert had killed for the first time. He experienced no remorse or sorrow for what he had done, only exhilaration and relief.

John joined the U.S. Air Force, completed training as a radar technician and was posted to Offutt Air Force Base in Bellevue, Nebraska. Judy and Leonard Eberle lived right beside the Air Force base. On September 18, 1983, their 13-year-old son Danny went out on his paper route as he did every day. It was Danny's misfortune to cross paths with a monster.

By now, John Joubert was driving a 1979 Nova. In an instant, he clamped one hand over the boy's mouth while his other hand held a knife to Danny's throat. Danny was forced into the trunk of the Nova, driven to a secluded area and stabbed four times in the chest. John bit the dead boy's legs before dragging his body into a field adjoining the road. The experience left him hungry. It was almost morning. John drove to a restaurant and ate a hearty breakfast.

When Danny failed to return home from his paper route, his parents pinpointed the last paper he had delivered. They searched the area and found their son's bike leaning against a fence. Days later, Danny's stabbed and bitten body was found in the field.

Airman John Joubert was ecstatic. He was acting out his fantasies and enjoying every minute of the kill and the aftermath. Murder is news and John revelled at being in the news. He would kill again within three months.

On December 2, 1983, Chris Walden, 12, left his home for the few minutes walk to the Pawnee Elementary School he attended. John forced the boy into his Nova and drove away. Beside an isolated dirt road some distance from town, John choked and stabbed Chris until he was dead.

The monster returned to the air force base and, as if by magic, was transformed into mild-mannered, pleasant Airman John Joubert. He soaked up every detail of the latest infamous murder. Now there was more talk than ever about the killings. It was difficult not to connect the Eberle and Walden murders. The victims were so young, the killings so senseless.

Certainly Barbara and Warren Weaver were well aware of the madman in their midst. They warned their young son of the potential danger, never dreaming that it would be Barbara who would cross the monster's path.

On January 11, 1984, just a little over a month after Chris

Walden's murder, Barbara was at work as a preschool instructor at the Aldersgate United Methodist Church. At about 8:15 a.m. she noticed a Chevy Citation circling the church. Barbara paid little attention until the vehicle stopped in front of the church. A young man came to the door. It was bitterly cold out, but Barbara's instinct told her to open the door only a crack. She wondered if this could be the man who killed children. That's what made her decide to memorize the Citation's license plate - 59-L5154.

The man shivered in the cold. He asked, "Can I use your phone?" Barbara lied, "There's no phone here." Suddenly the man growled, "Get back inside or I'll kill you!" Barbara threw open the door and raced outside past the stranger. She ran, fell, cut her hand on the icy road, but made it to the nearby home of Pastor David Kelly.

Nancy Kelly called police. Barbara was able to give them the licence number of the Chevy Citation. It didn't take long to trace the vehicle to a car dealership. Airman John Joubert had been given a loaner while his Nova was being repaired.

Less than two hours after Barbara Weaver's harrowing ordeal, John was located in his room at the air force base. It was over. When questioned about the threat to Barbara, he confessed to killing little boys.

John stood trial for the murders of Danny Eberle and Chris Walden. He was found guilty of both murders and sentenced to die in the electric chair. Since then he has been returned to Maine, where he was found guilty of murdering Ricky Stetson.

Psychological tests revealed that John Joubert has an IQ of 123, considered to be in the superior range. He is presently on Death Row in Nebraska State Prison.

STEVE JUDY

The clean-cut 12-year-old with the wide grin explained that he was a Boy Scout and was selling cookies door to door. The lady of the house smiled and beckoned for the youngster to enter. When the lad innocently inquired if her husband was at home, the woman replied that he was at work.

Steve Judy flashed a jackknife, held it to the terrified woman's throat and forced her into a bedroom. Once there, he stabbed her over and over again. Then he raped the hapless woman. When the blade of his knife snapped in her sternum, he ran to the kitchen looking for another weapon. The woman, bleeding profusely, staggered to a bureau to fetch a small hatchet her husband kept there.

Steve returned just as the woman found the hatchet. He grabbed it and swung wildly, severing the woman's left index finger and splitting her head open.

This remarkable woman underwent brain surgery and survived the attack. Steve was quickly apprehended and incarcerated in a mental institution for juveniles. After spending only nine months in the institution, he was released into the care of foster parents.

Steve continued to be in and out of trouble for the next nine years. His most serious brush with the law occurred when he beat and almost killed a woman in a Chicago suburb. Only the intervention of passers-by saved the woman's life. The 20-year-old was sent away for another of his many short stints in prison. In March 1977, he was paroled after serving only 20 months. A month after his release, Steve robbed a woman and spent another year in prison.

On April 28, 1979, two men searching for wild mushrooms along White Lick Creek outside Indianapolis, Indiana, stumbled across several articles of women's clothing near the bank of the creek. As they followed the trail of clothing, they came upon the nude body of a woman. Her legs rested on the creek bank, while the rest of her body was submerged.

Within minutes, the area was swarming with Indiana State Troopers, who went about securing the crime scene. Det. Sgt. Jerry Conner interviewed the two men who had found the body and then proceeded to walk downstream from the location where the body had been discovered. Later, he would say he was looking for any other clothing belonging to the dead woman. What he found was far different. Conner took about 100 paces when he came across the body of a little girl tangled in the weeds in the creek.

Officials were still absorbing this horrendous discovery when detectives, who had continued to walk downstream, came across another child's body. The small boy had washed up on a sandy outcropping. Police scanned the area. From where they stood beside the little boy's body, they were able to see the body of yet another child. What monster had snuffed out the lives of four individuals and what reason could anyone have for killing three children, all under six years of age?

A preliminary examination of the bodies revealed that the woman had been raped and strangled. The children had no marks of violence on their bodies. All three had drowned in the swirling waters of White Lick Creek.

From a bankbook found at the scene, the woman was identified as Terry Chasteen. The three little victims were her children. Terry regularly drove her children to a baby sitter's before continuing on to work at a local grocery store. She hadn't shown up for work that day.

Terry had a boyfriend who was genuinely shocked to learn of her death. He cooperated fully with investigating officers and it was he who was asked to officially identify the bodies. On the way to the mortuary, he shouted out to accompanying police, "That's Terry's car!" By blind luck, the victim's distinctive bright red vehicle had been found.

Terry's boyfriend later identified her body and those of her three children, Misty Ann, 5; Stephen Michael, 4; and Mark Lewis, 2. Terry was only 22 years old at the time of her death and was divorced from the children's father, who was in the U.S. Navy.

Police solicited the public's assistance. They asked anyone who had been near Highway 67 and White Lick Creek that morning to contact the Indiana State Police. Scores of calls were received. One caller reported that he and his young son had driven across the bridge over White Lick Creek before 8 a.m. They had noticed a distinctively painted red and silver pickup truck parked down an access road.

Police put out a bulletin to adjoining states describing the conspicuous vehicle. But it wasn't necessary. Once again, by coincidence, the truck was located. The same man who had spotted the red and silver pickup called police the day after the murder. His young son had seen the vehicle parked near a neighborhood construction site.

Police quickly learned that the truck belonged to Steve Judy, who was well known to Indianapolis police. Steve was taken into custody and questioned. It had taken less than 36 hours to home in on their chief suspect.

Initially, Steve, on the advice of his lawyer, wouldn't talk about the crime. Authorities went about building a case against the vicious young criminal. Tests proved that Steve's blood type was compatible with semen stains found on Terry's clothing. Threads taken from Steve's clothing matched threads from Terry's blouse. Casts of tire tracks lifted from the murder scene were the same as the tire tracks of Steve's pickup truck.

Steve Judy testified toward the end of his trial. From the witness stand he related how he stopped Terry Chasteen. It was simple. He pointed to her tire, indicating that she was having a flat. When she stopped, he pulled up and offered assistance. At the same time, he offered to look under the hood of her car. That's when he ripped out the ignition coil. When the car wouldn't start, he offered to give Terry and her children a lift.

They travelled a short while before Steve pulled off the road and parked near White Lick Creek. In an obvious attempt to save her children, Terry didn't resist. She was forced to walk down to the creek. Steve told the children to go downstream and play. He then commanded Terry to remove her clothing. She complied in silence and was raped. Suddenly, she screamed hysterically. Steve ripped away a piece of her clothing and stuffed it in her mouth before strangling his helpless victim.

The children ran toward their mother's screams. One by one, Steve picked them up and threw them in the creek, where they drowned. Steve Judy begged the court to execute him.

Sitting in the courtroom was a woman who would later testify against the accused man. The witness had no index finger on her left hand. She was the woman who had survived the vicious attack on her life nine years earlier.

On March 8, 1981, Steve Judy's wish was granted. He was executed in Indiana's electric chair.

EDMUND KEMPER

Some time ago I travelled to the tiny village of
Bovingdon, England, to research the unbelievable case of
Graham Young. Young poisoned his own family in 1963,
when he was only 14 years old. Released from Broadmoor
nine years later he proceeded to poison his colleagues at his
place of employment in Bovingdon. After causing two deaths
and many bouts of illness, he was taken into custody. In
1972 he was tried for murder, convicted, and is presently in
prison.

The Young case received worldwide publicity, as it went
to the very heart of major social questions the western world
had been grappling with for years. Should our judicial system
emphasize rehabilitation or punishment? Does capital punishment ultimately save lives?

At the time, I believed that the bizarre case of the obsessive poisoner who had fooled psychiatrists and lawyers into
releasing him to kill again was an isolated incident. I was
wrong.

At approximately the same time another young man, age
15, was following the same path as Graham Young. The
methods of killing were different, but the dates, the motives,
and even the mental ability of the two murderers are so similar they stretch coincidence to the limit.

The other boy's name is Edmund Kemper. This is his
story.

Edmund was born on December 19, 1948 in Burbank,
California. His father was a huge man, towering six feet,

eight inches, while his mother, Clarnell, stood an even six-feet. The Kempers had three children — Susan, the oldest; Edmund, and Allyn. Edmund's parents argued incessantly. The more heated of these arguments usually culminated with Mr. Kemper leaving home for long periods of time.

There is no evidence that either parent ever physically abused their son. Edmund, as the only boy in the house, may have felt some rejection by his mother, who probably identified him with her husband. Eventually, in 1957, Mr. Kemper left his wife and never returned. Clarnell was to go to work to support her three children. She would marry twice again in a futile attempt to find companionship and a father for her children.

In the meantime, Clarnell moved to Helena, Montana, where she obtained employment as a secretary with the First National Bank. She made a new home for her three children, but Edmund was miserable. He longed for his father, and visited him at every opportunity at his new home in Los Angeles. Mr. Kemper had remarried. Edmund may not have been the most welcome of guests with the new Mrs. Kemper.

At the age of 10, Edmund, who was a tall, big-boned boy, began exhibiting some strange traits. He enjoyed taking the arms, legs and heads off his younger sister's dolls. When he was only 13 years old, Edmund shot a dog belonging to another boy who lived nearby. Young Kemper had been well schooled in the use of firearms by his father, who prided himself in having been a member of the Special Service during World War II. After the incident with the dog, neighboring children mocked and made fun of Edmund. From then on Edmund Kemper had no close contact with anyone other than his mother. Their relationship was strange in many ways. Edmund always brought his troubles to his mother, who seemed concerned, but their discussions usually ended in shouting matches, with one or the other storming out of the house.

Shortly after Edmund killed the dog, he cut the head off the family pet, a Siamese cat. This time he was terrified at what he had done, and quickly buried the cat in his backyard.

In September 1962, Edmund went to live with his father in Los Angeles. He was ecstatic. For a few months he led a happy, normal existence. At Christmas, Mr. Kemper visited his parents on their farm at North Fork, California.

Most 15-year-old boys would look forward to a visit with grandparents down on the farm. Not Edmund. He suspected his family of subterfuge. For the first time in his life Edmund's instincts were correct. His father left him on the farm and returned to Los Angeles. Edmund felt rejected, cast aside, and, above all, bored. His grandparents meant well, but they were old and set in their ways.

Grandfather Edmund Kemper was 72 and retired. He still did some farming on his eight-acre spread. Maude Kemper, at 66, spent her spare time writing juvenile stories. Being something of an artist, she illustrated her own work. All of this was an idyllic situation for the elderly couple, but was utterly boring for 15-year-old Edmund. His grandfather detected the unrest in the young lad and tried to help. He presented Edmund with a rifle to shoot gophers and rabbits. At school in the nearby town of Tollhouse, Edmund did well, making from C-plus to B-minus in all his subjects.

The school term ended and Edmund went to Helena to visit his mother and her third husband. In two weeks he was back on the farm with his grandparents. There was a marked change in Edmund's behavior. He now appeared even more withdrawn and sullen. The change was so evident that his grandfather wrote to Edmund's father especially to tell him that the visit with his mother had not done the boy any good.

Later, Edmund was to reveal that his feelings towards his grandparents vacillated from gratefulness for what they were doing for him to resentment. Edmund resented the fact that his grandparents often mentioned how much it was costing them for his room and board. Sometimes his grandmother reminded him of his mother who Edmund felt was the most domineering woman in the world.

Occasionally, deep in thought, Edmund would stare off into space. The weird habit bothered his grandmother. She always shouted at him to bring him out of his reverie. Maude Kemper had no way of knowing that her grandson was fantasizing about murdering her.

On August 27, 1963, Edmund was sitting at the kitchen table proofreading one of his grandmother's stories. Slowly he began to stare off into space. As usual his grandmother shouted at him, bringing him back to reality. Edmund then nonchalantly mentioned that he was going out to shoot some rabbits. He picked up his .22-rifle and went out on the porch. Edmund raised his .22 and took careful aim at the back of his grandmother's head. The bullet travelled through the screen door and into his grandmother's skull. Did Edmund Kemper feel remorse at what he had done? Was he terrified at the consequences? Edmund raised the gun and twice more shot his grandmother in the back. He then dragged the body into the elderly couple's bedroom. Just then a car chugged up the driveway. It was his grandfather. Edmund raised the rifle until the back of the old man's head was in his sight. He squeezed the trigger ever so gently just as his father had taught him. His grandfather fell to the ground never knowing what had killed him.

Edmund went to the telephone and called his mother. His first words to her were "Grandma's dead and so is Grandpa." His mother, understandably shaken, composed herself enough to get the story of the killing from her son. She pleaded with him to call the police. Edmund put down the phone and minding his mother like a good boy should, he called the sheriff's office.

When questioned by police Edmund had a hard time explaining his motive. He had often thought of killing his grandmother, because at times she had annoyed him. His grandfather was another story. Edmund had performed a mercy killing. You see, had the old man discovered his wife's body, it was quite possible he would have had a fatal heart attack. Edmund had mercifully spared his grandfather a great deal of grief.

Psychiatrists who examined Edmund discovered two things. Their subject had an I.Q. of 136, indicating superior intelligence and they felt he was a paranoid schizophrenic. Still only 15 years old, Edmund was declared insane. On December 6, 1964, the ominous doors of Atascadero State Hospital closed behind him. Ironically, half-way around the world in England, 15-year-old Graham Young had already been in Broadmoor for over a year. Both boys would gain their freedom to kill again.

Once in the huge hospital which specialized in sex offenders, Edmund appeared to make a complete adjustment. He responded to treatment exceptionally well. So well, in fact, that eventually Edmund worked in a psychology lab testing other patients. Even in the confines of the institution he led something of a double life. To all outward appearances he was the well adjusted mental patient making an extraordinary recovery. His other life consisted of delving into every detail of sexual perversion garnered from fellow inmates. Edmund's curiosity knew no limits. He wanted to know it all.

After five years at Atascadero, Edmund was enrolled in a community college, where he earned straight A's. In the meantime his mother, now Clarnell Strandberg, had moved to Santa Cruz, where she worked at the University of California as a secretary. Clarnell made one close friend, Sara Hallett, while employed at the university. The previous five years had been most pleasant for Clarnell. She didn't have to worry about or argue with her son Edmund.

Now the lumbering six foot, nine inch giant was paroled to his mother. Edmund worked at menial tasks, saved his money and bought a car. He coerced his mother into getting him a University of California sticker for his vehicle, ostensibly so he could park on the campus.

Edmund had a plan. California law had a unique loophole, which Edmund proposed to use to his advantage. On his lawyer's advice he was examined by two different psychiatrists. Both doctors gave him glowing positive reports. Their recommendations were interspersed with words such as "normal," "adjusted" and "no danger to society." These two reports were placed before a superior court judge, who then ruled that Edmund's juvenile record be sealed forever. This meant that Edmund could apply for any job without having to reveal his previous record. He could serve on a jury, or join the army. Why, Edmund could even legally purchase guns.

Edmund Kemper had killed both his grandparents at 15. Now the slate was clean. He had fooled all the experts. Edmund had what amounted to a licence to kill again.

It wasn't long before Edmund and Clarnell were taking part in their monumental shouting matches. Edmund drifted from job to job, never approaching a task which would tax his intellectual abilities. He drank some beer at local hang-outs and cruised around in his Ford. For no apparent reason, he purchased a few knives and guns and stashed them in the trunk of his car.

The university campus was located a little way from Santa Cruz.

Most students lived in the town and hitchhiked to the campus. During the day and early evening it was customary to see both male and female students catching lifts to class. One day Edmund got up enough nerve to stop for a girl hitchhiker. He noticed that the girl glanced at the University of California sticker on his car before jumping in. It was easy.

After that initial triumph, Edmund not only picked up girls near the campus, but roamed all over the state picking up female hitchhikers. He didn't do anything to the girls, just talked. For two years the young giant spent his every spare moment giving lifts to young girls.

Edmund fantasized about possessing a girl. Later he was to state that possession to him meant not only sexual posses-sion, but a type of total ownership that only death could bring.

On Sunday, May 7, 1972, Edmund Kemper was hunting — hunting for a human victim. He found two. Near Berkeley he picked up two Fresno State College coeds. The two friends, Anita and Mary Ann, were hitching a ride to Stanford University. From the time they stepped into Edmund's car they were never seen again.

Edmund pulled a 9-mm Browning automatic from under the seat of the Ford Galaxie. Anita and Mary Ann were terrified. Edmund found a deserted rural road. Both girls knew they were about to be raped. Mary Ann tried to talk Edmund out of it, but without success. Edmund sized up the two girls, who didn't seem to be overimpressed with what he thought were his daring actions.

Finally Edmund told them he would drive them to his mother's house, but in the meantime Anita would have to be placed in the trunk. All the while Edmund had made up his mind to kill both his captives. With no choice in the matter, Mary Ann allowed herself to be handcuffed. Anita, looking in to the barrel of the Browning automatic, was led to the trunk. She got in. In the front seat of the car the insane giant stabbed the 105-lb. girl repeatedly until she was dead. He then opened the trunk and proceeded to stab Anita until she lay still in death.

Edmund drove home with the two bodies in his car. First he washed up, then returned to his vehicle and carried Mary Ann's body to his room. Fully aware of his actions, and without panic or remorse, Edmund dissected his victim. He returned to the car for the second body and repeated his insane ritual. Wrapping the sections of human remains in plastic bags, Edmund drove into the Santa Cruz mountains and buried the two girls. Their heads were thrown over a ravine. Edmund drove home and fondled the girls' wallets.

Four months later, on September 14, a 15-year-old dance student named Aiko disappeared. Edmund had raped, suffocated and decapitated his victim.

In the months which followed three more girls, Cynthia, Alice and Rosalind, were murdered by Edmund Kemper. Parts of the various bodies were found. Some were identified, others were not. Investigating officials knew they were dealing with one killer, but had no idea who he was or why the mad killer struck in such a vicious manner. They also knew they were dealing with a necrophiliac and cannibal.

On Easter weekend, 1973, Edmund decided to kill his mother. The idea so excited him that he couldn't sleep. He

tossed and turned in bed until he gave into the uncontrollable urge which boiled within. At a little after 5 a.m., armed
with a knife and claw hammer, he entered his mother's bedroom and, without saying a word, bludgeoned her to death.
He then decapitated his mother. Later Edmund was to tell
police that the whole thing took less than a minute. Edmund
placed his mother's body in a closet, cleaned up the bedroom and left to have a few beers at a local hangout.

Somewhere in the dark recesses of his mind Edmund felt
that he had to create a reason for his mother's disappearance.
She was not the type of woman to leave her job and home
without good reason. Edmund thought about the problem all
day. As he drove home the solution came to him. If his
mother's best friend, Sara Hallett, dropped out of sight at the
same time, it would be logical to assume that the two women
had gone away together.

At around five that evening Edmund returned home and
opened a can of beer. The phone rang. Edmund picked up
the receiver. It was Sara Hallett asking for his mother.
Edmund explained that his mother was out, but had asked
him to invite Sara to dinner that evening. Sara was delighted
to accept. A few hours later the unsuspecting woman walked
into hell. Edmund throttled her to death, breaking her neck
in the process. He placed her body in the closet with that of
his mother.

On Easter Sunday, Edmund awoke and decided to flee.
He drove his car east to Reno, Nevada, where he rented
another vehicle from Hertz. Carefully he transferred what
amounted to an arsenal to the rented car. He drove for 18
hours without stopping.

When he arrived in Pueblo, Colorado, Edmund made up
his mind to call Lieutenant Charles Scherer, who he knew
was in charge of the investigation of the missing girls. When
the long distance call was received in Santa Cruz, Lt. Scherer
was not on duty. Edmund had a hard time explaining just
who he was and that this was no crank call. He was told to
call back. When one of the most despicable monsters who
ever lived called back at 1 a.m., he was told that Lt. Scherer

would not be on duty until 9 a.m. He was informed that the police were not supposed to accept collect calls. The officer hung up.

At 5 in the morning Edmund tried for the third time. This time he contacted a policeman who was familiar with his case. He kept Edmund on the line until the Pueblo police took him into custody while he was still speaking on the phone. Edmund hardly had time to tell the police to go to his home where they would find the bodies of his mother and Sara Hallett.

When taken into custody, big Edmund Kemper directed police to gravesites which had not yet been uncovered. Police were astounded to learn that the monster they were seeking was this intelligent, lucid giant. Edmund resorted to his photographic memory to recount every detail of the eight lives he had snuffed out. He claimed that his reason for surrendering was to get the whole thing off his chest. To psychiatrists he suggested that possible repressed fears and anxieties had driven him to kill. None of this was new to Edmund. He had been through it all before when he had killed his grandparents.

Edmund Kemper stood trial for murder. He was found to be sane and guilty of eight counts of murder in the first degree. Edmund Kemper is now confined to a maximum security prison at Folsom.

HENRI LANDRU

Henri Landru was born in Paris on April 12, 1869, to honest, hardworking parents. His mother was a dressmaker who ran her business from her home on Rue de Puebla, and his father was a book seller. These occupations did not place the Landru family in the highest income bracket, but it did allow them to lead comfortable, if frugal, lives. Henri attended a school run by Jesuits, and was a good, hardworking, intelligent student.

At the age of 15 he was initiated into the delights of sex by the neighborhood prostitute, but despite these attractions, he had eyes only for the daughter of a neighbor who lived not far from him on Rue de Puebla. Her name was Marie Catherine Remy, and in his unique fashion Henri loved her. As a result of his affections she became pregnant, at which point Henri, coincidentally enough, left Paris and joined the French Army.

After three years of military service, Henri desperately wanted out. He wrote to Marie's father, who used his influence to get Landru a discharge. Henri came home, married Marie, met his two-year-old daughter, and got a job as an accountant. Within the next two years, the couple was blessed twice more. Now 26 years old, Henri found himself in a dead-end job, with three children and a wife to support.

In the years between 1900 and 1910, Henri tried his hand at swindling women, using any ruse to gain possession of their money and furniture. It didn't seem to matter what he did, he always got caught, and received a series of short jail sentences for fraud. In between sentences, Henri never forgot Marie — in fact, he remembered her to the extent of another bouncing baby daughter. The Landru family now totalled four children.

Henri's profession was that of con artist and thief, with no gainful employment other than the courting, wooing and fleecing of members of the opposite sex. He had a magnetic personality, but at this point in his life he had not yet perfected the fine art of escaping detection after the fact. From 1910 to 1914, he corrected this flaw in his operating procedure to a degree that put his frauds in the top professional category. He kept meticulous notes and records on every lady, her likes, dislikes, and habits. He categorized the potential degree of difficulty in fleecing them and how big a financial reward was waiting to be plucked. Six days a week, Henri left his wife and four children to go to his work.

Only Henri knew that he was busy building up another life and another role, which he entered fully and completely. Sometimes when he left his family, he would have to stay away for a few days. He always told Marie the length of his business trips, and if he was held up for any reason, he was always considerate enough to phone her. She never questioned his absences, nor did she inquire about the cyclical nature of his income. She had a general idea that her husband was in the used furniture business and had several warehouses which he visited. When he made a profitable deal the family shared in the good fortune, but when he had trouble putting together a lucrative transaction, the exchequer suffered.

Marie was a perfect wife for Henri Landru; she cared for her brood, but more important, she didn't have an inquisitive bone in her body. The family moved frequently; this too she took in her stride without question. She knew her husband would be home at least one day a week, for on that day Henri opened his huge desk and did his bookwork.

At the age of 45, Henri had grown a long, flowing beard that was without a doubt his most outstanding feature. He had a rather long body for a small man, which gave him the appearance of being taller than he really was. His pale complexion contrasted sharply with his bright red beard, and he was bald as a billiard ball, with large, powerful hands for a man of his size and build.

In order to guarantee a constant supply of ladies, Henri used the simple but effective method of placing matrimonial ads in the newspapers. He studied the best ads, and by trial and error he developed the wording that brought the best results.

On Bastille Day, July 14, 1914, the Landrus had just moved into another new home in Clichy. Henri had to go to work soon after they arrived in their new home, and this particular job was to be concluded in a most unique way. Using the name Raymond Diard, he had received a reply to one of his ads from Jeanne Cuchet. Jeanne fell into the exact category that rated an A in Henri's book. She had been married to a commercial traveller, who had unfortunately died of natural causes. She lived with her elderly parents and teenaged son, Andre. Best of all, she had a substantial nest-egg of 5,000 francs.

A tall, thin, plain woman, she was flattered and thrilled to be singled out, and soon became completely infatuated with Henri. An expert at his chosen profession, he knew the words, the topics and above all the manners that appealed to Jeanne. As Monsieur Diard he dined with her parents, careful to agree with her father's views on the conduct of war, and careful to have an extra helping of her mother's biscuits. This milieu was Henri's business office, and in it he labored as patiently and efficiently as any accountant. The couple announced their engagement, received congratulations from the family, and another plum of a set-up was ready to be plucked. The 5,000 francs would go a long way — wouldn't Marie be pleased at the successful conclusion of this piece of business!

In subsequent meetings with his fiancée, he let it be known that he was a qualified engineer who ran a small business currently making lighter flints. Lovestruck Jeanne's life had changed in three short months. It was too bad that her son Andre didn't take to Raymond; but never mind, he would doubtless grow to love him as much as she did. What a trusting man Henri was, thought Jeanne. He insisted that he put his money and hers together in the bank. The happy couple moved into a little apartment, and as soon as the money was safely placed in the bank, Henri cleaned out the account and took off.

Months later, quite by accident, Henri bumped into Jeanne, who was tossing flowers at the feet of passing soldiers during a military parade. One of the flowers landed at his feet, and when he looked up it was into her eyes. It was a tribute to his ingenuity and her stupidity that he was able to make up a story that placated her. He admitted to her that he had lied — he was really married and had two daughters — his divorce would become final any day now — the day he left her he had received word that his wife had balked at the divorce and was coming to Paris with his two daughters — he had held her money for her — it was safe in a Swiss bank.

Bluebeard was able to pull it off, and the pair took up where they had left off months before. In November, three months after his reunion with Jeanne, Henri rented a house in the country. It was a villa called The Lodge at 46 Rue de Mantes in Vernouillet, a small town just outside Paris. Henri took Jeanne to this villa. He usually only worked for profit, and there was nothing further to be had from Jeanne but her life. While lying in bed with Jeanne, Bluebeard leaned over, placed his large hands firmly on her neck, and strangled her to death. He then left for Paris with her bankbook. He had noticed that she had managed to save a paltry 400 francs since her last plucking, and it was not difficult for a man of his experience to extract it from the bank. The next day he was back at Vernouillet, with a body on his hands.

The unheated lodge was cold and damp, and when Henri arrived he was altogether uncomfortable, but repeated trips to the woodhouse soon warmed him up. He piled the logs high in the stove, and the fire caught on his first attempt. Next, operating according to his prearranged plan, Henri cleaned out the bathroom tub, which was in the cellar. Revolted as he was at handling Jeanne's body, he managed to place it into the tub. Ditchdiggers don't necessarily like digging ditches, but it's their job. And this was Henri's. With crude household implements Henri managed to dissect the body in the tub. As he proceeded, he decided he would never be this ill-prepared again, but after all, this was only his apprenticeship. If butchers learned how to dress game, he could learn to become as efficient as a butcher.

Over the next several days, Henri lugged his gruesome cargo piece after piece up the stairs and placed it ever so carefully in the stove. Black smoke billowed out of The Lodge's chimney, and the smoke was accompanied by a repulsive odor. The wind carried it to every nook and cranny of Vernouillet. Later, many villagers stated that they had noticed the smoke, and more particularly the offensive smell. Some even said it smelled like roast beef. One villager complained to an official, who knocked on Henri's front door to question him about the terrible smell emanating from his chimney. Henri told the official that the chimney was defective and promised to have it fixed immediately. This seemed to satisfy the official, and he went away.

Soon afterwards, while walking on the streets of Paris with the signs of war all about him, Henri was accosted by Jeanne's son Andre, in one of those chance meetings which plague murderers.

"Monsieur Diard, where is my mother?"

Henri had to shift into high gear in a hurry. Again it is a tribute to his guile that he convinced the lad that his mother and he were living together in Vernouillet, happy and contented. He placated Andre by telling him that his mother was planning to send for him, and now that they had met in this way he wanted Andre to accompany him to Vernouillet. Henri always liked to put a bit of frosting on the cake. "She is pregnant," he told her anxious son.

They arrived at Vernouillet; Jeanne, it seemed, was not in. Henri offered Andre something to eat. While the young man sat at the table Henri's strong hands firmly clasped his neck and squeezed the life from his body. This time the operation went more smoothly. Henri had bought a hacksaw, meat cleaver and mallet, so it was not long before the black smoke and offensive odor billowed forth from the chimney once again.

In December 1916, Monsieur Diard closed The Lodge at Vernouillet and left it forever.

It is one thing to swindle women one at a time, but it is quite another to be playing many roles simultaneously. Henri always kept extensive notes to remember which lady knew him under which name. He couldn't afford a mistake, because sometimes he had to deal with bank officials, using his many aliases without the slightest hesitation. He even got into the habit of talking to himself, using the alias of the moment in order to implant the proper name in his mind. On many occasions he would rush from one apartment to another, consulting his notebook to refresh his memory as to which name and personality he had to assume.

In the summer of 1917, Henri rented a house in Gambais, not far from Paris. He picked it carefully. The house adjoined a cemetery; there were no inhabitants for miles around. Using the name of Paul Fremyet, he purchased a good stove and connected it to the existing smokestack. Then he set about enticing more women, making sure that they turned over their worldly belongs to him before they turned over their lives. In all, Henri Landru strangled and burned eleven people — young Andre Chuchet and ten gullible women.

One of his victims, Anna Collomb, had invited her sister, Madame Pillot, to Gambais to visit the man she was soon to marry. After returning to Paris, Madame Pillot never heard from her sister again, though she wrote to her at Gambais. In desperation, she wrote to the mayor of Gambais, who answered that he believed he had located the house mentioned in her letter, but that no one had ever head of her sister's fiancé, Monsieur Fremyet. The mayor stated that the tenant of record of the house in question was a Monsieur Dupont. He volunteered that he had received another inquiry about the house from the sister of one Madame Celestine

Buisson. The writer of the letter was Mademoiselle Lacoste, and the mayor suggested that Mme Pillot might find it useful to contact Mlle Lacoste.

The two ladies did meet and compare notes. No one could mistake that red beard. Diard, Fremyet, Dupont, Cuchet, the names went on and on. Landru was readily traced and arrested. The police found him trying to destroy a notebook in which he had the names and addresses of all his victims.

One woman, Fernande Segret, visited the house in Gambais and lived to tell about it from the witness stand. For some unknown reason the mass murderer put the pretty Fernande in the same class as his wife, Marie Catherine. They lived as husband and wife, and she claimed he was normal sexually and in every other way. There was nothing perverted or sadistic about Landru, nor did he ever cheat or swindle her, as she had no worldly goods. But relatives and swindled ladies kept coming forward, and from these women and the detailed files Henri kept in his desk at Clichy it was estimated that he had had intimate relations with close to 300 women in the five years before his trial.

On February 24, 1922, Henri Landru, now known throughout the world as Bluebeard, admonished his keepers for offering him a mug of rum and a cigarette. "You know I neither drink nor smoke," he said. The tired old man of 52 was still receiving over a 100 letters a day from women offering everything from a lock of their hair to proposals of marriage. His loyal and faithful wife visited him in jail, and it was only when he refused to see her that his ties with her were finally severed.

His keepers tied his hands behind his back as was the custom, and Henri walked steadily to the guillotine, taking his brief instructions from the executioner. Then his head tumbled into a basket of bran that had been placed in position for that purpose.

ALLAN LEGERE

This is beautiful Miramichi country, tucked away off the beaten path in New Brunswick. Max Aitkin, who achieved fame and fortune as Lord Beaverbrook, was brought up in the north shore town of Newcastle. Ted Williams, the celebrated outfielder with the Boston Red Sox, was one of hundreds of sportsmen who sought out this small portion of paradise to fish the Miramichi River for the finest salmon in the world.

Well over 100 years ago, my grandmother and grandfather settled across the bridge from Newcastle in the adjoining town of Chatham. The young immigrants from Austria made Chatham their home for the rest of their lives. They had seven daughters and one son. One daughter, my elderly aunt Addie, lives today in my grandparents' original home. She was there through the seven months in 1989 when the reign of terror that was Allan Legere swept through the Miramichi.

As I sit in the kitchen of the homestead where my mother and my aunts played as children, it is difficult to imagine that an entire section of this province was caught in a grip of fear only a few short years ago. Back in 1989, as summer faded into fall and the leaves of the trees along the Miramichi burst forth in breathtaking hues of reds and golds, the entire nation would learn about a cruel killer, a man with an uncontrollable urge to mete out a terrible retribution upon innocent and vulnerable victims.

It all really began three years earlier, on June 21, 1986.

John and Mary Glendenning finished the day's work in their general store in Black River Bridge, about 20 miles outside Chatham. They walked across the yard to their home, as they did most days. Although Black River Bridge is little more than a sprinkling of homes on a back road, the Glendennings, John, 66, and Mary, 61, had prospered over the 30 years they had been in business. Everyone in the region knew their store.

The Glendennings were reported to keep large sums of cash in their home. You wouldn't call it gossip. It was the sort of rumor that is harmless unless it is heard by the wrong types. Thirty-eight year old Allan Legere, Scott Curtis, 20, and Todd Matchett, 18, planned on stealing that money. Several different versions of what took place in the Glendenning home on that pleasant summer night have been told by the participants. There is no doubt about the outcome.

The three masked men crashed into the Glendenning home. By the time they left, John had been viciously beaten to death. Mary had been badly beaten, but survived the attack. The men made off with the Glendennings' safe containing some $45,000. The empty safe was later recovered.

The two younger men were well-known in the area as petty thieves. Legere, by far the most experienced criminal, was a professional break and enter man with a long police record dating back to his teens. The three men were soon traced, apprehended and speedily tried. Matchett and Curtis both pleaded guilty and received life sentences. Allan Legere went to trial, was found guilty of second degree murder and was sentenced to life imprisonment with no possibility of parole for 18 years.

The brutal murder and the ensuing trial caused a sensation along the Miramichi. Still, it was a local crime, a botched robbery. The perpetrators were behind bars. Life goes on. In time, Mary Glendenning recovered, although acquaintances tell me that even after this length of time she still suffers from the effects of the blows she received to her head.

On May 3, 1989, Allan Legere was escorted from the Atlantic Institution, a maximum security facility in Renous,

N.B. to a Moncton hospital to have his ears checked. Although handcuffed and chained, Legere managed to shed the restraints, dash out of a bathroom past his guards and escape. Citizens along the Miramichi didn't know it at the time, but seven months of living in fear were about to begin. Twenty-five days later, they would learn of the rage within the soul of Allan Legere.

Annie Flam was a 75-year-old merchant in Chatham. She had been a fixture in her grocery store on Water St. longer than most people could remember. Annie lived with her sister-in-law Nina in a section of the premises attached to the store. Surely the two women deserved to be left alone to live out their lives in peace. But such was not to be the case.

On the night of May 28, Annie Flam was raped and beaten to death. Nina was likewise sexually assaulted and beaten. She survived the attack. The old Flam residence was set on fire. Nina, badly burned, managed to crawl downstairs, where she was rescued by a passer-by. She would later relate in vivid detail how the cruel man had entered their home and attacked them. Because the intruder had worn a balaclava, Nina was unable to describe his face.

Could Allan Legere have been responsible? It had been 25 days since his escape. Could he have made his way from Moncton back to his hometown? People remembered the Glendenning killing. There were similarities, yet it seemed too incredible. Why would a man facing years in prison if captured return to the area where he was born and was known by sight? There were reports of a shadowy figure being seen stealing food and slipping away into the woods. Allan Legere was certainly a suspect. Police poured into the area, but Legere, as if by magic, remained at large.

On October 13, the madman struck again, this time in Newcastle at the home of Linda and Donna Daughney on Mitchell St. The town fire station is on the corner of Mitchell and Jane Streets. It was a fireman who first spotted smoke emanating from an upstairs window of the Daughney residence. The fire was quickly extinguished before it could engulf the bodies of the two sisters. Linda, 41, and Donna,

45, had been sexually attacked and beaten to death. Police dogs and helicopters were used in the hunt for their murderer. There was little doubt they were looking for one man - Allan Legere, now a suspected serial killer.

Newsmen travel the globe to cover major fast-breaking stories. Rick Maclean, the 32-year-old editor of the Miramichi Leader, could walk the distance from his office to the Daughney home in under two minutes. It was a unique opportunity to cover the story, capture the fear of the community and get into the mind of Allan Legere.

Now, three years later, as we walked the short distance to the Daughney residence, Maclean explained that, in the towns and villages along the Miramichi, the average citizen had lived in a state of fear unlike anything they had ever experienced. Little else was discussed. Day after day, his paper featured the three recent murders with the built in anticipation that more would follow unless Legere was captured. At the time Maclean had no way of knowing that diagonally across the river from his office window, the killer would strike again.

Father James Smith was uncharacteristically late to conduct mass at the Nativity of the Blessed Virgin Mary Church. Parishioners gathered around the church, waiting for the 69-year-old priest to make his way across the yard from the rectory. Finally, someone peeked into the window of the rectory. Father Smith had been beaten to death. But death had not come with any degree of speed. An examination of the murder scene and the post mortem revealed that the priest had been tortured. His face had been carved with a knife which hadn't penetrated more than a quarter of an inch. He had been repeatedly kicked so viciously that his entire rib cage had caved in.

Was no one safe from the madman who seemed fully capable of outwitting over 100 police officers? Jeeps sped up and down the Miramichi. Helicopters flew overhead, scanning the woods, while dogs led search parties through heavy brush. Many citizens installed floodlights in their backyards.

Father Smith's 1984 Olds Delta 88 was found abandoned

near the train station 50 miles away in Bathurst. Authorities had correctly deduced that the fugitive had caught a train to Montreal. Perhaps he would never be apprehended. He might have been successful in crossing the border into the United States.

Allan Legere, now the most wanted man in the country, had checked into the Queen Elizabeth Hotel in Montreal. He was relaxing.

Seven days after Father Smith's murder, the urge to return to the Miramichi compelled Legere to take a train to St. John. It was a blustery cold night. Legere commandeered a taxi driven by Ron Gomke. As he stuck a sawed off .308 into Gomke's ribs, he announced, "I'm the one they're looking for. I'm Allan Legere."

The taxi driver did as he was told and headed for Moncton. Near that city's famed Magnetic Hill, Gomke, fighting the deteriorating road conditions, went off the highway into a ditch. Legere flagged down a passing motorist. By sheer coincidence, the driver happened to be Michelle Mercer, an RCMP officer on her way to her native province of Prince Edward Island.

Michelle stopped and offered Legere and Gomke a lift. Once they were headed for Moncton, the wanted man introduced himself and made Michelle aware of his .308. Although she was told to take the Chatham exit, weather conditions were so bad that Michelle missed the exit and ended up south of Moncton near Sussex.

Michelle Mercer's mind was racing. She pointed out to Legere that fuel would soon be a problem. He agreed and allowed her to pull into the Four Corners Irving gas station. Legere took the keys of the car and pumped gas into the vehicle. He then stepped the few feet inside to pay for his purchase.

Unknown to Legere, Michelle Mercer had a second set of keys. In a flash, she was speeding down the highway. Within minutes she located a phone and reported her experience. Roadblocks were immediately set up.

Legere cursed as the car vanished down the road, but he

still had one more card to play. At the side of the gas station, he spotted Brian Golding working on his Mack flatbed tractor trailer. Never one to miss an opportunity to introduce himself, the wanted man said simply, "I'm Allan Legere. Let's get going." His rifle spoke volumes.

Near Newcastle, the big vehicle was spotted on a road never travelled by flatbeds. The police were notified and were soon directly behind Legere, lights flashing. Golding hit the brakes and jumped out. A few seconds elapsed before Legere stepped down from the cab of the truck. "I'm Allan Legere," he said.

The hunt was over.

Legere was charged with four counts of murder. He was positively linked to three of his victims through genetic fingerprinting, better known as DNA. This relatively new investigative tool was utilized by matching the genetic structure of Legere's hair and blood to that of semen samples found on his victims at the crime scenes. He was also identified as the man who had attempted to sell the Daughney sisters' jewelry in Montreal. In addition, he had left his bloody footprints in Father Smith's rectory.

Legere was found guilty of all four murders and sentenced to life imprisonment with no possibility of parole for 25 years. Since his conviction, he has been moved out of New Brunswick to the super maximum wing of the Ste Anne des Plaines prison outside Montreal.

Notorious Allan Legere will long be remembered along the Miramichi. Rick Maclean's book, *Terror's End*, is the definitive study of the drama which held an entire province in fear. Mary Glendenning often suffers from bad headaches as a result of the injuries she sustained from her beating. Nina Flam, who refuses to discuss her horrifying experience, moved to Halifax, but still comes back to visit the area she called home for so many years.

The Chatham business community has placed a globe in the new local library in memory of Annie Flam. Across from Father Smith's church, a home for the elderly has been renamed Father Smith's Manor.

As I left my Aunt Addie, she remarked, "I'm not afraid anymore." She could have been expressing the feelings of the entire Miramichi.

JOHN LIST

John List planned it all in meticulous detail. He called the children's school advising them that his three children would not be attending class for some time. He cancelled newspaper, milk and mail deliveries. You see, John List had decided to disappear. First, he would kill his entire family.

Quiet, religious John was 45 years old in 1971 when everything seemed to turn sour in his life. He simply couldn't continue to make payments on the two mortgages he had placed on his huge, 18-room mansion at 431 Hillside Ave. in fashionable Westfield, New Jersey. His accountancy salary didn't come close to covering his reserved but comfortable lifestyle.

Wife Helen was a disappointment. She adamantly refused to attend church regularly. His daughter Patricia even talked about going into the acting profession. John's rather fanatical religious beliefs were definitely not being adhered to by his family.

There were choices. He could declare himself bankrupt or seek assistance from welfare agencies, but John couldn't bear to think of the shame and disgrace that these avenues held for him and his family. After all, he was a highly-respected accountant who had once been vice president of a bank. He had taught Sunday school at the Lutheran church, which he attended regularly. No, in John's mind there was only one proper thing to do and that was to send his entire family to heaven.

Calmly, John went about the details of his plan. It was

November 9, 1971. He loaded his 9 mm pistol and his .22 calibre revolver. John shot his wife Helen in the back and dragged her body to the ballroom. He then made his way up to the third floor and shot his 85-year-old mother, Alma.

John wanted to move the body down to the ballroom, but it was too heavy. He decided to place his mother's corpse in a closet, but found the dead weight difficult to manipulate. James Moran, who was then chief of police of Westfield, says, "When we went upstairs, we found Alma List's body halfway in a closet. We figured that whoever killed her gave up trying to get her in."

John drove to Westfield High School, where he picked up his 16-year-old daughter Patricia. He killed her with a single shot in the back. Patricia's body was carried to the ballroom and placed on a sleeping bag beside the body of her mother. Frederick, 13, was picked up from his after-school job. Once in the house, he too was shot in the back and placed on a sleeping bag in the ballroom. John List, Jr., 15, arrived home from soccer practice. He had a few moments of awareness before he was shot nine times from both of his father's weapons. His body was placed in a row beside those of his mother, sister and brother. The killing was over. There was no one left.

The diabolical mass murderer cleaned the blood-spattered kitchen to the best of his ability. He stood amidst the bodies of his family and prayed for their deliverance. Then he sat down and wrote a letter to his pastor, the Rev. Eugene A. Rehwinkel. Pertinent excerpts of this letter follow.

"Dear Pastor Rehwinkel:

"I am sorry to add this additional burden to your work. I know that what has been done is wrong from all that I have been taught and that any reasons that I might give will not make it right. But you are the one person that I know that while not condoning this will at least possibly understand why I felt that I had to do this.

"1. I wasn't earning anywhere near enough to support us. Everything I tried seemed to fall to pieces. True, we could have gone bankrupt and maybe gone on welfare.

"2. But that brings me to my next point. Knowing the type of location that one would have to live in, plus the environment for the children, plus the effect on them knowing they were on welfare was just more than I thought they could and should endure. I know they were willing to cut back, but this involved a lot more than that.

"3. With Pat being so determined to get into acting I was also fearful as to what that might do to her continuing to be Christian. I'm sure it wouldn't have helped.

"4. Also, with Helen not going to church I knew that this would harm the children eventually in their attendance. I had continued to hope that she would begin to come to church soon. But when I mentioned to her that Mr. Jutze wanted to pay her an elder's call, she just blew up and said she wanted her name taken off the church rolls. Again this could only have an adverse result for the children's continued attendance.

"So that is the sum of it. If any one of these had been the condition, we might have pulled through but this was just too much. At least I'm certain that all have gone to heaven now. If things had gone on who knows if this would be the case.

"Of course, Mother got involved because doing what I did to my family would have been a tremendous shock to her at this age. Therefore, knowing that she is also a Christian I felt it best that she be relieved of the troubles of this world that would have hit her.

"After it was all over I said some prayers for them all - from the hymn book. That was the least I could do.

"One other thing. It may seem cowardly to have always shot from behind, but I didn't want any of them to know even at the last second that I had to do this to them.

"John got hurt more because he seemed to struggle longer. The rest were immediately out of pain. John didn't consciously feel anything either.

"Please remember me in your prayers. I will need them whether or not the government does its duty as it sees it. I'm only concerned with making my peace with God and of this

I am assured because of Christ dying even for me.

"P.S. Mother is in the hallway in the attic - 3rd floor. She was too heavy to move.

"John."

John turned on some lights, locked the doors of his home and drove away. A month passed. Light bulbs burned out. Neighbors, who later confessed they hadn't known the Lists very well, became suspicious. Finally, they called police.

Chief James Moran spoke to me from his home, "I've handled scores of murders over the years, but nothing like this. We forced the back door and walked through some rooms to the ballroom. The smell was terrible and there they were, four bodies all neatly placed in a row. They were blackened and partially decomposed. I will never forget the sight."

Police found John List's car at Kennedy Airport on December 7, two days after the discovery of the bodies of his family. But John wasn't found or traced. Moran says, "We didn't have the remotest idea where he had gone. He had no real friends and no one really knew the man."

John's past was ordinary in every way — strict religious parents, high school, university, a stint in the army during World War II and, later on, service in the Korean War. As the admitted perpetrator of New Jersey's most infamous crime, he was sought on three continents. All tips and clues led nowhere. John List had apparently committed the perfect murder, not once, but five times.

After the murders, John made his way to Denver, Colorado, where he changed his name to Robert P. Clark. For a while he eked out a living as a cook, but in 1977 gravitated to his original profession of accountancy. Soon he was earning $400 per week. He met his second wife, Delores, at a Lutheran Church gathering. The quiet, introverted Robert was a good and devoted husband.

In 1985, a friend showed Delores Clark a newspaper account of an old New Jersey murder. The photo of John List which accompanied the article bore an eerie resemblance to her husband Robert. Delores dismissed the whole thing as ridiculous.

In 1988, the Clarks moved to Richmond, Virginia. Robert Clark attended Lutheran services, puttered in his garden, watched TV and melted into the woodwork. But modern technology caught up with List. The old unsolved New Jersey murders were televised on the syndicated program, America's Most Wanted. Forensic sculptor Frank Bender, working from 18-year-old photos of List, produced a model of the wanted man's head. Bender ingeniously created an uncanny likeness of John List, aged 18 years.

Sure enough, the same neighbor who had shown the newspaper account to Delores Clark three years earlier, recognized the sculpted head. She had a relative call the program.

John List was traced to an accounting firm in Richmond. Robert Clark denied being the wanted man, but a fingerprint check of old army records on file in Washington proved that he was indeed John List.

In May 1990, 64-year-old John List stood trial for murder, almost two decades after he had eliminated his entire family. He was found guilty of all five murders and was sentenced to five consecutive life terms in prison. When the judge passed sentence on List, the courtroom broke out in applause.

HENRY LEE LUCAS

Is Henry Lee Lucas one of the greatest con artists and liars the world has ever known or is he the world's most prolific serial killer?

Henry will always be remembered as the man who, on various occasions, claimed to have murdered 150 people, then 300 people, and at the height of his "confession period," 600 during an eight-year spree of robbery, rape and murder.

To lay credence to Henry's claims, in many of the killings he had an accomplice, one Otis Toole, who was easily located to corroborate Henry's wild stories. Otis was on Death Row in Stark, Florida.

Henry's early life makes Dickens' poor houses seem like resorts in comparison. He was brought up by a mother who was a prostitute and an alcoholic father. His father had lost both his legs in a railroad accident. The Lucas family lived in the backwoods of Virginia, where Henry's mother took relish in performing the sex act with her customers in front of her young son.

At age seven, Henry suffered a severe eye injury which resulted in the loss of his left eye. It was replaced with a glass eye which, to this day, gives him a somewhat sinister appearance.

In 1960, Henry stabbed his mother to death. He was found guilty of murder in the second degree and was sentenced to 20 to 40 years imprisonment. On August 22, 1975, after spending 15 years behind bars, he was released. Henry tried married life, but that didn't work out. He took off and it was during this transient period that Henry met Otis Toole.

Otis was a big mean transvestite who took a liking to Henry and brought him home to live with his mother. It was here that Henry met Otis' niece Becky, 12, and his nephew Frank, 9. The unlikely foursome drove throughout the States in Henry's dilapidated Olds. Sometimes, they scavenged for empty pop bottles along the highway. Desperate for gas money, Henry often sold his blood.

The foursome broke up. Becky and Henry ended up at a sort of mission for the destitute near Wichita Falls, Texas. After spending some time there, Becky disappeared. An elderly widow, Kate Rich, who lived nearby, also disappeared. Henry was a suspect in the Rich disappearance and was picked up by the local sheriff.

It was while incarcerated that Henry got his bright idea. He decided to "confess" to hundreds of murders throughout the States and Canada. He now says he started confessing because he was being tortured in jail.

First he confessed to killing Becky Powell and Kate Rich, but he didn't stop there. He began confessing to other murders, abetted by investigating officers who often talked about the crime en route to murder scenes, revealing many details about the victim's clothing, personal characteristics and date of the murder. Most times, Henry seemed confused about the exact location, but a few times the officers actually pointed out the crime scene. On these occasions, the media reported that Henry had related details about the crime which only the murderer could know.

Sometimes Henry would travel by helicopter to the crime scene. At the height of his confession period, it was tough to get an interview with Henry. When I phoned the Georgetown Jail around that time, Sheriff Jim Boutwell told me, "Henry is away visiting a crime site today."

One can't help but believe that in Henry's world eating restaurant food and travelling in air conditioned vehicles was far better than sitting in the Georgetown Jail.

Could the sham sustain itself?

Two things assisted Lucas in his role as the self-confessed

177

super serial killer of all time. One of his confessions was given directly to Sheriff Boutwell, who became convinced that Henry was the killer of an unidentified young girl found in Williamson County, Texas. As a result of his convictions, Boutwell applied for and received funding from the Dept. of Public Safety to establish a Henry Lee Lucas Homicide Task Force. From that time, Henry was flying high.

The air-conditioned vehicles couldn't wait to take their star killer on his macabre missions. Law enforcement officers flocked to the Georgetown Jail.

To cap his unbelievable confessions, Henry implicated his old buddy, Otis Toole, comfortably ensconced on Death Row in the Stark, Florida penitentiary. When told of Henry's confessions and that he was being implicated in them all, Otis figured he had nothing to lose. He confirmed every single murder. Otis went a bit further. He volunteered that the reason Becky Powell was never found was simple enough. He had eaten her.

It couldn't go on forever. Responsible journalists delved into details of Henry's confessions. They found that Henry had claimed that he and Otis had murdered people in 1978. There is strong evidence the two men hadn't met until 1979.

Then there was the Adam Walsh case.

Adam, the six-year-old son of John Walsh, was kidnapped from a Florida shopping centre and murdered in 1981. While a desperate search was underway for Adam, Otis Toole confessed to his murder. Otis said that the body would never be found because he had eaten the child.

Adam's body was eventually found, which didn't add to the credibility of Lucas' corroborating witness. John Walsh went on to spearhead changes in the laws of several states, so that missing children could be more easily traced. He is presently host of the highly-rated TV program, America's Most Wanted.

In hindsight, it is rather improbable that Henry and Otis, travelling with two youngsters, roamed the country robbing, raping, mutilating and killing as many as three victims every week.

Finally, even Henry grew tired of the deception, supposedly because the gruesome pictures he constantly had to view made him sick. He turned full circle, claiming that he hadn't murdered anyone, except, of course, his mother. Once again, Otis agreed. It had all been a hoax.

In 1986, Texas Attorney General Jim Mattox issued a comprehensive report on the Lucas affair. In essence, the report states that Henry's confessions concerning Becky Powell and Kate Rich appear authentic. All the rest are extremely doubtful. The report castigates the Texas Rangers for perpetuating the deception by insisting that Henry had killed hundreds of people.

Presently, Henry Lee Lucas is confined to Huntsville prison's Death Row.

Many feel that he has put himself in jeopardy of meeting his end by lethal injection for a murder he didn't commit.

Otis Toole has had his death sentence commuted to life imprisonment.

Did he kill three or three hundred? Despite the irrefutable evidence that Henry and his pal hoodwinked law enforcement officers from all over the States, there are those who still believe he is the most prolific mass murderer the world has ever seen.

As for Henry, he claims he is finally telling the truth. He never killed anyone, except his mother.

Henry had a close call in 1990. Tried and convicted of one of his many confessed murders, he was scheduled to be put to death on December 3. Two days before the sentence was to be carried out, a state appeals court indefinitely delayed the execution of Henry Lee Lucas.

THE MAD BUTCHER OF KINGSBURY RUN

Many believe that serial killers are a recent phenomenon. Nothing could be further from the truth. Serial killers, the most heinous of all criminals, have always been out there, preying on the unwary.

On September 5, 1934, a man walking on Euclid Beach, about eight miles from downtown Cleveland, stumbled across a young woman's nude body partially buried in the sand. The girl had been decapitated. Her description was checked against reported missing persons, but she has never been identified.

At the time, police had no idea that they were dealing with the first in a series of murders, which would later be called the Kingsbury Run murders, named after the rather ugly ancient creek bed running through the heart of Cleveland.

A year later, on September 23, 1935, the bodies of two men were found at the foot of East 49th St. and Kingsbury Run. Both bodies were nude, headless, and had had their penises removed. The heads were recovered separately, buried some distance from the bodies. Several clues were found at the murder site — a blue jacket, a shirt, cap, flashlight and some rope. All were sent to a police laboratory for analysis.

Attempts to trace these items failed. To some it appeared that the clues had been left by the killer as red herrings to frustrate investigators. A fingerprint check identified one of the bodies as Edward Andrassy. The other was never identified.

Edward's past was thoroughly investigated in the hope that something would be uncovered which would lead police to the murderer. Edward had been a transvestite who frequented local bars. He sometimes posed as a doctor and had been arrested for examining female patients. Four days before his decapitated body was found, he had left his rooming house at 8 p.m. and had not been seen alive after that time.

Two things puzzled police. A type of preservative had been used on the remains of the headless body found on Euclid Beach. The same preservative had been applied to the unidentified man found more recently. Another connecting link was the skill with which all heads had been removed. Was it possible that a madman was loose, systematically killing and decapitating both male and female victims?

Four months after the two bodies were found, a woman reported that a basket of meat had been left in the alley behind 2315 East 20th St. The basket proved to contain the right arm, lower torso and thighs of a woman. Thirteen days later the legs and left arm of the woman were found behind a derelict building on Orange Ave. The head of this victim was never found, but a fingerprint check identified her as Mrs. Florence Polillo, a 42-year-old alcoholic prostitute.

Florence had walked out on her husband 13 years earlier. Andrew Polillo travelled from Buffalo to identify the various parts of his long lost wife's body. Weeks were spent delving into Florence's past, but all efforts failed to uncover her killer.

The Mad Butcher of Kingsbury Run, as he was now called, struck three more times in the same year. On June 5, 1936, two young boys found a human male head wrapped in a pair of men's pants. Next day, a railroad worker found the matching torso. Once again, a degree of skill had been utilized to separate head from body. Police were still attempting to identify this latest victim when, two months later, another decapitated body was found. This time, the head was only 15 feet from the body and the crime scene indicated that the murder had taken place where the body had been found. Why had the Mad Butcher changed his pattern of delivering bodies to selected locations?

On September 10, beside a hobo jungle on Kingsbury Run, a man's torso was found bobbing in a stagnant pool. The body had been emasculated with the same surgical skill as previous victims. The head was never found.

One can only imagine the effect this series of strange murders had on the general population of Cleveland. The Mad Butcher of Kingsbury Run was the main topic of conversation in the community. Visitors shunned the city. Vagrants and hobos travelled in groups. The city of Cleveland was held in the grip of fear.

The Mad Butcher took a holiday from his macabre profession until February 23, 1937, when a female body turned up on the beach close to where victim number one had been found. As the arms and head were never recovered, identification proved to be impossible.

A coroner's report issued after this latest murder pointed out the similar conditions of the various victims' bodies: "It is the peculiar dissection of the bodies which groups these cases together. All show that the heads were severed from the bodies through the intervertebral disc by means of a sharp knife. Cases four, seven and eight, showed further that the bodies were cleanly dismembered at the shoulder and hip joints, apparently by a series of cuts around the flexure of the joints and then by a strong twist, wrenching the head out of the joint cavity and cutting the capsule.

"The torsos were further sectioned through the abdomen, the knife being carried in cases four and seven through the intervertebral discs. Case number four was further mutilated by disarticulating the knee joints roughly, fracturing the mid portion of the bones of the lower legs and slashing the abdomen down through the pubic bones. All the skin edges, muscles, blood vessels and cartilages were cut cleanly.

"The procedure followed by these cases suggests to us that the dissection was done either by a highly intelligent lay person or, as is more likely, by a person with some knowledge of anatomy, such as a doctor, a medical student, nurse, orderly, butcher, hunter or veterinary surgeon."

The bodies kept turning up bearing the Mad Butcher's unique signature. On July 6, 1937, portions of a man's body were pulled out of the Cuyahoga River. During the remainder of 1937-1938, four more bodies were found near Kingsbury Run. On August 16, 1938, the last murder took place and the nightmare that had haunted Cleveland came to an abrupt end.

From time to time, suspects were arrested, but all were released when they proved to be innocent. Special police units were formed to track down the butcher, but these too failed. Many deranged men confessed to the serial killings. These confessions proved to be false.

In January 1939, Cleveland's Chief of Police George Matowitz received the following letter, which is believed to be authentic. It was postmarked Los Angeles, California: "You can rest easy now as I have come out to sunny California for the winter. I felt bad operating on those people, but science must advance. I shall astound the medical profession, a man with only a D.C.

"What did their lives mean in comparison to hundreds of sick and disease-twisted bodies. Just laboratory guinea pigs found on any public street. No one missed them when I failed. My last case was successful. I know now the feeling of Pasteur, Thoreau, and other pioneers.

"Right now I have a volunteer who will absolutely prove my theory. They call me mad and a butcher, but the truth will out.

"I have failed but once here. The body has not been found and never will be, but the head minus the features, is buried on Century Blvd., between Western and Crenshaw. I feel it my duty to dispose of the bodies as I do. It is God's will not to let them suffer. (Signed) X."

The Mad Butcher of Kingsbury Run was never heard of

again. The series of killings which took place in Cleveland has never been solved.

CHARLES MANSON

Over 25 years have passed since that night when the rage within Charlie Manson's soul was unleashed inside the home of director Roman Polanski and his pregnant wife, movie actress Sharon Tate.

When small time thief and pseudo folk singer Charlie Manson was paroled from Terminal Island in San Pedro, California in 1967, no one was aware that the 5-foot-2 misfit with the magnetic personality would commit crimes so horrible they are remembered over 25 years later.

There was Charlie, 32, free at last, after serving almost seven years in prison. It was the era of love and peace, peace and love; homeless girls wandered the country in search of a meaning to life. LSD helped. It was an era custom-made for Charlie Manson, with his guitar and charismatic personality.

Gravitating to San Francisco, Charlie's inner circle of sub-culture followers grew in number. Mary Brunner, Lynette (Squeaky) Fromme and Patricia Krenwinkel became known as 'Charlie's girls.' They slept, travelled, stole and begged together. They purchased an old bus and scoured the countryside. They were like family.

New recruits joined the Manson family. Susan Atkins, a 19-year-old hellion, came aboard. Robert Beausoleil, a 20-year-old actor, who sometimes lived with Gary Hinman, became a Manson follower. Diane Lake, 14, who was later renamed Snake because of her distinctive movements during intercourse, joined the family in their nomadic existence. Tex

Watson was an avid Manson disciple. Later, Tex would prove to be a valuable and loyal member of the family.

Growth in the family was not derived solely from outsiders. Some of the girls became pregnant. Susan Atkins had a child. Mary Brunner gave birth to Charlie's baby.

In 1968, Charlie and his followers made their headquarters at the Spahn movie ranch, a dilapidated group of buildings near Los Angeles. The sect had evolved from love and peace to Satanism, hate and revenge. Charlie would send out groups of his followers to change the world, make it a better place in which to live.

In July 1969, Gary Hinman had a falling out with Charlie. Although Gary had always allowed members of Charlie's family to crash at his house, he was never a committed member of the sect. When Gary, who reputedly had money hidden in his house, steadfastly refused to devote himself to Charlie and his children, he signed his own death warrant.

Robert Beausoleil and a couple of the girls paid Hinman a visit. Gary wouldn't give them the time of day. Charlie showed up and, in a fit of rage, stabbed Hinman in the head with a sword, almost severing his ear. Then he left. Beausoleil and the girls bound Hinman with rope. When they phoned Charlie for instructions, they were told to kill their captive.

Hinman was stabbed twice in the chest and died on his living room floor from loss of blood. Charlie's girls wrote "Political Piggy" on the wall in Hinman's blood, after which they returned to the Spahn ranch and sang songs. Within two weeks, police had matched a fingerprint in Hinman's home to Robert Beausoleil. He was picked up and charged with murder.

On the night of August 8 and early morning of August 9, 1969, Charlie's followers went on a mission. They were well-equipped. Inside their vehicle they had placed a pair of bolt cutters and a quantity of nylon rope. Linda Kasabian, Susan Atkins and Patricia Krenwinkel jumped in. Tex Watson drove. Charlie instructed: "Leave a sign. You girls know what to do. Something witchy." On the way, Tex told the girls they were going to kill everyone in a house once owned by Doris Day's son, Terry Melcher.

Tex drove up to 10050 Cielo Drive, then leased by director Roman Polanski. Polanski was on a roll. His movies in the '60s included Repulsion and The Fearless Vampire Killers, as well as the runaway hit, Rosemary's Baby. On this night, he was in Europe.

His wife, actress Sharon Tate, 8-1/2 months pregnant, was at home entertaining friends: coffee heiress Abigail Folger, hairstylist Jay Sebring and Voityck Frykowski.

It was Steve Parent's misfortune to have picked that particular night to visit the Polanskis' caretaker, Bill Garretson, in a separate dwelling on the estate. Steve was in his car, just about to pull away, when he spotted Tex Watson.

According to later testimony, Steve said, "Hey, what are you doing here?" Tex thrust his .22-calibre revolver into the open driver's window. As Steve said, "Please don't hurt me," Tex pulled the trigger five times. He probably thought he had killed the caretaker. Inside his house, Bill Garretson heard nothing. He would not hear a sound the rest of the night.

Once inside Polanski's house, Tex accosted Frykowski. He shouted, "I'm the devil! I'm here to do the devil's business!" The girls were instructed to secure Frykowski with nylon rope. Abigail Folger was found reading in bed in her room. Sharon Tate was lying in bed in another room. Jay Sebring, fully clothed, sat on the bed talking to Sharon. All the occupants of the house were gathered together in the living room.

It was killing time. Jay Sebring was shot by Tex for suggesting that the gang should allow Sharon to sit down. After all, she was pregnant. While Sebring lay on the floor, unconscious, Tex kicked him in the head.

Abigail and Sharon were tied around the neck with nylon cord. One end of the cord was tossed over a beam. Susan Atkins pulled the rope taut. Abigail and Sharon had to stand straight up or strangle. Tex announced that they were all about to die. He ordered Susan to kill. She complied, stabbing Voityck Frykowski repeatedly. When Frykowski continued to struggle, Tex clubbed the wounded man with his gun and shot him. Frykowski made it outside before being killed on the lawn. Later, 51 separate stab wounds were found on his body.

Sharon and Abigail frantically struggled to free themselves. Abigail was successful. She ran to the back door. Patricia Krenwinkel stabbed at her wildly, but Abigail warded off the blows, her hands and arms now horribly cut. Tex spotted the melee. He ran over and cut Abigail's throat and abdomen.

Outside the house, Linda Kasabian stood watch. She observed Steve Parent's body in his vehicle. She saw Frykowski stagger out, screaming for help. It certainly was an action-filled night. Linda wondered how much money would be taken from such a nice home. Inside, the killing continued. Sharon Tate, unattended for a few moments, freed herself. She started toward her front door, but was seen by Patricia Krenwinkel. Patricia solicitously assisted Sharon to a chair. Then Susan Atkins held her, while Tex Watson stabbed her to death. The three members of Charlie's family took turns stabbing the body.

It was quiet. Tex decorated the bodies with nylon rope. Susan wrote the word "PIG" in blood on the door. Only 30 minutes had elapsed. It was so very quiet. Everyone was dead. Sharon's black kitten meowed forlornly amidst the silent bodies.

Charlie would be delighted. As they drove, the family members changed out of their bloody clothing. Blood soaked garments and knives were tossed out of the car. Tex's revolver was thrown into a ravine.

Back at the Spahn ranch, the children of evil reported to Satan. He was pleased. They were tired. Everyone slept well.

Next morning, the scene of death was discovered. Horror swept Los Angeles. America — and ultimately the entire world — was made aware of the ritual-type massacre that had taken place in exclusive Benedict Canyon.

Charlie and his children were ecstatic at the publicity his crime was receiving. It had been a commendable job, but messy. That very night they would do it all again, but Satan himself would lead the way.

Linda Kasabian drove the '59 Ford to the home of grocery chain store owner Leno LaBianca, 44, at 3301 Waverly Dr. His wife, Rosemary, 38, was in bed when Charlie Manson appeared in the living room waving a sword at her husband. Charlie tied the LaBiancas standing up back to back.

Charlie walked out of the house. His family, waiting in the car, was ready for action. It was killing time again.

Tex Watson, Leslie Van Houten and Patricia Krenwinkel were given their instructions. After the job was completed, they were to hitchhike back to the ranch. Linda Kasabian and Charlie sped off.

The killing squad did their work efficiently. They led Rosemary into the bedroom, where they stabbed her to death. Leno was killed in the living room. Neither victim panicked until the very end. Tex carved the word WAR on Leno LaBianca's chest. Using the dead man's blood, they wrote DEATH TO PIGS on the walls. On the refrigerator door, Patricia wrote HEALTER SKEALTER. The killing squad then bathed and raided the fridge. Killing was hard work, but it was worth it. The LaBiancas' house was quiet. The family left.

Rosemary's children by a previous marriage called on the house of death and the second night of horror was made known to the world. The ritualistic aspects of the two killing sprees linked them forever. They became known as the Tate-LaBianca murders.

As the days turned into weeks without the killers being apprehended, famous movie actors such as Warren Beatty, Peter Sellers and Yul Brynner established a reward of $25,000 for the apprehension and conviction of the killers.

Weeks turned into months. The family kept busy. They stole gasoline and robbed indiscriminately. One man, Shorty Shea, 40, somehow found out details of the Tate-LaBianca killings. Charlie's clan, led by Steve Grogan, tortured, killed and buried Shorty in the desert.

By the end of September, members of the Manson family

were being rounded up for minor crimes. Many were in and out of jail on various charges. Fingerprints recovered at murder scenes were checked against suspects. Snitches were placed in cells. A myriad of evidence pointed to the family as perpetrators of the Tate-LaBianca murders. Finally, the family's leader was taken into custody.

The world was shocked. These suspects were young girls from middle class American families. They likened their leader to Jesus Christ and displayed no remorse for what they had done. Tex Watson was a high school track star from Texas. Leslie Van Houten had been a small town high school princess. Yet these same young people had stabbed a pregnant woman and stuck a fork in the stomach of a man they had just killed.

Somewhere in the deep recesses of his mind, Charlie Manson believed that the blacks of the world would rise against the whites. He would be the catalyst, the trigger that would change the world. Instead, his madness was directly responsible for nine known deaths.

The Manson Family received various prison sentences for their part in the summer of horror. Their leader was sentenced to death on eight counts of first degree murder, but his sentence was commuted to life imprisonment during the short time when the state of California abolished capital punishment.

Now, 25 years later, Charlie, Squeaky Fromme, Robert Beausoleil, Susan Atkins and Patricia Krenwinkel are still in prison. Leslie Van Houten has obtained a university degree in psychology and literature and is still serving her time. Tex Watson remains in prison, where he has sired three children via conjugal visits.

Linda Kasabian, who testified for the state in return for immunity from prosecution, is now living in New Hampshire. Diane Lake, who also testified for the state, is believed to be working for a large corporation in California.

LUIS MONGE

Almost everyone is familiar with the saga of Gary Mark
Gilmore and his execution before a Utah firing squad on
January 17, 1977. With Gilmore's death capital punishment
returned to the United States after an absence of nine years,
seven months, and 14 days.

Gilmore's execution grasped the notorious mantle of "last
man to be executed in the United States" from a far less
known murderer. Unlike Gilmore, Luis Jose Monge was not
an habitual criminal. In fact, for all but a very short period of
his life, Monge was a good husband and an ideal father. Yet
his crime was a horrible and disgusting one.

After the death of his parents when he was 11, Luis was
sent from his native Puerto Rico to Brooklyn, N.Y., where he
was raised by assorted relatives. He left school after complet-
ing Grade 10 and took a series of jobs until he was 22, when
he joined the Army Air Corps. While stationed at Lowrey Air
Force Base near Denver, Colorado, Luis met Dolores Mitla.
The young couple married in 1944.

Luis received his discharge and became a successful
insurance salesman. He always wanted a large closely knit
family. Dolores agreed. By 1961 Luis and Dolores were the
proud parents of seven boys and two girls.

Luis Monge was a happy, rather handsome middle-aged
man who loved his wife and children. His home, while not
lavishly furnished, was more than adequate. No one could
honestly say that the large family went without any of the
necessities of life.

Luis was somewhat of an athlete and loved to coach his children at various sports. The large family almost made up a team. Luis enjoyed playing baseball and football with his boys and table tennis and volleyball with the girls. When he wasn't actively participating in sports with his family, Luis sang in his church choir. He attended mass regularly.

Despite his outward appearance of tranquility and contentment, Luis was a troubled man. Unknown to the members of his family he had developed a deep rooted sexual attraction for one of his own daughters. Seven-year-old Janet loved her father. She loved to be kissed and hugged, but sometimes her father invented special games just for her. The child became afraid and told her mother.

Dolores was appalled upon hearing of Janet's suspicions. She couldn't believe her ears. She faced her husband with the dreadful accusation. Luis quickly told his wife of his problem. Crying in shame he swore that he would be able to control himself and would never again touch his child in an improper manner. Dolores believed Luis, but warned him that if such an incident ever occurred again she would leave him.

Years passed and Luis was able to control his unhealthy sexual urges. In April 1961, Luis Monge dropped out of sight. Dolores reported him missing. As suddenly as he disappeared he reappeared two months later. He had been in New Orleans and told his family that he had suffered from amnesia. They accepted his explanation, and soon life was as it always had been. Luis was once more the loving husband and father. Once again the family played sports together and partook of formal Sunday dinners.

But Luis had lied to his family. His unnatural feelings towards his daughter had resurfaced. Rather than succumb to these feelings he had run away. Now, two months later, he had overcome his strange infatuation toward his daughter. It was safe to return home.

By 1963 Luis' family had increased. He now had 10 children, with an eleventh due that August. The oldest was 18.

On Friday, June 28, 1963, the Monge family were sleeping

peacefully in their beds. All except Luis. The urge to touch his daughter Janet overtook the tormented man. Janet, now 13, was no longer the child her father fondled years before. She lay sleeping in an upstairs bedroom with her 16-year-old sister, Anna. As if in a trance, Luis climbed the stairs and entered the girls' bedroom. He sat on the edge of the bed. Slowly his hands reached under the bedclothes. Luis Monge, loving husband, and devoted father to 10 children, was in a state of sexual excitement.

Suddenly Anna sat bolt upright in bed. She shouted, "What are you doing?" Luis tried to placate Anna, but she wouldn't listen. He fled from the room.

Luis Monge paced the floor of his living room. In a single moment he had lost the love of his family. His wife would have nothing more to do with him. He had run away once, but that was no answer this time. It was too late. His family would hate him. Outsiders would learn of his shame.

Luis Monge, loving husband and devoted father, decided to kill his entire family and himself as well.

He picked up a large poker and slowly entered his wife's bedroom. Dolores didn't move as several blows rained down on her head. Then, acting in a deliberate manner, Luis picked up his stiletto and stabbed his 11-month-old baby to death. He neatly placed the body of the baby beside his wife.

Thomas, 4, was the next to die. He too was placed in bed with his mother and baby sister. Freddie, 6, his father's favorite, was clubbed to death with the poker and placed with the other bodies.

Luis had intended to kill all his family and then kill himself with carbon monoxide in his garage. Later, he couldn't explain what made him stop. Possibly the whimpering of his favorite child, Freddie, brought him to his senses. Whatever the reason, Luis picked up the telephone and called the police: "I just killed my wife and three of my kids. You'd better come over before I kill somebody else."

Within minutes police arrived and were greeted by the macabre sight of the four bodies neatly arranged in bed. Taken to a police station, Luis revealed many of the facts that are related here. Psychiatric examination indicated that he was legally sane. Throughout his questioning by police and psychiatrists, Luis insisted that he wanted to die for his crimes as fast as possible, and not bring further shame and disgrace to his family.

All seven of Luis Monge's surviving children, accompanied by an uncle and aunt, visited their father before he stood trial. Each one in turn embraced their father and told him that they forgave him for what he had done. They reasoned that their father was suffering from a mental illness. Later, the family was allowed to have Sunday dinner with Luis. It was like old times. Luis held court as his loving family showed their respect for the head of the house.

Eventually Monge was found guilty and sentenced to death. On March 20, 1964, he was transferred to Death Row in Colorado State Prison, where he lingered for three months. On June 2, Luis Monge was escorted to the gas chamber by Warden Wayne Patterson. Meanwhile, in Denver, Gov. Love remained near his telephone. He had promised to grant a last-minute reprieve if Monge requested it. As Luis entered the gas chamber, he glanced at the telephone, but he didn't hesitate.

At precisely 8:04 p.m. sodium cyanide pellets were dropped into receptacles containing acid. Luis Monge breathed deeply and slumped into unconsciousness.

It would be nine years before Gary Gilmore would defiantly utter his last words, "Let's do it." Luis Monge was no longer the last man to be executed in the United States.

WAYNE NANCE

Missoula, Montana is in the heart of Big Sky Country, where the Marlborough man mounts his trusty steed and gallops off into the fading sunset. It was also the home of Wayne Nance, serial killer extraordinaire.

Wayne was born in 1955 to Charlene and George Nance. Charlene worked as a waitress, while George was employed as a trucker. The family lived in a trailer park just outside town.

As a small boy, Wayne was often in minor scrapes, but excelled in school. Sometimes he displayed a hair trigger temper and occasionally fought with his school chums. Still, no one gave a second thought to his often unwarranted outbreaks. Other little boys have temper tantrums. They don't turn out to be serial killers.

Wayne sailed through grade school. In high school he displayed a deep interest in Satanism, which was a popular topic with many teenagers in the '70s. Other than belaboring the subject with schoolmates, Wayne didn't make waves.

Donna and Harvey Pounds were poor, hardworking and religious. Donna worked part-time at the Christian Book Store in Missoula. Harvey was employed in the shoe department at Yandt's Men's Store, but his real interest was religion. He was a deacon of the Bethel Baptist Church and had just been appointed pastor of a church in nearby Stevensville. The Pounds had three children; a son, Kenny, in the army, and two daughters, Karen, 20, and Kathy, 12, living at home with their parents. All were excited at their father's appointment.

The anticipation of a new beginning was to change forever on April 11, 1974. Karen and Harvey were at work. Kathy was in school. Donna was home alone.

The intruder was wearing rubber gloves. He had found Harvey's .22 calibre Luger and encountered Donna in the master bedroom. The man had come prepared. From his black gym bag he extracted lengths of clothesline, which he used to tie Donna's arms and legs to the posts of her bed. After raping the defenceless woman, he untied her and led her down to the family's unfinished basement. Donna was forced to crawl under the stairwell. Her attacker retied her arms and legs. Then he coolly shot her five times in the back of the head.

Harvey came home from work, discovered his wife's body and called police. A bloodstained surgical glove found behind the Pounds' home, along with the cords dangling from the bedposts, were removed for laboratory analysis.

Wayne Nance was a neighbor of the Pounds. He knew where Harvey kept his .22 Luger. When a witness claimed to have seen someone who looked like Wayne near the Pounds' home on the day of the killing, Wayne was questioned. He denied any connection with the crime, stating that he hadn't been feeling well that day and had stayed home from school. He was alone all day.

Detectives searched his home and discovered a black gym bag and a bloodstained pair of underwear, which had recently been washed. The bloodstain, although identified as human, could not be classified. No matching clothesline cord was found in the house.

Wayne was a serious suspect, but nothing of a concrete nature was found to connect him with the murder. When detectives learned that Harvey may have been involved with another woman, he too fell under suspicion, but again authorities met a blank wall. There was no direct evidence connecting either man with the crime. Both took polygraph tests. Harvey's results were inconclusive. Wayne's indicated that he was telling the truth and had no guilty knowledge of the crime.

Two months after Donna Pounds' murder, Wayne graduated from high school. A few days later, he joined the navy. When he was charged with possession of marijuana for the second time, he was given a general discharge. After having served two years, Wayne moved back into the trailer in Missoula with his parents. For a while, he kicked around town, but soon took a night job as a bouncer at a western bar known as The Cabin. By day, he worked at Conlin's Furniture Store as delivery and set-up man for their products.

It should be pointed out that Wayne was well liked. Sure, some folks called him weird, with his odd collection of knives and all, but generally speaking, as the years sped by, no one took much notice of Wayne Nance.

Many employees of The Cabin were pleased when Wayne started to date a girl named Robin, who just happened to be passing through town. In time, Robin moved in with Wayne and his father. Unfortunately, Wayne's mother had been killed in a car accident while under the influence of alcohol. According to Wayne, on September 28, 1984, Robin left town after being his woman for the best part of the summer.

Almost three months later, on the afternoon of Christmas Eve, a wildlife photographer tramping through the woods outside Missoula spotted a human foot sticking out of the earth. An autopsy indicated that the unidentified female had been dead for approximately three months. No one had been reported missing from Missoula during that time span. Much later, this body was identified as Robin.

On December 12, 1985, Mike and Teresa Shook and their three children — Matt, 7, Luke, 4, and Megan, 2 — had finished their evening meal when someone knocked at the front door and entered their house, barking out commands. By the time the intruder left, Mike Shook lay stabbed to death on the floor. Teresa was raped and stabbed in the chest. She, too, was dead. The killer then set the house on fire. Miraculously, the fire didn't spread and the three children were found by a friend the next morning, unconscious and in critical condition from smoke inhalation. All three would survive.

Down at Conlin's Furniture, Wayne was considered the best delivery man in their employ. He was obliging to all the salesladies and in particular, the store manager, Kris Wells. Wayne had a crush on Kris and she knew it. She went out of her way not to encourage his flattery. She even discussed Wayne's infatuation with her husband Doug. They agreed that it was harmless. They were wrong.

On a brisk fall night in September 1986, Kris and Doug returned to their home around midnight. After Kris retired for the night, Doug thought he spotted someone outside. He went out and discovered Wayne Nance. Incredulous, Doug asked him what he was doing there. Wayne explained that he had been driving by the house and thought he had spotted a prowler. He suggested Doug get a flashlight and take a look. As Doug turned to enter his home, he was struck a severe blow on the back of his head. Bleeding profusely, Doug fell to the floor and saw Wayne, wild-eyed, lunging in his direction. Doug was able to rise and struggle with his attacker. From the bedroom, Kris heard the commotion. She rushed to Doug's side in time to see Wayne pull a revolver out of his pocket. He shouted, "Get back. I've got a gun!"

Kris backed off. Doug sank to the floor. Although weak, he didn't lose consciousness. Kris begged Wayne to tell them why he was doing this. He said that he wanted money to get out of town. Wayne forced Kris to tie her husband's hands and feet. He then tied her hands behind her back and carried her down the hall to the bedroom. Once there, he tied her hands to the bedframe and returned to Doug.

Wayne untied Doug's legs and forced him down into the basement. He struck Doug on the back of the head and tied him by the neck to a post. He then left to check up on Kris. He soon returned. Doug, barely conscious, was horrified when Wayne straddled his legs and slowly stuck an eight-inch knife into his chest just below the heart. Doug Wells thought he was about to die but, despite the beating, loss of blood and the stab wound, he did not lose consciousness. He watched as Wayne removed the knife from his chest.

When Wayne went upstairs once again to check on Kris,

Doug managed to free himself and locate his own Savage 250 rifle. He staggered upstairs and made a noise, knowing it would attract Wayne. As his adversary appeared in the hallway, Doug fired. The slug ripped through Wayne's side, but the fallen man was able to crawl on his hands and knees. Doug swung his rifle, striking Wayne on the head and back over and over again until he finally shattered the rifle's wooden stock. Wayne was able to get out his own revolver. Doug swung his rifle at the revolver just as Wayne fired, deflecting the shot directly into Wayne's head. Wayne fired again. This time, the bullet struck Doug in the leg just above the knee. Despite this added wound, Doug rained blow after blow on Wayne's head until Wayne was nothing more than a bloody hulk cowering in a corner. Doug disarmed Wayne and told the now-freed Kris to call 911. He lay down on the bed, convinced he was about to die.

Both men were rushed to hospital. Wayne died soon after he arrived. Courageous Doug Wells miraculously survived.

I have related here the four murders officially attributed to Wayne Nance. Several other unsolved murders, which took place around Missoula during the many years Wayne lived in the area, are believed to have been perpetrated by him.

Because Kris and Doug Wells experienced the horror of being attacked by a serial killer, they often attend sessions at Quantico, Virginia, where the FBI maintains a Behaviorial Science Unit studying serial killers.

CHARLES NG

Mark Twain immortalized Calaveras County with his humorous tale of a frog who refused to jump because its stomach was full of buckshot. The Celebrated Jumping Frog of Calaveras County has delighted readers for over 100 years. The famed author had no way of knowing that the isolated area 250 kms. northeast of San Francisco would make headlines around the world in 1985 as the scene of a series of the most horrendous crimes ever committed in the United States.

No one paid much attention to the odd couple who lived together on a ranch outside the tiny town of Wilseyville. One was a big man with a bushy beard, who liked to strut around in army fatigues. He explained away the cinder block bunker on the three-acre ranch as being a survival capsule in case of nuclear attack. Leonard Lake didn't even cause any raised eyebrows in Calaveras County. Neither did his slight, 25-year-old Chinese friend, Charles Ng, who hardly spoke to anyone.

Lake, a former U.S. Marine, had served a stretch in Vietnam, but didn't see any action. In the summer of 1982, he met Ng, whose background was far different. Ng was born and educated in Hong Kong and later attended a private school in England. After graduation in 1977, he returned to Hong Kong, where he worked for a short while as a teacher. A year later, he travelled to San Francisco and attended Notre Dame College. In 1979, he left Notre Dame to join the U.S. Marines.

Ng orchestrated a robbery of firearms from a Marine armory and was sentenced to 14 years imprisonment. This sentence was later reduced to three years. In 1982, he was released from prison and teamed up with Leonard Lake. It was to be an unholy alliance.

On Sunday, June 2, 1985, in San Francisco, a slight Chinese man walked out of a lumberyard hardware store without paying for a $75 vice. A clerk alerted Officer Daniel Wright, who happened to be close by. Wright immediately spotted the man putting the vice in the trunk of his Honda Prelude. At the same time, the young man spotted the police officer and took off on foot with Wright in pursuit. Wright was unable to catch his man. When he returned to the car, he was met by a bearded man, who identified himself as Robin Stapley.

It's all a mistake, Stapley said. He thought I had paid for it. Wright peered in the trunk of the car. Spotting a tote bag, he inquired as to its contents. Stapley said, "I don't know. It must belong to that young fellow who was with me."

Wright opened the bag and found a .22 calibre automatic pistol equipped with a silencer. He informed Stapley that silencers were illegal and that he would have to accompany him to the police station. Stapley readily consented. At the station he claimed to have no connection with the silencer. He said he didn't know his companion, Charles Ng, that well, but had planned to hire him to do some work around his ranch.

Abruptly, Stapley asked for a glass of water. He gulped down a pill with the water. Within a few seconds, he collapsed. Police officers were sure their suspect had suffered a heart attack. Rushed to hospital, Stapley was found to be brain dead and was placed on a life support machine. A few days later, he was removed from the machine and died.

A police check revealed that one Robin Stapley had been reported missing five months earlier. Since then, his pickup and camper had been in a slight accident, having collided with a tractor. The accident had been reported. A Chinese man was driving the missing Stapley pickup truck.

Police now did a computer check on the Honda Prelude. It belonged to Paul Cosner, a San Francisco used car dealer, who had been reported missing seven months earlier when he went out with the Honda to deliver it to a customer. Meanwhile, a fingerprint check on the man on the life support system in the hospital proved that he was not Robin Stapley, but Leonard Lake.

A check with the National Crime Information Computer revealed that Leonard Lake had jumped bail. He had been charged with burglary, possession of explosives and illegal automatic weapons, and had been hiding out in his isolated Calaveras County ranch since 1982. Apparently Ng had been his companion since that time.

Police realized that they were not dealing with a simple case of shoplifting, but quite possibly a series of killings. Lake and Ng were now directly connected to two missing persons: Robin Stapley and Paul Cosner. There would be more.

Equipped with search warrants, police drove to the Lake ranch. They observed what appeared to be an average clapboard house. Adjacent to the house was Lake's survival bunker. Inside the house, officers found handcuffs and chains. In the bedroom, they observed eye bolts screwed into the ceiling.

Officer Irene Brunn spotted a new VCR in a corner. She had recently investigated the disappearance of a family in San Francisco. Deborah and Harvey Dubs and their 16-month-old son had simply vanished. Neighbors had noticed a young Chinese man removing furniture from the Dubs' apartment. Among the missing items was a VCR. Officer Brunn had been able to locate the store which had sold the VCR and to obtain the serial numbers. It was the machine found in Lake's home.

Meanwhile, outside the house on a hillside, police officers made gruesome discoveries. Tiny particles of bone and baby teeth were found on the ground. The door to the bunker was forced open. Water, canned goods and firearms were scattered about. A trap door led underground. Enlarged photos of several girls in various stages of undress lined the walls. A filing cabinet held video cassettes. It is from these cassettes that we know the diabolical nature of the alleged killers and the fate of their hapless victims.

One of the cassettes depicts Deborah Dubs bound on a chair. Another shows Kathleen Allen, 18, who had disappeared from a supermarket in 1985, being forced to disrobe and ordered to do anything Lake desired. On the same tape, Brenda O'Connor, who disappeared with her husband Lonny and their infant son, is handcuffed and bound in chains. She is begging for the welfare of her baby and is told by the two men that they have given the baby away. Then, one of the men, whom police say is Charles Ng, cuts off her bra when she refuses the order to undress.

While a total of 60 officers gathered evidence of the mass slaughter of men, women and children, an all-points bulletin was issued for Charles Ng. He had become one of the most wanted men in the world, sought by the FBI, Scotland Yard, Interpol and the RCMP.

More horrors were uncovered. Two 500-page diaries belonging to Lake were found on the property. In them, he described torture, rape and murder. He also philosophically commented that females were nothing more than sex slaves meant to succumb to his every desire.

During the search for fragments of bodies, investigators learned that Ng's one friend, Michael Sean Carroll, and his girlfriend, had been missing for a month, and Carroll's driver's licence was found in Lake's house.

The gruesome search continued. Several missing persons were positively identified as having met their deaths at the Lake ranch. In all, it is believed that at least 25 murders took place there.

Where was the only living person who had allegedly taken part in the slaughter? Where was Charles Ng?

In the weeks following the horrible discoveries near Wilseyville, Ng made his way to Detroit, crossing the border into Windsor. From there he travelled to Chatham, then to Sudbury, and on to Calgary, Alberta.

On a pleasant July day, a month after Ng ran from Officer Wright in San Francisco, security officers George Forrester and Sean Doyle spotted a man shoplifting in a Calgary Hudson's Bay store. When accosted, Ng pulled a .22 calibre pistol from his belt. Two shots were fired. Doyle was superficially wounded in the hand, but the men succeeded in disarming the shoplifter. Ng was quickly identified as he was carrying his authentic driver's licence on his person.

Ng was tried and convicted of assault, robbery and illegal use of a firearm, all charges pertaining to offences which took place in Calgary. He was sentenced to four-and-a-half years imprisonment.

Ironically, Ng, who faces several murder charges in the U.S., is protected from extradition by Canadian law, which stipulates that because there is no death penalty in Canada, the prisoner may not be extradited to a state where the death penalty exists, unless the requesting state provides assurances that the death penalty will not be implemented.

Since California has the death penalty, this left a suspected mass murderer in a Canadian prison, affording him the right to fight extradition upon release from prison and to avoid standing trial for murder.

Despite the legal ramifications, Ng was returned to California. However, his lawyers have managed, by using every ploy at their disposal, to keep their client out of court. As this is written, he is still in custody but has not been tried for murder.

DENNIS NILSEN

In 1942, pretty Betty Whyte of Fraserburgh, Scotland, married handsome Olav Nilsen. Their courtship had an aura of glamor. After all, it was wartime. Olav was stationed in Scotland with the Free Norwegian Forces. The couple, who would divorce in 1948, had three children: Olav, Dennis and Sylvia. No one knew then that quiet, well-behaved Dennis would become the most prolific mass murderer in the history of English crime.

Dennis joined the army in 1961, at the age of 16. He spent most of his army career in the Army Catering Corp., where he learned skills which were, in later years, to assist him in the most unusual way imaginable.

While in the service, Dennis discovered two things. He was sexually attracted to men. His comrades never learned of his secret desires, for Dennis was well aware of the ridicule heaped upon homosexuals by rough, tough army personnel. In fact, Dennis often led his colleagues in demeaning those men who appeared to be effeminate. Dennis also learned how to drink in the army. It was the one way he had of joining in, becoming one of the boys.

Eleven years later, Dennis was discharged from the army, having attained the rank of corporal. In 1972, he took a 16-week course at the Metropolitan Police Training School in North London and became a police officer. While serving with the police force, he was a practising homosexual. Unlike army life, Dennis found no camaraderie in the police force. At the end of their shifts his fellow officers went home to their families. A lonely, brooding man, Dennis left the force after one year.

For a while, Dennis was employed as a security guard, but found the work boring. Eventually, he obtained a position as clerical officer with the Department of Employment, where he would remain as a valued and conscientious employee for the next eight years.

In his spare time, Dennis picked up male companions at pubs, particularly the Wellington IV in Hampstead and the Salisbury in St. Martin's Lane. He took them to his room, but these encounters, though numerous, were of a passing nature. Dennis had no meaningful relationships, no real friends.

In 1975, Dennis received a bit of a windfall. His father whom he never knew, died in Noway, leaving him £1000. Around this time, Dennis met David Gallichan at a pub. He ended up taking the 20-year-old blond boy home with him. Next day, they decided to live together. Within days of paying one month's rent in advance, Dennis and David moved into a pleasant flat on the ground floor at 195 Melrose Ave. French windows opened onto a long garden at the rear of the flat.

The relationship provided a period of relative contentment for Dennis. He was a faithful lover, but the same could not be said of young Gallichan. It was Gallichan's promiscuity which precipitated the breakup. When both men began bringing home extracurricular lovers, the writing was on the wall. In 1977, the pair parted. Dennis Nilsen was devastated. About the only thing Dennis had left was his loyal mongrel bitch, Bleep. A year passed. He and Bleep spent the Christmas season of 1978 alone and lonely. Dennis spent Christmas Eve in a drunken stupor.

On December 30, Dennis picked up a lad at the Cricklewood Arms. They spent the night together at Dennis' flat on Melrose Ave. Next morning, Dennis looked at the nude, sleeping body beside him. How pleasant it would be to have a friend over New Year's. Silently, Dennis picked up his own necktie from the floor where he had dropped it the night before. He slid it under his new friend's neck and squeezed until the struggling boy went limp. Dennis noted that the boy was still breathing. He quickly filled a bucket of water and dunked the rasping boy's head into the water. After a few minutes, he was dead.

Years later, Dennis would relate that he bathed his victim in the bathtub, even washing his hair. The clean body was placed in the bed. Then Dennis went for a walk to clear his head. Slowly a plan formed in his tormented, twisted mind. He purchased a cooking pot, but put it away when he got home.

Dennis dressed the body in new clothing he had purchased for himself and laid it out on the floor. That day Dennis slept peacefully, getting up in the evening to watch TV. Next day he pried some floorboards from the living room and shoved his companion's body under the floor, after covering it with dirt from the garden.

A week later, Dennis retrieved the corpse, washed it once again in the bathtub and performed indignities to the body. It was then once again placed under the floorboards. Seven months later, the luckless youth's body was burned in the garden. Dennis had successfully obliterated his first victim. The body has never been identified.

After keeping a body for seven months and then disposing of it, Dennis was amazed at the ease of it all. No one seemed to miss the victim. Five months later, Dennis struck again. Ironically, his second victim was a Canadian on holidays in London.

It was Kenneth Ockendon's misfortune to meet Dennis the day he was to fly home to Toronto. Kenneth was having lunch when Dennis struck up a conversation with him. Later, the two men went sightseeing, before making their way to Dennis' flat for something to eat.

Back at the Central Hotel, Kenneth's baggage remained unclaimed. He never checked out. Dennis strangled Kenneth to death that same night. The Canadian tourist was reported missing. For a while, his mysterious disappearance was noted by the London papers, but he was never traced to civil servant Dennis Nilsen.

In the next few years, Dennis was to kill ten more young men. With the exception of his Canadian victim, none were missed. Most were wandering homosexuals. Dennis liked to wash the bodies and keep them around his flat, not only to satisfy his necrophilic desires, but also for their mere physical presence. He often dressed the bodies and propped them up on chairs to watch TV. On occasion he spoke to them and played them his favorite records. Only four of the 12 men killed at Melrose Ave. have been identified. Other than Ockendon, they are Martyn Duffey, Billy Sutherland and Malcolm Barlow.

Dennis was now killing at a rapid rate. To make room under the floorboards, he dissected some of his victims. Other victims were dissected and placed in suitcases, which were stored in an outside shed, together with various deodorants. Still, Dennis was having difficulty disposing of the bodies as fast as he was killing. At one point, in 1980, he had six bodies in various stages of dissection, both in the flat and outside in the shed.

In December 1980, Dennis built a huge bonfire beyond his garden in a vacant lot. A couple of old tires atop the fire served to disguise the odor. Dennis was housecleaning, destroying bodies.

Good thing, too. Dennis had never been a good tenant. In fact, he was a born complainer. As a result, he had often been asked to move by the agents acting for the owners of the building. In desperation, they located another apartment for their troublesome tenant and threw in £1000 as compensation for the inconvenience. It was an offer Dennis couldn't refuse. He moved into a self-contained attic flat at 23 Cranley Gardens. One can only imagine his feelings as the moving van pulled away from Melrose Ave. He had terminated 12 young lives and no one was the wiser.

Dennis Nilsen was not finished, but the business of disposing of bodies was not as easy at it had been at his previous dwelling. There was no garden, no floorboards and no shed. But Dennis was not to be denied. In the ten months between March 1982 and January 1983, he killed three more times. Each body was dissected. Individual parts were boiled in large pots on the kitchen stove. With flesh boiled away, the remaining bones were dumped in the garbage and taken away by the garbage collector.

Larger body parts, such as the skull and leg bones, were placed in bags, which were stored in a tea chest placed in the corner of the living room. A red cloth over the tea chest transformed the grave into an attractive table. Excess flesh, as well as some organs and hair, were flushed down the toilet. And that's how Dennis came to the attention of police.

The toilet clogged. Tenants complained and were told not to use the facilities until the trouble was repaired.

On Saturday, February 5, 1983, plumber Mike Welch showed up at 23 Cranley Gardens. Mike checked the pipes leading out of the house. There didn't seem to be any problem there. He checked outside the building, but couldn't correctly diagnose the difficulty. Mike advised one of the tenants to call an outfit named Dyno-rod. However, nothing could be done until after the weekend. Unknown to all, Dennis Nilsen was busy dissecting a body all that weekend.

On Tuesday, Michael Cattran, an engineer with Dyno-rod, arrived at 23 Cranley Gardens. He went down a 12-foot manhole outside the house and discovered the cause of the malfunction — strange looking pieces of flesh. Police were called.

When Dennis Nilsen returned home from work that night, Scotland Yard inspectors were waiting for him. He made no attempt to deny his guilt. When his flat was examined, plastic bags yielded two torsos, two boiled heads and four arms. The tea chest contained various bones.

Dennis Nilsen admitted to 15 murders. He was tried on six counts of murder and two counts of attempted murder. Dennis was found guilty of all charges. He received eight life sentences with a recommendation that he serve not less than 25 years.

SUSI OLAH

The tiny Hungarian villages of Nagyrev and Tiszakurt were unlikely locales for murder, but from 1909 to 1930, a series of murders took place in the two villages which made headlines throughout Hungary and all of Europe.

The villages were isolated agricultural communities. In the winter, they were snowbound. The closest railroad was 25 miles away. You get the idea. What went on in the two villages was no one's business but the natives.

The male inhabitants worked hard and played hard. They were forever sloshed on the rather vile wine they produced, mainly for their own consumption. For relaxation and to give a boost to their faltering egos, they often beat up their wives. That is, until Susi Olah arrived on the scene in 1909.

Susi was stout, short and not that good looking. In fact, she was a carbon copy of most of the other ladies who were forever cleaning, cooking and having babies. Susi followed the midwifery profession and was in great demand. Her popularity wasn't due entirely to her dexterity around those with expanding tummies.

You see, the farms in the area were small, the soil poor. In most cases, a peasant couldn't expand his farm because rich men's large estates and imposing walls shut off any expansion. The laws were stacked against the peasants as well. Upon the death of the head of the family, offspring would inherit only a fraction of the father's land. Clearly, the more children born to a family, the grimmer the future. Pregnancy and childbirth were not always happy occasions in Nagyrev and Tiszakurt.

Susi gained in popularity when she added abortion to her midwifery repertoire. One has to keep in mind that doctors were not available in the villages. On occasion, when Susi lost a patient, the only official, a sort of modern medicine man, examined the body. This gentleman always attributed the cause of death to pneumonia, consumption, heart failure and other common fatal maladies.

Of course, this couldn't go on forever. Susi was concerned about the number of women dying while she performed abortions. That's when she got her great idea. Arsenic. Wonderful, deadly arsenic was the solution to all her problems. Why not let the women give birth and poison the infants after birth? The results would be exactly the same as an abortion without any risk to the mother.

No sooner said than done. Susi soaked arsenic laced flypaper in water. The subsequent solution, placed in the unwanted baby's milk proved to be deadly. Business boomed. Susi's reputation as a purveyor of death spread throughout the two villages. For the equivalent of a few dollars, you could purchase a bottle of the solution and, quick as a Gypsy's fiddle, the unwanted child was gone.

Now, Susi wasn't the only midwife in the area. Her competitors became jealous of her success. Word drifted back to Susi that the competition was restless. Not to worry. Susi held a meeting with the four other midwives. She explained that they shouldn't compete against each other. To solve their mutual problem, they should divide the territory. Everyone agreed that it was a super idea. They arranged to meet again at Susi's home.

A few weeks later the midwives met for the second time. Susi served tea and the most delicious petits fours. Shortly after the meeting, one of the ladies took ill and died. Funny thing, after every meeting one of the women took mysteriously ill and went to her great reward. So much for the competition.

Susi's fame and power grew. She had a husband and son of her own. Up to this point, they add little to the strange tale of the arsenic slinging midwife. Unfortunately, Susi grew tired of her husband. He died suddenly, supposedly of pneumonia. Susi's son smelled a rat. Armed with a revolver, he faced his mother on the village's main street. He aimed and fired. Susi stood unharmed as her son fell to the ground in agony.

The villagers were impressed. Susi apparently had the power of life and death. What they didn't know was that Susi, anticipating the problem with her son, had laced his dinner with arsenic. Suffering stomach pains, his aim was off and, quite by chance, he was overcome by excruciating pain the instant after he fired. Susi's son recovered, but so fearful was he of his mother that he fled the territory, never to return.

The long suffering women of the two villages had a bona fide heroine. Susi became their confidante and leader. The dominance of men over women in the villages gradually disappeared. Under Susi's guidance, an unwanted husband was easily dispatched via her ever faithful arsenic. The stout women of the village, once stuck with unloving husbands, took on lovers. If hubby objected, a little meeting with Susi usually straightened him out - permanently. She didn't charge much for her service, normally the equivalent of $25. For those ladies in better financial circumstances, the price rose to about $200. Kindhearted Susi often dispensed her deadly concoction at no charge to those who didn't have the ability to pay.

For years Susi serviced the women of the area. Men died, women took on new husbands and lovers. A sort of secret sisterhood existed between the women, with Susi acting as high priestess. She expanded her operations, dispensing her "medicine" to women who wanted to rid themselves of the elderly.

Of course there were rumors, insinuations and downright suspicions, but they were all put on hold with the outbreak of World War I. The men of the villages went away to war. Some were killed. The survivors returned to the villages. Shortly after their return, seriously wounded former soldiers took ill and died.

The first news of the drama taking place in the villages reached the outside world when a Mrs. Bulenovenski reported that her 77-year-old mother, Mrs. Purris, was missing. A few weeks later, the elderly woman's body was found beside a river bank. Clearly discernible wheelbarrow tracks were found leading to and from the location of the body. When the wheelbarrow was located, it was traced to Mrs. Bulenovenski.

Well, the goulash hit the fan. Mrs. Bulenovenski was tried, found guilty, and sentenced to life imprisonment. The cat was out of the bag. Now the men of the village knew that evil forces were at work. The women, on the other hand, for the first time realized that one of their own could be punished.

In July 1929, a new pastor came to the village of Tiszakurt. No sooner was the man of the cloth installed in his new pulpit than he heard rumors about Mrs. Ladislas Szabo, who had recently buried her aged father and uncle. The pastor decided to pay Mrs. Szabo a visit. He explained his suspicions to the dear woman, who broke into tears at the mere suggestion that she had had anything to do with the recent deaths.

Between sobs, the woman served the pastor a spot of tea. Almost immediately, he was seized with convulsions. A vacationing doctor and a stomach pump saved the pastor's life. He never bothered Mrs. Szabo after that.

Someone who has never been identified informed police in Szolnok, the closest city, that Mrs. Szabo had certainly murdered her father and her uncle. The police popped up in Tiszakurt one fine day and questioned Mrs. Szabo in the street in front of her neighbors. The terrified woman confessed, implicating several other women, including Susi Olah. The suspects were questioned. Five women broke down and confessed. They were all taken into custody and the entire group removed to Szolnok.

Susi refused to talk and was released. She made her way to her home village and visited several of her women friends.

She told them to keep their mouths shut. Unknown to Susi, the police had let her go, hoping that she would lead them to the other conspirators. The scheme worked. All the women were taken into custody. All except Susi.

When the police called at her home, there was no answer. They found the mass murderer in a clothes closet. She had hanged herself.

Thirty-one women were placed on trial in Szolnok for the arsenic poisonings which had taken place in Nagyrev and Tiszakurt. The trials took place that summer and spring of 1930. The pressure was too much for five of the accused. They took their own lives. Others were found guilty and given jail sentences of from five to 20 years imprisonment.

Today, in the two villages, it is difficult to find a home which wasn't affected by the diabolical wave of killings instigated by Susi Olah.

JOEL RIFKIN

When we conjure up thoughts of the modern serial killer, we picture a derelict wandering the countryside, stealing, raping and killing at random. Many serial killers fit this mold, but the man known as the Long Island Serial Killer was quite different.

Joel Rifkin was brought up in a middle class neighbourhood, had loving parents and a better than average education. Something went drastically wrong. Joel, his mother Jeanne and his sister Jan, lived together at 1492 Garden St. in East Meadow, Long Island. They were a close-knit family. Jeanne mourned her late husband Ben, who had succumbed to prostate cancer some years before Joel began his diabolical exploits.

Back in 1959, when the Rifkins learned they couldn't have children, they adopted newborn Joel. Three years later they adopted Jan. Shortly after Jan's adoption, they moved to Garden St. in East Meadow, where, for all intents and purposes, the children were raised in a middle class environment. Jeanne, whose hobby was gardening, soon found that Joel shared her interest. It wasn't unusual to see mother and son laboring over their showplace garden on sunny summer afternoons. Jeanne had high hopes for her son, whose IQ tested at 129. He would be a doctor or a judge. Joel would one day make the Rifkin family proud.

When the apple of his mother's eye started high school, it was evident that he wasn't a personality kid. There was nothing you could put your finger on. Joel just wasn't well liked.

In addition, he was skinny and awkward. Other kids soon learned that they could tease Joel and make him the brunt of their practical jokes without fear of reprisal. Despite his unhappy social life, Joel graduated from East Meadow High in 1977 with better than average marks.

Now watch their son soar, thought Jeanne and Ben Rifkin. For a short while it appeared that Jeanne's aspirations for her son would bear fruit. Joel enrolled in State University at Brockport, but two years later he dropped out and moved back home with his parents. Joel tried a local college. He lasted only a few years before abandoning his studies to pursue menial jobs at minimum wages. None of these jobs had any permanence. Joel was a ship without a rudder. Jeanne couldn't fathom her son. Maybe he just needed more time to settle down than other boys. Soon Joel would find his niche, just you wait and see.

Joel aspired to be a writer, but didn't write much. He tried his hand at photography, but soon lost interest. He drifted from job to job. In time, Jeanne stopped cleaning his room or making his bed. She agreed with him when he explained that a man required some privacy. Joel's room was his alone, off limits to other members of the family.

Ben Rifkin, respected volunteer of many community charities and services, committed suicide by taking an overdose rather than linger through the last weeks of his painful illness. Ben left a note, asking his Jeanne to forgive him. He was 68. It was February 20, 1987. His son Joel was 28 years old.

Unknown to members of his family, Joel had, since high school days, sought out the favors of prostitutes. He would drive into Manhattan in his mother's Toyota and cruise the streets for hours. Joel was fussy. He preferred petite girls. From $30 to $50 changed hands and willing girls performed their skills in Mrs. Rifkin's car. The money he spent on women left Joel perpetually broke. After all, he seldom worked at any job that brought in more than the minimum wage.

The summer after his father's death, Joel brought joy to

216

his mother's heart when he announced that he planned to be a landscaper. He had a natural talent for the work and intended to further his education, this time in a field he really enjoyed. He enrolled in the agricultural program at State University at Farmingdale. Initially, as with most things, Joel did well and actually obtained a job which lasted almost a year as a result of his specialized studies in horticulture. Running true to form, by the spring of 1989, Joel had lost interest and left both school and his position. He placated his mother by assuring her that it was now time for him to go into the landscaping business on his own. Jeanne helped him purchase a 1978 Chevy van and a trailer.

Because of his rather impressive credentials, Joel was successful in obtaining several contracts to take care of local estates. The future looked bright for a time, but it didn't take long before Joel was neglecting lawns, showing up late for appointments or not showing up at all. Soon, contracts were cancelled. Coincidental with his business failure, Joel neglected his personal appearance. He wore dirty clothing and let his unkempt hair grow long.

It is difficult to pinpoint what drove Joel Rifkin to murder. For years he had been denied a normal social life. Worse still, he had often been ridiculed by fellow students and later by colleagues. Shunned by girls, he had sought out prostitutes to satisfy his sexual urges. But it wasn't enough.

Little is known of Joel's first two victims. Their bodies have never been found. Joel has told police that he picked up two prostitutes, one in 1989 and one in 1990, and had sex with each before strangling them. He dissected their bodies and disposed of the body parts in New York Harbor and in the ocean off New Jersey. Years later, he couldn't remember the exact locations.

Joel purchased two old Mazda pickups for his almost non-existent landscaping business. No one, not even his family, took much notice of Joel's coming and going. After all, that's what landscapers do; they travel from job to job. No one pays much attention. Joel even rented space to store his trailer and other equipment. Whether he planned it or not, he now had adequate transportation to move bodies, a place to store them and an occupation which allowed him freedom of movement without being conspicuous.

In May 1991, Joel picked up Barbara Jacobs. Barbara, 32, was a well-known prostitute with a drug problem. She worked hard on Manhattan's Lower East Side to earn the money to support her habit. The petite Barbara fit the pattern of Joel's victims. Her body was found in a garbage bag near the Hudson River on July 14, 1991.

Whatever brake mechanism had restrained Joel Rifkin in the past was now out of control. It was 31-year-old Yun Lee's misfortune to be spotted by Joel as she was walking the streets, looking to turn a trick. A few words of conversation and the tiny prostitute made a deal. Her body was found on September 23, 1991, squeezed into a steamer trunk floating down the Harlem River.

Unlike Joel's previously known victims, Mary Ellen DeLuca had never been arrested, although she was a known drug user. Mary Ellen left her home in Valley Stream periodically to live on the streets of New York, but she always returned to her parents' home. On September 1, 1991, she left their residence and never returned. Somewhere along the way, she crossed paths with Joel Rifkin. On October 1, Mary Ellen's body was found by a man searching through a dump near West Point, the famed military academy. The body was not identified until much later when Joel was arrested. Ironically, Mary Ellen's parents continued the search for their missing daughter long after she had been found and buried.

Joel Rifkin had become a killing machine, yet he was able to function in society without any discernible change in his personality. Both his mother and sister had no hint that the young man living under the same roof was spending his nights prowling the streets of New York seeking out a certain type of prostitute. His method was simple, his supply of victims plentiful and the time to perform his strangulations was unlimited. After his killings, Joel would park his Mazda outside 1492 Garden St. and carry a trophy from his latest victim's body into his bedroom. Items such as a piece of jewelry or a garment would serve to remind Joel of that particular night's work. Like many other serial killers, Joel was a trophy collector.

Around this time in his career, Joel found that it wasn't always convenient to dispose of a body immediately after a kill. Sometimes he stored bodies at his rented space and disposed of them later. This method proved to be tedious. Joel decided to try something new. He purchased four 55-gallon steel drums.

Around Christmastime, Joel picked up a prostitute, strangled her and placed her body in one of his drums. The last he saw of the drum, it was floating down the Harlem River. This particular victim has never been found. The innovative disposal method proved so satisfactory that Joel decided to make use of all his drums. It wasn't until May 13, 1992 that a sanitation worker sighted a steel drum floating in a creek in Brooklyn. A skeletal leg was sticking out of the drum. This unfortunate girl has never been identified.

In January 1992, Joel used his third drum. Twenty-eight-year-old, four-foot 11-inch Lorraine Orvieto had gone down the pike from college graduate and successful business-woman to confirmed crack cocaine user. She gravitated to prostitution to support her habit. Lorraine had always kept in touch with her middle-class family, but just before Christmas 1991, the phone calls stopped. In July 1992, a fisherman came across a steel drum with Lorraine's skeleton inside.

Around the same time that Lorraine Orvieto was murdered, Joel claimed another victim, Maryann Hollomon, 39. Her body was found in a steel drum off Coney Island. Joel had used up his fourth and last drum.

One must remember that while bodies were floating in steel drums and others were scattered and hidden in woods and bushes, Joel was functioning as a somewhat erratic landscape gardener. No one even mildly suspected him of wrongdoing, nor was anyone aware that a serial killer was at large. Several of the bodies had not been recovered. Some of the girls were listed as missing. Given their addiction to dope and their profession, there was the distinct possibility, if not probability, that they had moved out of the greater New York area.

Iris Sanchez, 25, was strangled and shoved under a mattress near John F. Kennedy International Airport. Her body lay there undiscovered for over a year. Anna Lopez, 33, the mother of three children, was murdered on May 25, 1992. Her body was transported upstate to Putham County and deposited in woods off Interstate 84. Unlike some of the other victims, Anna's body was found within 24 hours by a trucker who entered the woods to relieve himself. Although she was a prostitute and heavy drug user, Anna had always kept in touch with her family and her children. When she failed to contact them, they were sure she had met with foul play. A month and a half later, Anna's family learned of the unidentified woman found in Putham County. At last they knew the fate which had befallen their missing daughter.

As the summer of 1992 drew to a close, Joel killed again. The body, which Joel later admitted cutting into several pieces, has never been identified. It was recovered from a suitcase floating in the East River. Joel also claims to have killed another young woman at this time, but police have as yet been unable to locate the body.

In the fall of 1992, Joel picked up and murdered Mary Catherine Williams, a 31-year-old former cheerleader from the University of North Carolina. Life hadn't been easy for Catherine. Shortly after leaving university, she married, but the marriage had lasted only a few years. Catherine headed for the Big Apple to pursue an acting career. The frustration of being out of work most of the time drove her to cocaine. When the money ran out, she turned to prostitution, and that's how she met up with Joel Rifkin. Catherine's decomposed body was found in Westchester two months later. She was buried as an unidentified Jane Doe in a pauper's grave. Catherine was the only victim Joel couldn't remember killing.

Leah Evens was the daughter of a Manhattan Civil Court judge and a graduate of Sara Lawrence College. Upon graduation, Leah had difficulty finding employment. Like many other young women in similar circumstances, she took a job as a waitress in Manhattan. Leah and a colleague lived together for a few years and had two children, Julian and Eve, before he walked out on the relationship. Leah became despondent and sought to relieve her depression with the use of drugs. Before long she was hooked on crack and was forced to turn to prostitution. On a few occasions, she was arrested for soliciting.

On February 27, 1993, Joel Rifkin paid Leah $40 for sex. Then he strangled her and transported her body in his Mazda pickup over 60 miles to Northampton. Joel buried Leah's body in a shallow grave, which was only discovered three months later when wild vegetable pickers spotted a hand sticking out of the earth. It wasn't until Joel Rifkin was apprehended that authorities learned how Leah Evens had ended up buried in the lonely field.

The murder of Jenny Soto, a 23-year-old prostitute, was indelibly etched in Joel's mind. She didn't die easily. Joel would later state that Jenny struggled ferociously for her life. When her body was found, her fingernails were broken. Underneath some of them was the skin of Joel Rifkin. He had dumped her body in the Bronx at the edge of the Harlem River.

Although Joel's memory of events has in the main been fairly accurate, it has not always been completely reliable. He claims to have murdered Julie Blackbird, 31, who was plying the oldest profession on the streets of New York when she encountered Joel. He has been unsuccessful in leading authorities to her body.

It was a pleasant warm night in June 1993, when Joel cruised New York's Allen St. in his mother's Toyota looking for another victim. He spotted 22-year-old Tiffany Bresciani, who needed a fix badly. Tiffany had left her folks back in Louisiana in 1987 to make her mark as a dancer. Seven years later, she was selling her body to obtain money for drugs. Joel Rifkin paid her $40 for sex before strangling her in his mother's car. He drove the body back to East Meadow, lugged it into the garage and placed it in a wheelbarrow, where it was to remain all weekend in the midsummer heat.

In the wee hours of Monday morning, June 28, as his mother and sister slept, Joel transferred the body, which by now was giving off a putrid odor, into the covered bed of his Mazda pickup. Joel pulled out of the driveway and made his way to the Southern State Parkway. He was travelling at the speed limit when he caught the attention of a patrol car. The Mazda's rear licence plate was missing.

Police officers flashed their red light and attempted to pull the Mazda over to the side of the road. Much to their surprise, the driver seemed to ignore them. The officers tried their siren. Still the stubborn driver didn't respond. He neither increased nor decreased his speed. Frustrated, the police activated their loudspeaker, "Pull over to the side of the road!" When they failed to get a reaction, the officers requested backup. Their quarry didn't attempt to get away. He simply wasn't obeying police commands. Soon there were three patrol cars following the driver of the Mazda pickup.

Suddenly, the driver of the pickup stepped on the gas and swung off the main road in an attempt to pull away from the officers on side roads. The ploy didn't work. The Mazda veered out of control and hit a utility pole.

By now, six police cars had joined the chase. The officers approached the Mazda. Inside, Joel wasn't hurt, nor was he armed. They searched him for drugs, but found none. The more experienced officers recognized the pungent odor permeating the area around the Mazda as that of a dead body. Their suspicions were confirmed when they pulled back a blue tarp and gazed at the partially decomposed corpse of Tiffany Bresciani.

Joel was arrested and taken into custody. He answered questions calmly and lucidly. Yes, he was a landscaper who was temporarily without clients. Yes, he had been riding around with a body which he had planned to drop off at some secluded spot. Rather nonchalantly, Joel informed the officers that he had murdered a total of 17 or 18 women over the past few years. He related the horror stories as if he were reciting a nursery rhyme. Emotionless, he informed the amazed police that all his victims had been prostitutes with whom he had had sex before strangling them.

Once he started talking, Joel cooperated fully with police. He directed them to several bodies which had not been found at the time of his arrest. A search of his room uncovered the trophies which proved that his recital of murder was accurate in most details. Items such as Leah Evens' driving licence and employee identification card were found in his room. Police discovered Catherine Williams' credit cards, pictures of Jenny Soto's boyfriend, as well as credit cards belonging to Anna Lopez. And so it went. Joel had surrounded himself with bits of clothing, jewelry and other mementos belonging to his victims.

In his wake, Joel left grieving families to mourn the loss of their loved ones. The insignificant Joel Rifkin, now referred to in the press as the Long Island Serial Killer, gained a degree of infamy by becoming New York State's most prolific mass murderer. At this writing, he is in custody at the Nassau County Correctional Facility, awaiting his trial for the murder of Tiffany Bresciani.

DANNY ROLLING

Sonja Larson really wanted to live on campus, but all the dorms at the sprawling University of Florida campus in Gainesville were occupied. The 18-year-old education student settled for an apartment at the Williamsburg Village Apartments just a few minutes walk from the university.

Sonja's roommate, architecture student Christina Powell, 17, drove down from Jacksonville. Both girls were looking forward to the next semester. They were exuberant young women, who tragically had only hours to live. Another girl was to join them in a few days to share the apartment. Her delay in arriving saved her life.

Unknown to all, an evil presence was about to descend on the university, an evil so repulsive that officers who have investigated hundreds of homicides over careers which have spanned decades were to state that they had never witnessed a crime scene to equal the horror of the one which greeted them when they entered the girls' apartment.

On Thursday, August 23, 1990, Sonja phoned home to let her father know she had arrived safely in Gainesville. Three days later, on Sunday, Christina Powell's sister and brother knocked on the apartment door, but received no response. They summoned a policeman, who entered the building with the aid of a janitor. When the officer opened the door he was repulsed by the putrid odor of decaying flesh. The sight before him repelled his senses. He closed the door abruptly, barring Christina's brother and sister from entering.

The bodies of the two girls were nude and posed in such

a way as to set a macabre scene. The killer had not had sex with either victim, but had extensively mutilated their bodies. Both girls had been stabbed to death, most probably on the previous Thursday night or early Friday morning.

The university community was reeling from the horrendous murders on Monday when Christa Hoyt, an 18-year-old student, failed to report at her part-time job. Christa was the overnight clerk at the Alachua County sheriff's office. She was interested in crime and planned on a career as a crime lab technician. When she didn't show up by 1 a.m. for her midnight shift, her superior had a deputy check her off-campus apartment. Christa lived alone since her roommate had moved out just a week earlier.

The deputy entered the apartment and was chilled to the bone by the posed scene before him. Christa had been decapitated and her head had been placed on a shelf.

Tracy Paules was a 23-year-old political science student, who had been out of town that weekend, visiting with her boyfriend's parents. She arrived back at the Gatorwood Apartments in Gainesville on Sunday night. She and the rest of the 34,000-student population were well aware of the double murder. But Tracy didn't have the concern of other girls living alone. She shared her apartment with Manny Taboada, a six-foot, two-inch, 200-pound fellow student. Tracy and Manny were not romantically involved, but were good friends.

On Monday, Tracy talked to several friends about the murders. By Monday afternoon, the news of the third victim had become common knowledge. Tracy was worried, but she did have big Manny for protection. On Monday night, a friend became concerned when Tracy didn't answer her phone. Next morning, a janitor, using a pass key, entered the apartment. He found Tracy and Manny. Both had been stabbed to death while they slept.

Detectives ascertained that all five victims were most probably killed during a 72-hour time span. The killer had lingered in the three apartments. In the case of Christa Hoyt, he had stripped her of her clothing, bound her with duct tape and stabbed her to death. Her body had been horribly mutilated after death.

The killer then went about cleaning the body with a germicide. The absence of blood at such a violent crime scene was unusual and gave an eerie appearance to the stage setting the killer obviously took some time to create. Detectives believe that the murderer would have been unable to clean the floor of blood stains. They feel he must have used some sort of drop cloth, which has never been found.

Investigators are reluctant to reveal details of the crimes, but it is known that the diabolical killer used mirrors to heighten the horror for the first people to come across the staged settings he had constructed.

The murderer of the five students had taken the time to obliterate his fingerprints from anything he had touched in all three apartments. This attention to detail was unusual and was frustrating to detectives. He had virtually cleaned the apartments of all clues which could be used to trace his identity.

An attempt was made to connect the four female victims. All were attractive brunettes who were excellent students, but other than attending university, they had nothing else in common. The occupants of the three apartments did not know each other.

Fear gripped Gainesville, as law enforcement agencies stepped up the hunt for the killer. Initially, part-time University of Florida student Ed Humphrey was a major suspect. A few days after the series of murders, Humphrey was picked up after he had severely beaten his 79-year-old grandmother. Ed had known Tracy Paules and had lived close to her apartment. He turned out to be a madman, but he wasn't the Gainesville serial killer. Humphrey is presently confined to a state mental institution and is no longer considered a suspect in the case.

Stymied in obtaining a speedy solution to the murders, police proceeded to employ routine and time consuming methods of investigation. It was this plodding which brought Danny Rolling to their attention.

Danny was a big man who had served time in three states, as well as an Alabama mental institution. Three months before the Gainesville murders, he had shot his father, retired police officer Lt. James Rolling, in the head. Father and son had argued. Danny had wrested a gun from his father and, after shooting him in the head, had kicked the fallen man. He then shot his father in the stomach. Lt. Rolling survived. That same night, Danny held up a couple he knew in Shreveport, Louisiana, relieving them of $30 and some food.

Danny made his way to Florida. On September 7, only 10 days after the student murders, he held up a Winn-Dixie supermarket in Ocala. Police were called and a car chase ensued, in which Danny wrecked the stolen Mustang he was driving. The desperate man was taken into custody. A Colt revolver and ammunition were recovered from the vehicle.

Police had no idea that Rolling was in any way connected with the Gainesville murders. In a routine manner they were obtaining hair samples and blood from prisoners arrested since the murders. Although authorities are not revealing details, it is believed that DNA "fingerprinting" has placed Rolling in the Gainesville victims' apartments.

Danny Rolling has been found guilty of the attempted murder of his father and of several other crimes he committed both before and after the Gainesville tragedy. He is serving a life sentence for these crimes in Florida State Penitentiary.

Since being incarcerated, Rolling has confessed to the murders of the five Gainesville students and has been sentenced to death. He currently resides on Florida's Death Row.

MICHAEL RYAN

Hungerford, England, a town of 4,000 inhabitants located about 100 km east of London, was an unlikely location for the worst mass murder in the annals of English criminal history. Not that much had ever happened in the quaint little market town.

Michael Ryan, 27, had an obsessive mother who doted on him. The 60-year-old Dorothy Ryan worked as a waitress and always saw to it that her Michael had a few bob for spending money. For her trouble, Michael often rewarded her with a slap across the face. Despite the abuse, Dorothy continued to cater to her son. After all, he was the man of the house now. His father had died of cancer two years earlier at the age of 80.

Michael quit school and drifted from one menial job to another. As a teenager, he displayed an extraordinary interest in guns. He belonged to two gun clubs and practised target shooting several times a week. Along with his passion for weapons, he favored the Rambo look and often wore army battle fatigues. He lied a lot, making up stories which everyone knew were blatant falsehoods. Michael loved to tell of his experiences as a paratrooper, dramatic tales, but all the product of his imagination.

No one will ever know what snapped in Michael Ryan's mind that summer day in 1987, but we do know the results all too well. It wasn't a spur of the moment thing. He planned his attack, assembled weapons, donned battle fatigues and even took target practice the day before the massacre.

Wednesday, August 19, 1987, started out as a normal market day in Hungerford. Stalls brimmed with fresh fruit and vegetables. The streets filled with shoppers. Susan Godfrey, got up early, gathered her two children, Hannah, 4, and James, 2, for what had been planned as a day in the country. The 32-year-old housewife left her home in nearby Reading and drove to Savernake Forest, a few miles outside Hungerford, where she found an ideal location for a picnic. Susan had no way of knowing that she was only minutes away from becoming the first victim of a madman intent on killing anyone he happened to meet.

In town, Michael slowly dressed in his U.S. Army fatigues. He fondled his Chinese copy of a Kalashnikov AK 47 assault rifle. In addition, he placed a 9 mm Beretta in his pocket along with hundreds of rounds of ammunition. In the trunk of his car he had stashed three other handguns. They rested beside his hunting knife, bandages, gas mask and flask of whiskey.

Michael Ryan had planned well. He drove his silver Vauxhall Astra to Savernake Forest, where he came upon Susan Godfrey and her children. For reasons known only to himself, he spared the children, but marched Susan into the woods some 100 meters distant. A volley of gunfire roared through the countryside. Michael shot Susan 15 times in the chest.

An hour later, the two Godfrey children were found wandering on the road. When taken to their grandmother's house, Hannah told her, "The man shot our mummie and he has taken the car keys and James and me can't drive the car so we are going home."

Michael had only begun his odyssey of terror. He drove toward Hungerford to Froxfield, where he pulled up to the gas pumps at the Golden Arrow garage. After filling his Vauxhall, he aimed his rifle at cashier Kakaub Dean and fired. The terrified woman dropped to the floor amidst a shower of broken glass. Michael walked through the door of the cashier's enclosure and pointed his rifle at the woman cowering on the floor. She could only whimper, "Please don't kill me!" She trembled in fear, eyes shut tight, as she heard the hammer of her attacker's rifle fall four times. The weapon had jammed, saving Kakaub's life.

Michael jumped in his car and drove away in the direction of Hungerford. Kakaub dialed 911. Police were already searching for Susan Godfrey's body in Savernake Forest. Other officers responded to Kakaub's call. Still others were dispatched from surrounding communities. A madman was shooting people.

Michael returned to his home at 4 South View to procure more ammunition. Constable Roger Brereton drove his patrol wagon down South View and recognized the killer about to pull away in his car. Brereton rammed Michael's Vauxhall. Michael responded by shooting the defenceless police officer dead.

Dorothy Ryan witnessed a portion of her son's wild rampage and begged him to put down his weapons. Michael shot and killed her before setting fire to the house. He then proceeded to shoot at houses on his own street. Several occupants were wounded. Two elderly residents, Roland and Sheila Mason, were getting ready to go out shopping. They were killed in their own home.

One of the wounded crawled to a phone and called a friend, 51-year-old George White. George jumped into his Toyota and rushed to South View. When he arrived at the scene, he was shot and killed instantly.

The carnage continued. Michael Ryan was literally shooting at anything that moved. Ken Clements was walking his dog and actually got to talk to the gunman before he too came under a barrage of gunfire.

Firemen arrived to fight the flames at 4 South View. They were spotted by Michael, who began shooting at them. The firefighters were forced to take cover. As a result, three additional houses caught fire and were destroyed.

The shooting continued. Michael made his way to Fairview Rd. Abdur Khan, a retired shopkeeper, and Douglas Wainwright, in town visiting his police officer son, were both shot dead. Michael stood in the street. As cars approached, he blasted the drivers. If he noticed any movement, he whirled and fired. The critically wounded lay where they fell. The less seriously hurt crawled away.

Eric Vardy, Francis Butler, Marcus Barnard, Jack Gibb and Sandra Hill had the misfortune to cross Michael's path. All were shot to death. Myrtle Gibb and Ian Playle both died of their wounds later in the hospital.

Around 3 p.m., the janitor of John O'Gaunt School, Michael's alma mater, called police to tell them that Michael Ryan was approaching the building. Within the hour the school was surrounded by police officers. Adjoining residences were evacuated. Because British police do not normally carry guns, there was a delay while weapons were brought in from a town 40 miles away. A helicopter hovered over the school. The drama unfolding in Hungerford was now being watched on TV in living rooms across the country.

Police cautiously approached the building and confirmed that their armed adversary was confined to the top floor. A negotiating team made contact with him. They were amazed at his calm demeanor. Michael expressed some remorse at having killed his mother.

At 7 p.m., a single shot echoed through the school. Michael Ryan had taken his own life. In his wake 16 people lay dead and 15 others were wounded. Surviving relatives of Michael Ryan had his body cremated and the ashes spread without a marker of any kind. No one felt that he deserved more.

ARTHUR SHAWCROSS

Arthur Shawcross was a Vietnam veteran with a problem. Upon returning to civilian life he was in and out of trouble, serving some time in prison.

In 1972, Art and his wife Penny resided in Watertown, New York. On the afternoon of June 4, 11-year-old Jack Blake followed Art wherever he went. Art took shortcuts through remote fields, but still, according to Art, the youngster followed him. Finally, Art lost his temper and struck the boy a vicious blow to the head. Jack fell to the ground. Art walked away. Three days later he returned to the scene and covered the boy's body with leaves and debris.

Three months later, Art was fishing when eight-year-old Karen Ann Hill strolled up to the river bank. The strange urges which motivated his evil deeds came to the fore once more. Karen Ann was raped and strangled. Art covered her body with stones and mud. But this time was different. He had been seen with the little girl.

Questioned by police in the presence of a public defender, Art was able to cop a plea. In return for his confession and revealing the location of the bodies, he was allowed to plead guilty to manslaughter in the case of Jack Blake. He was never formally charged with any crime concerning Karen Ann Hill.

Art was sentenced to the relatively light term of 25 years imprisonment. The enraged community was assured that without his cooperation the cases might never have been solved. At any rate, Art Shawcross would be out of circulation for a long long time.

Fifteen years passed. In March 1987, Art was paroled. The community of Watertown adamantly insisted that he not be paroled to their town. Art agreed. He didn't want to go to a place where he was thought of as a monster.

Art was paroled with a stringent reporting schedule and other tight restrictions to the city of Binghamton. While Art was in prison, his wife divorced him and he became a pen pal of Rose Walley. Rose visited the prison and, upon Art's release, the pair married.

When Binghamton police were advised of Art's presence, they often called on him while investigating criminal cases. Art requested a move, which was granted. The couple moved to Rose's home town of Delhi. When news got out that a double killer, who had somehow been released from prison, was in their town, the police and the public made it clear he wasn't welcome.

From Delhi they moved to Fleischmanns and from there to Elmira. No one wanted Art Shawcross.

Finally the authorities settled on Rochester. Surely, in a larger community, Art would remain anonymous. He obtained a job with Brognia Brothers, making salads which were distributed to schools and other institutions.

Despite being married, he acquired a girlfriend, Clara Neal, and often borrowed her Dodge to take long drives by himself. Rose knew of his attachment to Clara, but didn't seem to mind. She also tolerated Art's solitary fishing.

What no one knew, except those girls who were selling their bodies along Lake Ave., was that Art was a frequent visitor to Rochester's red light district.

In February 1988, Dorothy Blackburn was picked up by Art. They drove to an isolated area and parked. Buyer and seller dickered over price. When a price was agreed upon, sexual intercourse took place.

According to Art, during the lovemaking, Dorothy bit him. He retaliated by biting back. Art claimed that right then and there he decided to kill his companion.

He tied Dorothy's arms and legs and drove to one of his

favorite fishing holes. Once there, he strangled her and dumped her body over the bridge spanning Salmon Creek. It had been almost 16 years since Art had last killed. He liked the feeling. After it was all over, he put the entire episode behind him. In time, ice formed over the creek. Dorothy Blackburn ceased to exist.

When spring arrived in upper New York state, the ice covering Salmon Creek melted. A hunter discovered Dorothy's fully-clothed body.

In light of future events, it seems inconceivable that Rochester police had not been informed by parole authorities that there was a child killer in their city.

By merely driving a vehicle Art was in violation of his parole. By having a drink in a public place he could be returned to prison. Since they didn't know that such a man lived among them, Rochester police never routinely questioned Art when they investigated Dorothy's murder.

Art became well known in Rochester's red light district. Anna Steffen met Art in a bar on Lake Ave. They drove to a secluded area and proceeded to argue over Art's inability to perform. He strangled the girl beside the Genesee River and let her body slide into the water.

Eventually, Anna's body was discovered. Art did not enter the sphere of the investigation into her death.

Art's third victim was not a prostitute. She was a girlfriend of sorts — 58-year-old Dorothy Keller. Dorothy often visited Art and Rose, but Rose had no idea that the pair was making love at every opportunity.

In June 1989, while fishing, and after they had had intercourse, Art accused Dorothy of stealing his money. She denied the accusation and threatened to tell Rose of their relationship.

Art broke the hapless woman's neck with a piece of wood and then hid the body in bushes. Months later, Art visited the body, which had decomposed in the summer heat and was now nothing more than bones.

Six months after the murder, Dorothy's body was found by fishermen. Once again, Art Shawcross was not questioned. In fact, police did not connect this murder to the two previous killings.

In 1989, the death toll climbed. Patty Ives and Frances Brown brought his total to five.

When June Stotts became victim number six, news reports of a serial killer on the loose emanated from Rochester. Like the Green River killer, he preyed on prostitutes and operated in one general area. Many victims were dumped in and about the Genesee River.

Marie Welch braced herself against the brisk November wind swirling along Lake Ave. She felt herself fortunate when Art picked her up. Art made love to Marie and then killed her.

Darlene Trippi was Art's last victim of 1989. Art claimed she had to die when she laughed at his inability to perform. He stripped her body and deposited her clothing in a Salvation Army box.

Liz Gibson was killed because she accidentally broke the gear shift of Clara Neal's car.

June Cicero, victim number 10, laughed at Art, as had so many previous victims. For this, she too had to die.

It is beyond belief that this man roamed the district where prostitutes plied their trade without being seen picking up any of the women who were later reported missing. Art Shawcross, child killer, parolee, operated with immunity — an invisible killing man.

On January 3, 1990, Art drove out to Salmon Creek, parking only scant yards from where he had dumped June Cicero's body. He brought along his lunch. From his position on the bridge, he could just make out the form of the body enveloped in ice under the bridge. Art didn't notice the State Police helicopter as it swooped down the river. From the helicopter, police spotted the form of a body and the man in the car on the bridge.

As soon as Art sighted the helicopter, he drove away, but the vehicle was followed and Art was taken into custody. When questioned by police, he confessed to the most horrid series of murders in New York State's history. While in custody he confessed to an 11th murder, that of Felicia Stephens.

Art was tried for 10 of the 11 murders he confessed to having committed. His attorneys entered a plea of insanity but a New York jury thought otherwise.

Shawcross, now 46, was found guilty of 10 counts of first-degree murder. He was sentenced to 10 life terms to run consecutively with no possibility of parole for 25 years on each. He will be eligible for parole in 250 years.

GENE SIMMONS

Murder takes no holidays. The most horrendous mass murder ever to take place over the Christmas season occurred in Dover, Arkansas in 1987.

The first signs that retired U.S. Air Force Sgt. Gene Simmons led a strange life came to light years before when he was charged with sexually molesting his 16-year-old daughter, Sheila.

The Simmons family lived in Cloudcroft, New Mexico. When Sheila told her brother that their father had been sexually attacking her, he told friends, who in turn told their parents. Concerned parents informed school officials, who related the facts to police.

Eventually, an arrest warrant was issued for Simmons, but before it could be served, the entire family moved away. Sheila was pregnant with her father's child and later gave birth to a daughter. After a year of unsuccessfully attempting to locate Simmons, police dropped the charges against him.

May Novak, Gene's mother-in-law, begged her daughter to leave Gene. Rebecca Simmons simply couldn't. With a house full of children, how would she survive?

The family surfaced in Dover, Arkansas. Although retired from the Air Force, Gene worked at several jobs around Russellville over the years. In November 1986, Gene left his job at Woodline Motor Freight and took a part-time job with Sinclair Mini-Mart until December 18, 1987. He quit on that day, claiming that his wages were far too low.

When Gene Simmons, 47, walked into a law office in

Russellville shortly after Christmas, no one had any idea that a few days earlier he had killed his entire family. Kathy Kendrick, 24, a legal secretary, had once worked at Woodline Motor Freight. She had repulsed Gene's advances over a year earlier. Because of this or some other imagined grievance, Gene calmly shot her four times through the head.

He then moved on to the Taylor Oil Co., where he accidentally met James Chaffin. Without hesitation, he shot the 33-year-old Chaffin dead on a loading dock. Gene proceeded into the oil company offices and shot Russell Taylor, 38, the proprietor of the firm. Russell would survive the killing spree. Gene had at one time worked for Taylor and no doubt felt he had some score to settle.

A madman was on the prowl, settling imagined ills. Gene proceeded to Sinclair Mini-Mart. Without hesitation, he shot store manager David Salyer, 38, and employee Roberta Woolery, 46. Both would survive the senseless attack.

The shooting wasn't over. Gene made his way to Woodline Motor Freight. He shot and wounded 35-year-old Joyce Butts. Today, Joyce still has nightmares about the traumatic experience. She vividly remembers waking up 10 days after the shooting and being told that surgeons had successfully removed a bullet which had lodged near her heart.

Ten minutes after this last shooting, the building was surrounded by police. Gene gave up without incident, turning over two .22 calibre handguns to police.

Authorities proceeded to the Simmons' home. The Christmas tree was gaily decorated. Wrapped presents were under the tree. No Christmas presents had been opened for the very good reason that all the occupants of the house had been dead since before Christmas. Five victims were found in the house and were identified as one of Gene's daughters, his son, their respective spouses and one grandchild. All were still wearing overcoats, indicating to police that they were killed soon after they arrived bearing Christmas gifts.

Freshly dug earth was observed close to the Simmons home. There, in a 1.5-metre deep grave were the bodies of Gene's wife, four of their children, ages 7 to 17, and two grandchildren.

The horror story continues. In the trunks of two old abandoned vehicles near the Simmons house, two bodies were found. These tiny bodies had been wrapped in plastic garbage bags. They were later identified as Gene's grandchildren.

Ironically, after the last body was recovered and the killer behind bars, a letter written by Simmons' wife to her daughter shortly before her death was made public. In the letter, 46-year-old Rebecca Simmons wrote, "I am a prisoner and the kids are too. I don't want to live the rest of my life with Dad." She went on to say, "Dad has had me like a prisoner."

Rebecca revealed her life of isolation and fear in her dilapidated rural home. Her husband wouldn't allow her to have a telephone. He censored all mail and kept neighbors away. Rebecca attempted to explain, "You have to remember I've never had a job since I've been married, or before that either. I know I have to start somewhere. It would all be so much easier if it was just me."

Rebecca's attempt to escape the maniacal clutches of her husband came too late. Too late for Rebecca, 13 members of her family and two respected citizens of Russellville, Arkansas.

Gene was tried for the murders of Kathy Kendrick and James Chaffin. The Arkansas jury deliberated only one and a half hours before finding him guilty.

Believed to be the most prolific family mass murderer in U.S. criminal history, Robert Gene Simmons presently resides on Arkansas State Prison's Death Row, awaiting execution by lethal injection.

PETER SUTCLIFFE

Kathleen and John Sutcliffe's six children grew up and one by one moved out of the family home. Their eldest son, Peter, was the last to leave 57 Cornwall Rd. in Bingley, England.

Peter was ambitious, more ambitious than the gang he ran with. They only thought of nights at the pub and birds to pick up. If a legit bird wasn't available, there were always the pros, who, for £5, would show a man a good, if hurried, time.

But Peter was different. He had met Sonia Szurma, the daughter of honest Czech immigrants. Sonia's parents were impressed with hard-working Peter, who over the years held jobs as a furnace operator, grave digger and lorry driver. On August 10, 1974, on Sonia's twenty-fourth birthday, she became Mrs. Peter Sutcliffe.

Six months after his marriage, Peter, always attempting to better himself, took a driving course at the Apex School of Driving, eventually earning a Class One licence. The Sutcliffes and the Szurmas were pleased. Handsome, pleasant Peter was making his way in the world. He soon obtained a good position as a lorry driver.

What the family didn't know, what the entire country didn't know, was that something deep in the recesses of Peter Sutcliffe's mind was changing and festering and smoldering. He was developing a hatred of women, a hatred so strong that for five and a half years the mere mention of the Yorkshire Ripper sent shivers up and down the spines, not only of women, but of men as well. With the possible exception of Myra Hindley and Ian Brady, no killer was ever more hated than the Yorkshire Ripper.

On July 4, 1975, Anna Rogulskyj couldn't go to sleep until she satisfied herself that her kitten was safe and sound. The kitten was missing, but Anna felt that her boyfriend must have taken it to his apartment just a five minute walk away. Even though it was 1 a.m., she decided to set her mind at ease and travel the few blocks.

A man lurking the shadows asked, "Do you fancy it?" There was no doubt in Anna's mind what the question implied. She threw an answer over her shoulder, "Not on your life!" She hurried on and soon arrived at her boyfriend's door, but no amount of knocking could get a response.

Apprehensively, Anna retraced her steps. Again, the whispered innuendo, "Do you fancy it?" Anna increased her pace. The man walked faster and caught up to her, raining three blows on her head with a ballpeen hammer. He then lifted her sweater and slashed at her midriff. A window opened, a head stuck out, "What's the matter?" The attacker ran away and the head tucked back in. The window closed.

An hour later, Anna was found on the sidewalk. Rushed to Leeds General Infirmary, she was given the last rites of the Catholic Church. A 12-hour operation saved her life. Anna spent months in hospital, and had to learn to speak and walk again. She was unable to describe her attacker. Peter Sutcliffe, the Yorkshire Ripper, the man who would terrorize a nation, had struck for the first time.

Five weeks later, Peter and a friend, Trevor Birdsall, were driving from pub to pub. Peter spotted Olive Smelt, a 46-year-old cleaning woman, who habitually spent Friday nights in a pub with a female friend. Now Olive was walking home and took a shortcut down an alley. Peter stopped the car and told Trevor he was going to try and have a go. He rushed into the alley, caught up with Olive and struck her twice on the head with a hammer. He tried to cut her body with a hacksaw, but gave up when a passing car came along. He returned to Trevor in the car.

Trevor asked what had happened. Peter would only say that he had been chatting with that woman. Next day, Trevor read of the strange attack on a woman where nothing had been stolen and no sexual attack attempted. He was positive that the victim was the woman Peter had followed down the alley. He said nothing, told no one. Beating up the wife or girlfriend was the norm in his crowd. The old lady survived, didn't she? Olive Smelt was unable to describe her attacker.

In the fall of 1975, Peter was hired as a driver for the Common Road Tyre Co. in Bradford. This broadened his scope. Peter came to know Leeds' inner city Chapeltown section with its teeming watering holes and tough prostitute population like the back of his hand.

Wilma McCann sold her body whenever she could for the going rate of £5. It was her misfortune to be picked up by Peter Sutcliffe. A deal was struck. Peter drove to a secluded spot and spread his coat on the grass. Wilma lay down. That's when he struck her a vicious blow to the head and stabbed her 14 times in the chest and lower abdomen. Next morning her body was found by a milkman.

As the Sutcliffe family celebrated Christmas that year, no one had any idea that obliging Peter had attempted to kill two women and had succeeded in killing a third. He gave presents to his parents, his aunts, his brothers and sisters and his wife.

On January 21 of the New Year he killed again. Prostitute Emily Jackson routinely picked up a client. After a short drive, Peter asked Emily to hold a flashlight while he raised the hood of his car. As the unsuspecting girl pointed the torch, Peter struck her twice on the back of her head with a hammer. In a frenzy he stabbed his hapless victim 52 times.

Peter didn't kill for the remainder of the year, but in February 1977, he struck again. Irene Richardson's body was found near a park. She had been hit over the head with a hammer, stabbed in the neck and chest and had been horribly slashed across the lower abdomen. The newspapers of the district for the first time coined the phrase "Yorkshire Ripper."

Leeds detectives realized from the nature and physical characteristics of the wounds, that all three women had been murdered by the same man. One hundred detectives worked on the Richardson murder without coming up with any concrete results. Policewomen, dressed as prostitutes, roamed Chapeltown but the elusive Ripper didn't show.

Tina Atkinson was dead drunk when she picked up Peter and took him to her flat. As she sat on the edge of her bed, he struck her with his ballpeen hammer, after which he stabbed her repeatedly, slashing her across the lower abdomen. Peter drove away and tossed the incriminating hammer from his car. Two days later a man found the hammer in Cottingley Bridge. He used it for three years before finding out it was a murder weapon.

Jayne MacDonald and her boyfriend left the dance at Hofbrauhaus early so they could have some fish and chips on the way home. They lingered too long. By the time they had eaten, Jayne had missed her last bus home. The pair parted. Jayne made her way down Chapeltown Rd. with the intention of calling a taxi. Peter sneaked up behind her and struck her with his hammer. He dragged her off the street and performed his distinctive mutilations to the body.

Jayne was the Ripper's first murder victim who was not a prostitute. Whether this was a pertinent factor in the increased intensity of the Ripper investigation is not known. We do know that after Jayne's death, West Yorkshire's most famous detective, George Oldfield, was placed in charge of the investigation with one directive: Apprehend the Yorkshire Ripper.

Oldfield conducted a massive investigation. Four hundred citizens had been in the general area on the night of Jayne's murder. Three hundred and eighty were traced and cleared. One hundred and fifty two prostitutes were arrested. Over 3,500 statements were taken by police. None of these efforts produced one iota of useful information.

Late in the summer of 1977, Sonia and Peter Sutcliffe purchased a home at 6 Garden Lane, Heaton. With Sonia employed as a teacher and Peter on steady as a driver, the

Sutcliffes were definitely on the way up. There was even talk of a baby.

Peter had other thoughts in mind. After being in his new home for only a week, he took off for Manchester's red light district. Jean Jordan jumped into Peter's red Corsair without hesitation. He passed over the usual £5 note and then parked behind a high hedge near municipal allotments as he was directed by Jean.

The hammer crashed against the girl's skull again and again. Peter dragged the body into the bushes, but a car arrived and he left before mutilating the body. In the days following the attack, Peter was perplexed that headlines were singularly devoid of any mention of the Ripper striking for the first time in Manchester.

He correctly figured that the body had not been discovered, but this wasn't the reason Peter decided to return to the scene of the crime. He realized that he had left a valuable clue behind. Peter had been paid in crisp, newly minted notes. The £5 note he had given Jean was one of these traceable notes. Peter had to get it back.

Eight days after the murder, he returned to find Jean's body exactly as he had left it. He stripped the body, examining every garment, but could not find the £5 note. Frantically, he searched for Jean's purse in vain. He stabbed the body again and again, as if to quell the frustration at not being able to retrieve the only clue he had ever left behind.

Next day Jean Jordan's body was found. Five days later, her purse, with the £5 intact, was turned over to police.

The Bank of England quickly confirmed that the note was one of a large supply distributed by Midland Bank of Shipley, located just outside Bradford. They had been distributed four days before the murder and had been placed in pay packets for various commercial firms in the area. The new bills had been used by 30 firms employing over 7,500 men.

One of the companies was T. and W.H. Clark Ltd., the trucking firm where Peter was at the time employed as a driver. A month after Jean Jordan was murdered, two detectives knocked at the door of Sonia and Peter Sutcliffe at 6 Garden

Lane. Peter calmly told the officers that he was home on the evening of November 2 when Jean Jordan had been murdered. Sonia confirmed Peter's story. Peter had also been at home eight days later when the body had been mutilated. Once again, Sonia agreed. The officers left and reported nothing unusual to incriminate Pete Sutcliffe over the thousands of others being questioned.

Peter continued killing after spending another joyous Christmas season with his family and friends. In January 1978, he murdered prostitute Yvonne Pearson in his now familiar manner. Yvonne's body was not found for two months. On the last day of January, Helen and Rita Rytka, good-looking 18-year-old twin prostitutes, walked their regular beats. Helen was picked up by Peter.

The twins had an arrangement. After one completed her services, she would return to a certain location to check in with her sister. That way, through the course of the evening, they would see each other several times. On this night, Rita waited. Helen never returned. Her body was found three days later.

Someone had noticed a red Corsair in the vicinity where the body was found. Because Peter drove a red Corsair, he was once more visited by detectives. The obliging lorry driver explained that he was often in that area since he drove to work to pick up his lorry. Sonia confirmed that Peter hardly ever went out at night, which was true enough. He didn't go out often, but when he did, he killed women. Sometimes he would be gone only a half hour. The questioning detectives didn't know that Peter had already been interrogated by other officers concerning the £5 note. They left believing Peter's story. The two reports were never connected.

In May 1978, Peter cruised around with his friend Trevor. After dropping Trevor off at his home, he drove to Halifax and watched various people walking their dogs in a park. Finally, he spotted a young girl walking alone. He parked his car and accosted Josephine Whitaker, a 19-year-old clerk on her way home. Josephine was not a prostitute, but was simply in the wrong place at the wrong time.

Ten women had now been murdered at the hands of the Yorkshire Ripper. The police knew from saliva tests that the killer's blood belonged to group B, a rare type found in only six percent of the population. They knew precious little else.

George Oldfield received scores of letters from cranks, but firmly believed that one such letter was authentic. Tests on the envelope indicated that the sender was a group B secreter. Then, on June 20, 1979, the letter took a back seat to a tape recording received by Oldfield. The message on the tape was startlingly similar to letters written by the original Jack the Ripper 90 years earlier. George Oldfield was convinced that the tape was authentic.

Voice and dialect experts from the University of Leeds meticulously studied the tape and came to the conclusion that the voice had a "Geordie" accent, which is generally attributed to that area of northeast England immediately south of the Scottish border. Peter Sutcliffe did not have a Geordie accent. When a police directive was issued instructing officers to exclude anyone who didn't have a Geordie accent, Peter was off the hook.

The largest manhunt in the annals of British crime was now instituted. In all, over 150,000 individuals were questioned about the case. More than 22,000 statements were on file. The tape with the supposed Ripper's voice was played in public places, on the radio and even at soccer games. But nothing stopped Peter Sutcliffe.

In September 1979, Barbara Leach, a student at the University of Bradford, was slain in Peter's usual way. A short while later, while driving a Rover, Peter encountered 47-year-old Marguerite Walls in Farsley, a suburb of Leeds. Marguerite was strangled, a departure for the cunning Peter. He decided to throw the police off the trail by changing his tactics. He was right. Initially, the Walls murder was not attributed to the Yorkshire Ripper.

Peter's thirteenth and last victim was Jacqueline Hill of Headingly. She merely got off a bus and was followed by Peter until, in a darkened area, he struck her down with his hammer. She was his only victim in 1980.

On January 2, 1981, Peter took the precaution of taping old licence plates he had found in a junkyard over the plates on his Rover. He called Sonia and told her he'd be late. He then drove 30 miles to Sheffield, where he picked up prostitute Olivia Reivers. Peter parked in a dark area near a large stone building. Without warning, a police car pulled up. Sergeant Bob Ring and Const. Robert Hydes approached the Rover. Peter gave them a false name and told the officers he was merely parked with his girlfriend. Const. Hydes returned to his vehicle and checked out the plates with the national computer. The plates didn't belong to the Rover.

The officers returned to the car. After examining the Rover's licence plates, they found that they were taped over another set. The officers decided to take Peter and his girlfriend in for questioning. Olivia didn't realize it at the time, but the two officers had just saved her life.

Meanwhile, on the way to the police car, Peter asked if he could go around the corner of a building to relieve himself. He took the opportunity to throw his ballpeen hammer and knife behind a small storage tank.

At Hammerton Road police station Peter gave his correct name. He told police he had used the stolen plates because he was planning a robbery. He even told them he had been questioned as one of the individuals who had been paid with a new £5 note like the one found in Jean Jordan's purse. Peter was detained, but was still no more of a suspect than thousands of others who had been detained and questioned in the course of the massive investigation.

Next day, when Sgt. Bob Ring heard that the man he had brought in was being questioned by the Ripper squad, he decided to take another look at the spot where he had picked up Peter Sutcliffe. In particular, he searched the area where Peter had relieved himself. There, Bob Ring found a ballpeen hammer and a knife lying in a pile of leaves.

Word spread throughout the police hierarchy. This could be it. Inspector John Boyle conducted the questioning. He told the suspect he didn't believe his story. Early on in the questioning Boyle stated, "I think you are in serious trouble."

Peter replied rather cockily, "I think you have been leading up to it."

Boyle asked, "Leading up to what?"

"The Yorkshire Ripper," replied Peter.

"What about the Yorkshire Ripper?" the officer asked, hardly able to conceal his excitement.

The reply left little room for doubt. Peter said, "Well, it's me."

Peter Sutcliffe, 35, the man who had terrorized a country for five and a half years, confessed in detail to all his crimes. In May 1981, an English jury rejected his counsel's plea of insanity and found Peter guilty of 13 counts of murder. He was sentenced to life imprisonment and incarcerated at Parkhurst Prison on the Isle of Wight.

Since that time, due to mental deterioration and attacks on him by fellow inmates, he has been transferred to Broadmoor, an institution housing the criminally insane.

WAYNE WILLIAMS

Seldom has a city, its inhabitants and its officials come under such critical scrutiny as Atlanta, Georgia did between 1979 and 1981. Someone was systematically murdering the city's black children. As the number of victims grew, the case became known around the world as the Atlanta Child Murders.

On July 28, 1979, a woman pushed back shrubs and rubbish along Campbellton Rd. in Atlanta. She was looking for returnable bottles. The unwary woman recoiled in horror at the sight of a human leg sticking out of the foliage. Police were soon on the scene. They were in for a surprise. Barely one hundred yards from the first body, they uncovered a second victim. The boys were identified as Edward Hope Smith, and Alfred Evans, both 14.

In itself, two teenaged boys found shot to death on the same day in the same place was unusual. But there was more to come. Much more.

Six weeks after the bodies of Edward and Alfred were found, another 14-year-old boy disappeared. Milton Harvey had one possession he loved above all others and that was his bicycle. It was found abandoned along a dusty road. Investigators discovered that Milton had skipped school on the day of his disappearance because he was embarrassed to wear his worn-out tattered shoes. Three weeks later, his decomposed body was found in a dump in the Atlanta suburb of East Point, not far from where the first two bodies had been discovered.

Little Yusef Bell, 9, was running an errand for a neighbor when he dropped out of sight. His body was found by a vagrant in the heart of Atlanta. Four children had been murdered. All were poor and all were black.

In retrospect, the Atlanta police have been criticized for not intensifying their efforts to apprehend an obvious madman who, for some perverted reason, was killing black boys. Would more effort have been put into the investigation if the victims had been white?

The story soon drifted out of the local area. These killings were different from anything which had preceded them. The murders continued.

The Christmas season of 1979 passed without incident. The following March, 12-year-old Angel Lanier was found dead. She had been raped and strangled with an electrical cord. A pair of panties not belonging to the dead child had been stuffed down her throat. Angel's murder was a departure from the killer's usual pattern. For the first time, he had murdered a female, and for the first time, sex was involved in the killing.

A week later, 10-year-old Jeffrey Mathius left his home to pick up a pack of cigarettes for his mother. He was never seen alive again. Jeffrey's skeletal remains would be found months later.

Camille Bell, little Yusef Bell's mother, probably did more than anyone to bring the series of murders to the public's attention. She gave statements to journalists, accusing police of laxity in apprehending the killer. She insisted that one person was responsible and had to be apprehended before he killed again. Mrs. Bell's concern was well-founded. The killings continued, but now the terror which had enveloped Atlanta was being reported by the world press. Strange details concerning the murders became public knowledge. Some of the victims had been washed after they were killed.

Eric Middlebrooks, 14, was stabbed and beaten to death. Christopher Richardson, 11, disappeared on his way to a swimming pool. His skeleton was found eight months later. La Tonya Wilson, 7; Arron Wynche, 10; and Anthony Carter,

9, were murdered in quick succession.

The effect on Atlanta was devastating. Racial tension ran high. Rumors spread throughout Georgia. Some claimed a white man had taken it upon himself to wipe out black children. Others said the killings were not the work of one individual, but a diabolical scheme initiated by the Ku Klux Klan to kill black children so they would not grow up to propagate their race.

The city of Atlanta is reported to have spent a quarter of a million dollars a month conducting the extensive investigation. Funds poured in from the public and from private interested parties. Frank Sinatra and Sammy Davis, Jr., headlined a benefit concert at Atlanta's Civic Centre, raising $250,000 for the investigation. Schoolchildren and the public in general staged fund raisers. Actor Burt Reynolds contributed $10,000. Atlanta's first black mayor, Maynard Jackson, announced that the city had instituted a reward of $100,000 for the apprehension and conviction of the killer. Several corporations, with the help of heavyweight boxing champion Muhammad Ali upped the reward to half a million dollars.

Still, the litany of murder continued: Earl Lee Terrell, 11; Clifford Jones, 13; Darron Glass, 10; Charles Stephens, 12; Aaron Jackson, 9; Patrick Rogers, 16; Lubie Geter, 14; Terry Pugh, 15; Patrick Balazar, 11; and Curtis Walker, 13 — all under 16 years of age, all from underprivileged backgrounds and all black. By now, the list numbered 21 victims. Many thought the number to be far greater, claiming that other missing youngsters had fallen to the madman, but their bodies had not been found.

Ronald Reagan became president of the United States. He immediately allotted $1.5 million to help defray the cost of the investigation, as well as ordering the Federal Justice Department to assist in the case. That month, Jo Jo Bell, 15, and Timothy Hill, 13, were murdered by the Atlanta Child Killer.

On March 30 and 31, 1981, the bodies of Eddie Duncan and Larry Rogers were plucked from the Chattahoochee River. These two victims were a departure from the now well-patterned category of victim. Both were 21 years old and both were mentally retarded.

The task force solely devoted to apprehending the killer had interviewed and released scores of suspects during the course of their investigations. One such man was Wayne Williams, a rather unlikely suspect. Williams was a bright young man, who lived with his parents, both retired school teachers, on Penelope Rd. in north-west Atlanta.

As a high school student, Williams had constructed and operated his own radio station in the basement of his parents' home. Currently, he was active as a freelance newspaper photographer, media consultant and music producer. It was this latter activity which first connected him to the child killing case. Involved in promoting musicians, Williams had flyers printed outlining his credentials in this field. These flyers had been found on, or in the possession of, four of the victims.

Was it possible that Williams had lured victims with promises of recording dates and stardom? Williams also had access to the city's streets. He often roamed the streets in his station wagon, ostensibly looking for the opportunity to take saleable photographs. Williams often showed up at accidents and fires. He was well-known to police.

While Williams was being investigated, the bodies of Mike McIntosh, 23, and Jimmy Payne, 21, were pulled from the Chattahoochee in the same week in April. That same month, John Porter, 28, was found stabbed to death on the streets of Atlanta. In May, William Barrett, was discovered strangled to death in a ditch.

On May 22, 1981, three Atlanta police officers and an FBI agent were on stakeout duty at the South Cobb Drive Bridge over the Chattahoochee River. Suddenly, there was a splash in the water. The police saw automobile lights on the bridge. As the car sped away, they radioed another member of the stakeout team in a vehicle.

The chase was on. The car, a green station wagon, drove away, stopped, turned, and reversed its course, driving back over the South Cobb Drive Bridge. A second police car joined the chase. Two miles down the road, the station wagon was stopped by police. The driver was Wayne Williams. He was taken into custody, questioned and released. However, he was kept under close surveillance while the FBI dragged the river for a body. Two days later they recovered the body of 24-year-old Nathaniel Cater. Two weeks later, Williams was taken into custody and charged with Cater's murder, as well as that of Jimmy Payne.

Williams' murder trial lasted nine weeks. Prosecution attorneys produced microscopic fibres and dog hairs taken from the Williams' residence and car, which matched fibres found on victims. It was the state's theory that Williams hated his own race and killed so that they wouldn't become parents. It was also believed that he exulted in the challenge of outwitting the combined police forces attempting to solve the case.

Williams testified in his own defence. He claimed he was on the bridge at 2:45 a.m. looking for a female vocalist he wished to interview before she auditioned later that day. He swore he hadn't killed anyone, nor had he any knowledge of the murders.

A jury of eight black and four white citizens found Williams guilty of two counts of murder. He received two life sentences to run consecutively. After the sentencing, police announced that Williams was responsible for over 20 other murders, but it would serve no purpose to have him stand trial on those charges.

Not everyone is convinced of Williams' guilt. In 1987, an attempt to reopen the case, led by the mothers of several of the victims, was quashed. They believe that a ring of pornographic profiteers used the children before killing them.

Wayne Williams is presently serving his sentences at the Georgia State Correctional Centre in Jackson.

AILEEN WUORNOS

The woman waved her thumb in the air and struck an appealing pose as cars sped along one of Florida's sun drenched highways. Those who failed to stop had no way of knowing that they had just prolonged their lives. Others weren't as fortunate. They stopped and picked up 34-year-old Aileen Wuornos.

Aileen is unique. She is the only female serial killer in the United States. The phenomenon of taking three or more lives at different times in different locations has been strictly male dominated. All that changed when Aileen took up the killing profession.

Initially, Florida police had no idea that a serial killer was in their midst. The discovery of video store owner Richard Mallory's body in December 1989, was thought to be an isolated incident. Mallory's blood-stained Cadillac had been found a mile away two weeks before the gruesome discovery of his body.

I spoke to investigator Larry Horzepa of the Volusia County Sheriff's Office. He had no idea of the hornet's nest he was about to open when he was assigned the Mallory case. All that summer of 1990, Larry kept getting teletypes from other law enforcement offices in central Florida concerning murdered men. There was a striking similarity between the victims. They were all white middle-aged men who had been travelling alone. Their bodies had been found in wooded areas off main roads and all had been shot with small-calibre handguns.

The number of murders mounted. The occupations of the victims varied. There was a construction worker, truck driver, sausage company delivery man, missionary, retired police officer and a Florida state employee among the seven victims eventually attributed to Aileen.

Det. Horzepa says, "When we established that the bodies found in several counties were the handiwork of one individual, we joined forces with law officers in the other counties." A year after Richard Mallory's body was found, police received a break in the case.

Witnesses had seen two women running from a Pontiac Sunbird after they had crashed the vehicle through a fence. The damaged car belonged to Peter Siems, a missionary who had been missing since earlier that summer. With good descriptions of the two women, police released composite drawings to three tabloid TV shows. Citizens' tips pointed to one Tyria Moore, a domestic who had worked at a local hotel. The other woman turned out to be Aileen Wuornos.

Detectives found that Aileen had a long criminal record, which included disorderly conduct, armed robbery and prostitution. She was the constant companion of Tyria, whom she referred to as her wife. Authorities soon found out that the pair were lesbian lovers, who hung around rough tough bars in the Daytona area. Police staked out several such bars for two weeks. Sure enough, Aileen showed up at the Last Resort, a bar frequented by bikers. She was quietly taken into custody.

Aileen's lover Tyria had left her job and was picked up in Pennsylvania. Despite their relationship, it was believed that she had nothing to do with the murders. According to Larry Horzepa, "Moore had a full-time job at a hotel and worked a 40-hour week. They were lesbian lovers, but Aileen hitchhiked alone and met Moore after working hours."

Moore broke up with Aileen because she feared for her own life. She told authorities that on one occasion Aileen had told her, "I killed a guy today."

Aileen confessed to the murders of seven men who had picked her up while she was hitchhiking on the highway.

She told a heart-rending story about her youth, claiming that she was sexually abused as a child, pregnant at 13, and was actively selling her body by the time she was 15. She also stated that she had attempted suicide on six different occasions.

Aileen's uncle Barry, who would eventually travel to Florida to testify against his niece, disputed Aileen's claims of an abused childhood. He testified that Aileen came from an average home.

Det. Larry Horzepa obtained a search warrant for storage space Aileen had rented. Among her personal belongings he found several items she had taken from her victims, such as a police officer's badge, an alarm clock and fishing equipment. In some instances, she gave away items taken from her victims. No doubt she sold some of her loot, but robbery was not her primary motive.

Throughout her interrogation, Aileen absolved her lover of any complicity in the murders, adamantly stating that she had acted alone. She said that she sometimes posed as a woman in distress and at other times as exactly what she was — a prostitute looking for a customer. On some days she had turned as many as a dozen tricks and had never harmed any of her clients. She had only killed those men who had become physical with her or hadn't wanted to pay her. In her own words, she told Horzepa, "All I wanted was to get my money for sex."

Some of the tales told by Aileen about her early home life have been confirmed. She did become pregnant at the age of 13 and was sent to a home for unwed mothers. Her baby was taken away from her at birth. At the same time, her family received word that her father, a convicted child molester, had hanged himself in prison. From the age of 15, Aileen was on her own, making her living from prostitution.

Det. Horzepa, who was the first to question Aileen and was the first to hear her litany of death-dealing drives, finds it difficult to be sympathetic towards the multiple killer. He claims that Aileen went "from prostitution to murder for the cash the men carried on their person."

Recently, Aileen stood trial for the murder of Richard Mallory, the first of a series of murder trials she faces in the near future. She was found guilty and sentenced to death in the electric chair.

At her trial, Aileen took the witness stand in her own defence. She testified that she had killed her victims in self-defence. Det. Horzepa scoffs at this. "Some self-defence!" he says, "Several of the men were shot as many as four times in the back."

Aileen Wuornos awaits her second trial while residing on Death Row in Florida.

ZODIAC KILLINGS

In all the history of crime, no killer has ever written as many letters to newspapers and authorities as the infamous California murderer known as the Zodiac.

On December 20, 1988, David Faraday, a 17-year-old Vallejo High School student drove his father's 1980 Rambler into a secluded side road overlooking Lake Herman Reservoir. Beside him in the passenger seat was pretty 18-year-old Betty Lou Jensen. It was the young couple's first date. It would be their last.

David and Betty Lou had only been parked in the well-known lovers' lane for a matter of minutes when a man appeared at the side of the Rambler and ordered them out of the car. When they hesitated, he fired two shots through the car window. Once the youngsters were outside the vehicle, the gunman placed the barrel of his .22 calibre pistol behind David's right ear and fired. Betty Lou ran for her life, but it was no use. She took five slugs in her back and died where she fell.

Twenty minutes after the attack on the two students, a woman driving past the lane noticed them sprawled on the ground. She drove into Benicia, where she informed police. They arrived on the scene to find David Faraday still breathing. He died on the way to hospital.

Seven months passed before the killer struck again. Michael Mageau, 19, and Darlene Ferrin, 22, drove into the parking lot of the Blue Rock Springs Golf Course. This time, the gunman walked to the side of the vehicle and sprayed the unwary couple through an open window. Michael managed to stagger out of the car before falling to the pavement. Miraculously, although critically wounded, he would survive the attack. Darlene died in an ambulance while being rushed to a nearby hospital.

Thirty minutes after the couple was found in the parking lot, police received a phone call. A male voice declared, "I want to report a double murder. If you will go one mile east on Columbus Parkway to the public park, you will find the kids in a brown car. They were shot with an 8 millimeter Luger. I also killed those kids last year. Goodbye."

Police verified the facts mentioned in the phone call and were convinced the call was authentic. They knew they were dealing with a weirdo who preyed on couples in parked cars. He didn't rob his victims, nor were the attacks of a sexual nature. In fact, he gave no hint as to his motive, but authorities knew the man was cunning. No clues were left behind to identify him.

A month later, the three major newspapers in the San Francisco area received letters revealing details of the two attacks which only the killer could know. In addition, each paper received one third of a complicated cryptogram with the killer's demand that it be published on the front page of their newspaper. The cryptogram, which was made up of Greek and English letters, as well as triangles and circles, was turned over to U.S. Naval Intelligence where experts were given the task of decoding it.

A week later, the experts had not deciphered the killer's correspondence, but two high school teachers from Salinas were successful. Donald Hardin and his wife Betty managed to decode the message. Here is the letter as it was translated. Note the mistakes in spelling and other errors.

"I like killing people because it is so much fun it is more fun than killing wild game in the forrest because man is the most hongertue (dangerous) animal of all to kill something give eryetheyo a thrilling experience it is even better than getting your rocks off with a girl the best part of it I athae when I die I will be reborn in paradise and all the I have killed will become my slaves I will not give you my name because you will trs to sloi down or atop my collecting of slaves for my afterlife ebeo riet emeth hpiti."

The last four words of the message have no meaning to anyone to this day.

In the weeks which followed, the man with the strange urge to prove he was the killer wrote several letters to newspapers. For the first time he began his correspondence with the phrase, "This is the Zodiac speaking." The name stuck and forever after he has been known as the Zodiac.

On September 27, 1989, Zodiac struck again. Cecilia Shepard, 22, and Bryan Hartnell, 20, were attending Pacific Union College close to Vallejo. Bryan drove his Volkswagen to a pleasant spot beside Lake Berryessa to have a picnic. He and Cecilia were sitting beside the shore that evening when a man suddenly emerged from the brush. He wore a black hood which covered his entire head and carried a pistol in one hand and a knife in the other. The intruder had Cecilia tie Bryan's hands and feet. He himself bound Cecilia.

The hooded man uttered the terrifying statement, "I'm going to have to stab you people."

Bryan replied, "Well, then, stab me first."

Zodiac obliged. He plunged his dagger into Bryan's back six times and then proceeded to inflict ten stab wounds to Cecilia's back and four more to her chest.

When a fisherman found the two young people on the shore, they were still alive. Cecilia died in hospital two days after the attack, but Bryan survived and was able to tell authorities of his experience. As usual, Zodiac wanted credit. An hour after the attack, he called the Napa police, "I want to report a murder. They are two miles north of park headquarters. They were in a white Volkswagen Karmann Ghia. I'm the one that did it."

Two weeks later, Zodiac was at it again. Paul Stine was studying toward his doctorate degree at San Francisco State College. To finance his education, he drove a yellow cab at night. Paul picked up a fare in downtown San Francisco. Unfortunately, his passenger was Zodiac. The madman produced a nine-millimeter pistol and shot Paul directly in the temple, killing the 29-year-old student instantly. Before leaving the cab, Zodiac tore away a piece of Paul's shirttail. Three days later, the San Francisco Chronicle received a letter detailing Paul Stine's murder. As proof that the letter was authentic, Zodiac enclosed a small piece of his victim's bloody shirt.

Zodiac had deviated from murdering young couples. He was clever enough not to become a pattern killer. Ballistic tests proved that he had used a different weapon for each murder. His letters continued to arrive at the Chronicle building in San Francisco, some in English and some in cryptogram form. Several cryptograms were unsolvable, leading authorities to believe Zodiac was mocking them or simply having fun at their expense.

As time went by, other unsolved murders dating back to 1986 were attributed to Zodiac. If there was any doubt, Zodiac himself kept police informed by mail. He added postscripts to his letters. The last one received had the ominous notation: Me 37 SFPD 0.

Because Zodiac wasn't above writing provable untruths in his letters, it is difficult to know if his claim of 37 victims is a fact or an exaggeration.

The Zodiac killings and the unusual correspondence stopped as suddenly as they had begun. Police believe that a thrill killer such as Zodiac would never stop killing of his own volition. Many feel he must have died or been incarcerated in an institution where letter writing would be too risky.

Zodiac has never been identified and his known murders have remained unsolved to this day.